the essential guide to
cake
decorating

the essential guide to
cake decorating

whitecap

This edition first published in the U.S. and Canada in 2004 by Whitecap Books,
351 Lynn Ave, North Vancouver, British Columbia, Canada, V7J 2C4.

www.whitecap.ca

First published by Murdoch Books®, a division of Murdoch Magazines Pty Ltd.

Editor: Jane Price Editorial Director: Diana Hill
Designer: Vivien Valk Designer (cover): Annette Fitzgerald
Design Concept: Marylouise Brammer
Photographer: Robert Reichenfeld Photographer (cover): Ian Hofstetter
Stylist (special features): Mary Harris Stylist (cover): Katy Holder
Food Editor: Kathy Knudsen
Cake Decorators: Kerrie Walsh, Kathy Knudsen
Cake Decorators' Assistants: Jo Glynn, Maureen Dunn

Chief Executive: Juliet Rogers
Publisher: Kay Scarlett
Production Manager: Liz Fitzgerald

ISBN 1-55285-236-9

Printed by Toppan Printing Ltd.
PRINTED IN CHINA

IMPORTANT: Those who might be at risk from the effects of salmonella food poisoning ·
(the elderly, pregnant women, young children and those suffering from immune deficiency diseases)
should consult their GP with any concerns about eating raw eggs.

The publisher thanks the following: Paul Green, Alan Dunn, Joanna Farrow, Lindsay John Bradshaw, Anne Smith,
Nadene Hurst, Julie Springall, Adrian Westrope, Dan Tabor, Pat Trunkfield, Chris Jeffcoate, Jackie Kuflik,
Lisa Tilley, Corinne Mitchell, Anne White, Sarah Gleave, Caron Mathias, Tombi Peck.

OUR STAR RATING: When we test recipes, we rate them for ease of preparation.
The following cookery ratings are used in this book:
☆ A single star indicates a recipe that is simple and generally quick to make—perfect for beginners.
☆☆ Two stars indicate the need for just a little more care, or perhaps a little more time.
☆☆☆ Three stars indicate special dishes that need more investment in time,
care and patience—but the results are worth it. Even beginners can make these
dishes as long as the recipe is followed carefully.

THE FINE ART OF CAKE DECORATING

Several thousand years ago the ancient Greeks were baking cakes of fruit and honey with which to appease their gods and celebrate fertility and plenty. It is unlikely that they would recognise today's fabulous cakes, spread with rich icings of chocolate, eggs or cream, embellished with sugar flowers and tiny figures, or covered in a lattice of delicate piping, as a continuing history of the same celebratory food. Antonin Carême, one of the most renowned chefs of recent centuries, memorably remarked that there are five fine arts—sculpture, painting, poetry, music and architecture—and that the confectioner is the only artist to have mastered four of the five.

CONTENTS

Cake decorating through the centuries . . . 8
Glossary of terms 10
Equipment 14

CAKE BASICS 18
Before you start 20
Basic cake recipes 22
Basic icing recipes 32
Lining cake tins 38
Covering cakes with marzipan 40
Covering cakes with sugarpaste 42
Covering cakes with royal icing 44
Covering cake boards 46
Tiers and layers 48

WORKING WITH SUGARPASTE . 50
Adding colour 52
Decorative designs 54
Inlay, bas-relief and appliqué 56
Needlework designs 58

WORKING WITH ROYAL ICING . 60
Piping with royal icing 62
Basic piping 64
Pressure piping 66
Runouts 68
Runout collars 70
Embroidery 72
Lace and extension work 74

SUGAR FLOWERS 76
Simple filler flowers 78
Roses 80
Sweet peas 84
Poppies 88
Making a flower spray 90

MODELLING 92
Basic figures 94
Characters 96
Animals 98
Accessories 100
Backgrounds 102

GATEAUX 104
Chocolate decorations 116

CHILDREN'S CAKES 140

CHRISTMAS CAKES 192

WEDDING CAKES 226

CELEBRATION CAKES 264

Templates 288

Index 301

CAKE DECORATING THROUGH THE CENTURIES

Cakes have been baked and decorated for several thousand years, initially to appease angry gods and then as a celebration of special occasions. We carry this tradition with us into the third millennium.

Today's wedding cakes can be fantastic creations with several tiers.

Ribbon is often used to trim both cake and board.

It is very difficult to put an exact date on when baking, cake making and decorating began, although it is thought that the Babylonians taught the Egyptians the art of baking. A painted panel of around 1175 BC, depicting the court bakery of Rameses III, illustrates the preparation of several types of cakes, as well as some bread. There are also indications that confectionery sweetened with sugar was on sale in Egypt around 700 BC.

Today we serve specially decorated cakes to celebrate many different occasions: weddings, christenings, engagements, anniversaries, birthdays and Christmas. Christmas cakes have a long history and were baked by the rich in the eighteenth century as Twelfth Night cakes. A bean and a pea would be hidden and baked in the rich fruit mixture. Whoever found the bean was crowned 'king of the feast' and the finder of the pea 'queen of the feast'. But it is wedding cakes that have the longest tradition and the story of their changing development that best illustrates the history of cake decorating as an art.

CROWNING THE BRIDE

The tradition of creating special cakes for weddings reaches back to Roman times. A small and basic fruit cake would be made from food that was traditionally offered as an appeasement to the gods—rich fruit, nuts and tiny honey cakes. This cake would be crumbled over the bride's head so that the gods would bless her with abundance—the tradition known as 'crowning the bride'.

This tradition was brought to Britain by Julius Caesar in 54 BC and became part of local custom. At first, it was only wealthy families who could afford to adopt the practice, with poorer families scattering grains of wheat or corn over the bride, in the hopes of fertility.

Crowning the bride continued until a mere 200 years ago. Now the ritual has been split into two parts—rice or confetti is thrown over the bride to encourage fertility and each guest is given a slice of cake to eat or take home (girls were supposed to sleep with a slice of the cake under their pillows to induce dreams of future husbands).

THE FIRST DECORATIONS

Although they were not yet served at weddings, decorated cakes made their first appearance in England during the reign of Elizabeth I. Most were adorned with moulded almond paste. The food of this era was becoming exotic and extravagant, with the new culinary discoveries brought back from around the empire. Sweetmeats were served in dishes moulded from a form of pastillage. Extraordinary banquet centrepieces were brought out to amaze and delight noble guests.

At this stage, wedding cakes were baked as tiny separate cakes, more like buns with a sticky coating of almond paste. Some would be crumbled over the bride, some squeezed through her wedding ring, some eaten by guests and some thrown to the poor folk outside the feast. The remainder were built into a pile and set before the new husband and wife, who were expected to kiss over the pile of cakes. This would hopefully bless them with prosperity and many children. It would not be long before this unruly pile of sticky almond paste-covered buns would be converted into one large cake.

When Charles II returned from exile in France to reclaim the English throne in 1660, he brought with him a love of French cooking and some of his favourite French pastry chefs. It was these men who, finding the piles of almond buns unappetising and unattractive to their trained eyes, suggested they should be iced with a crust of sugar and then adorned with trinkets.

Once the idea of decorating the cake with trinkets had been embraced, there was a rush by all the great chefs of Europe to create more fantastical decorations. Competition was enormous, with every chef wanting to create something fit for the king's table. Sugar sculpting began in Italy in the seventeenth century: Giovanni Lorenzo Bernini used sugar to create works of art for special occasions. However, not until the 1760s were all the constituents of our present-day celebration cakes put together. The first edition of Mrs Raffald's book *The Experienced English Housekeeper* (1769) contains three successive recipes for a rich cake, marzipan and icing.

The most celebrated confectioner of this time was Antoine Carême. His book *Patissier Royal* is illustrated with engravings showing that he used a form of pastillage for his highly structured cakes and desserts. It is he who likened the art of the confectioner to that of the architect and, in fact, took many of his ideas from architectural drawings. A similar recipe for pastillage was given in the book *The Complete Confectioner* by Frederick Nutt, published in 1819.

In 1894 Ernest Schulbe first competed at the London Exhibition. He remarks in his book, *Advanced Piping and Modelling*, that at this time very little 'net or string work', as he described it, was done in Britain. Schulbe's book shows us that the modelling tools we know today were in use in the late nineteenth century, though made of bone rather than of plastic. Flowers were modelled in a similar fashion, including the use of stamens. The paste used was a mixture of marzipan and gum paste. Brass crimpers, very similar to those on sale today, were also used.

THE GROOM'S CAKE

Even after it became common practice to ice wedding cakes with sugar in the late seventeenth century, the cake would still be crumbled over the bride's head... the icing, in fact, making this ritual easier. The sugar would crumble and could be showered over the bride while the rest of the cake was left to be eaten. Eventually, the bride's family began to prepare two cakes for the feast: one for the crowning and one highly decorated creation to appeal to those who had discovered a taste for sugar icing. These became known as the bride's and the groom's cakes.

The tradition of crowning the bride continued until just before the reign of Victoria and it was then that the 'groom's cake', a dark fruit cake, was cut into pieces to be taken home by the guests. The 'bride's cake' (made from a lighter mixture but more highly decorated) would be served as a dessert at the wedding feast.

THE LAST CENTURY

Today's cakes can be eight feet high and covered in flowers, fountains of champagne, figures of the bride and groom or whatever else takes their fancy.

Since the early twentieth century, cakes have been raised in layers on pillars. Originally it was only royalty and high society who could afford these tiered cakes, with the rest of the country having single cakes decorated with perhaps a vase to add height to the display. The three-tiered round cake became traditional, representing the three rings—the

engagement, wedding and eternity rings. Soon the request for a three-tiered cake became fashionable among the style-conscious middle classes, even if there was more cake than was actually needed for the guests. Consequently, there was often a tier left over and, rather than use it immediately, it would be kept for the christening of the couple's first child.

Very little was published on cake decorating between the two World Wars. The Second World War, with its severe sugar rationing in the United Kingdom, reduced the number of books being published on the subject still further and icing practice became very difficult. Mashed potato was used to keep piping skills honed. One pound of icing would be used for a whole cake decorating class, for weeeks at a time.

Although there were sugar restrictions in the colonies during the War, they were not quite as stringent as in the United Kingom. Sugarpaste was the preferred covering of rich fruit cakes in countries like Australia and South Africa. But, in Britain, the master bakers continued with their favourite technique—royal icing. Ronnie Rock, one of the greatest craftsmen in this field, actually ground his own icing sugar to produce the magnificent piece he made for the first post-war exhibition in 1946. It is now displayed at London's National Bakery School.

The custom of the bride and groom cutting the cake together began in the 1930s when British cakes were encased in several layers of hard royal icing to hold up the pillared layers. Grooms would 'help' the bride cut the cake, using a sword or knife. In those days this would almost unfailingly have been a large hard white cake with some piped decoration. It would perhaps have been decorated with horseshoes (for good luck) and tiny bride's shoes (representing the giving away of the bride to the groom by her father and the idea of a possession—historically a shoe left on a piece of land symbolised ownership).

In the last thirty years, there have been many changes in the fashion for wedding cakes. Soft sugarpaste icing became popular and with it the creation of new techniques taken from needlework, such as smocking and ribbon insertion. Sugarpaste is often imagined to be a modern invention but, in fact, the first recipe for sugarpaste was published in 1609 in a book entitled *Delights for Ladies*. This paste was made from 'fine white sugar, starch and gum tragacanth', coloured and flavoured with pounded flowers.

It is this movement in trends for the decoration of wedding cakes that sets the fashions for styles of christening, birthday and anniversary cakes. Today we realise that with imagination and practice, almost anything is achievable.

Christmas cakes began life as Twelfth Night cakes.

Decorative royal icing lace can be used to edge cakes.

Today we celebrate many occasions with a cake.

GLOSSARY OF TERMS

Cake decorating, more than other forms of cookery, makes use of some specialised ingredients and equipment. Many of these can be found or improvised from articles already in the kitchen drawer. Others, such as cutters, are a good investment for future cakes. Some are known by alternative names.

Paint brushes are available in many different widths.

Cake pillars are used to separate the tiers.

ALBUMEN POWDER is powdered egg white and is recommended in many countries for making royal icing. It complies with food safety standards and gives consistent results, which can be difficult with fresh egg whites. Being able to measure the ingredients accurately makes royal icing simple. Albumen powders are available either as pure albumen or as an albumen substitute. Albumen substitutes are cheaper and can be used for most tasks, particularly coating, as they produce a slightly crumbly icing, which is easier to cut. Pure albumen powder is stronger and perfect for delicate designs. Pure albumen is a deeper colour than the substitute. When mixed with water the substitute will dissolve, but pure albumen forms a sticky mass and needs to be soaked for at least an hour to dissolve. Sieve both solutions before use.

ALMOND ICING is another name for marzipan.

APRICOT GLAZE is brushed over cakes to act as a glue before they are covered with marzipan. It is made by boiling apricot jam and water together until blended, then sieving to remove any lumps. The jam must be boiled to prevent any risk of mould forming between the marzipan and the cake. Apricot jam is used because its flavour complements the marzipan. Cheaper jams, which contain less fruit, are more suitable for making glaze.

BALL TOOL is a rounded tool used to gently curve and shape the edges of a sugar flower petal or other decoration. A selection of different sizes is useful, although a glass-headed pin stuck into a piece of dowel can be used instead of a small ball tool.

BAS RELIEF PASTE is another name for modelling paste.

BASKETWEAVE is a piping technique which requires a special basketweave tube.

BLOSSOM CUTTERS are used to make small flowers, often for filling out larger arrangements. They are tiny cutters, like biscuit cutters, used to stamp out the flowers from sugarpaste, flower paste or pastillage in one piece. They are bought in sets in metal or plastic. Some are of the plunger type, incorporating a spring-loaded plunger to curve the flower once it is cut.

BLOSSOM TINT is another name for petal dust, powder dust or dusting powder.

BRIDGEWORK is the basis for royal icing extension work and supports the lines of royal icing, keeping them away from the cake. It is the overpiped scalloping that lies under the vertically piped lines.

BRODERIE ANGLAISE is a decorative technique carried out on soft sugarpaste. Holes are cut or poked in the icing and thin lines of royal icing are piped around these holes to mimic broderie anglaise lace. The technique is also known as eyelet or Swiss work.

BRUSH EMBROIDERY is a textured decorative technique, whereby a piped royal icing outline is brushed inwards while still soft.

BUTTERCREAM is a beaten mixture of butter and icing sugar, in roughly equal quantities. It is one of the most simple icings and is often used to cover and fill children's cakes. It is easy to flavour and colour and can also be piped.

CAKE DOWELS are long thin solid cylindrical wooden pillars, pointed at one end. They are pushed into cakes to support pillars for holding tiered cakes. They are also useful for moulding and modelling.

CAKE PILLARS are decorative pillars used to cover or sit on top of cake dowels and separate the layers of tiered cakes. They are available hollow or solid and in a variety of materials including plaster, plastic and acrylic. They can be transparent or coloured.

CALYX is the collection of flower sepals that protect the bud as it develops. It is the small green star shape that is found where the petals join the stem. A calyx cutter is used for making the sepals of sugar flowers.

CLAY GUN is a modelling tool used to create lengths of softened modelling paste. The paste is placed in the gun and pushed down until it extrudes in a long line. The line can be circular, square or rope-like and effects are produced by twisting the paste.

CLEAR ALCOHOL such as gin, vodka or kirsch is used as a glue for securing sugarpaste to marzipan. Once the cake has been covered with marzipan and dried, the marzipan is brushed with clear alcohol and the sugarpaste pressed over the top. For children's cakes, use a sticky sugar syrup instead. Clear alchohol can also be used to secure soft paste decorations to soft icing.

CLING FILM is another name for plastic wrap.

COLLAR is a fragile royal icing runout that extends beyond the edge of the cake, giving it an impression of grandeur and importance. Collars can be positioned on round, square or many-sided cakes and made in one piece or several. The collar is runout with thinned royal icing on non-stick baking paper or acetate, following a template showing the size of the cake. Once dry, it is secured to the cake top. Collars can be made to cover just the corners of a square cake.

CONFECTIONER'S SUGAR is another name for icing sugar.

COPHA is another name for white vegetable fat or shortening.

CORNELLI WORK is a decorative piping technique, also known as scribbling, where royal icing is piped in close lines, changing direction constantly so the beginning and end of the line cannot be found. Very close in appearance to filigree work.

CORNFLOUR is used in cake decorating for dusting the work surface when rolling out flower paste and pastillage to prevent it sticking. It must be used sparingly as it can dry the paste out, but is finer to use than icing sugar.

CRANKED PALETTE KNIFE is a flat palette knife with an angled handle, useful for lifting dried runouts from paper.

CRIMPING is a decorative design carried out on soft sugarpaste. Special crimpers, which look rather like oversized tweezers, are used to press together small portions of the icing to create a border.

CRUST OVER is a term used when making runouts. A royal icing outline is piped onto non-stick baking paper or acetate and the sections of the outline filled in with thinned icing in various colours. After colouring each section, the icing is placed briefly under a heat lamp to 'crust over' before the next portion is filled, so that the different coloured icings do not run together. The crust refers to the hardening of the sugar under the heat.

CURVED FORMER is a piece of plastic that looks like a pipe cut in half lengthways. It is used to hold decorations in a curved position while they are drying. You could use a rolling pin, bottle or roll of cardboard instead, as long as the angle of curve is suitable.

CUTTERS are available for shaping flower petals or other decorative ideas. They often come in sets and can be bought in plastic or stainless steel.

DRESDEN TOOL is a decorating tool for drawing veins on leaves and petals. One end of the tool is fine and one broad.

DUSTING POWDER is another name for petal dust, blossom tint or powder dust.

EDIBLE GLUE is also known as sugar glue. It is used to glue together dry pieces of icing such as securing dried modelling figures to a dried cake. If both or one of the pieces of icing were still soft, they could be stuck with just water or egg white, so often edible glue is not necessary.

EMBOSSING is a decorative technique borrowed from leatherwork. A design is pressed into soft sugarpaste or pastillage. A special embossing tool can be bought, or you can use well-cleaned decorative buttons, cutlery, jewellery etc.

EXTENSION WORK is a decorative technique consisting of scalloped bridgework piped around the side of a cake with royal icing and fine lines piped to drop vertically from the bridgework. It is a technique for the experienced decorator.

FILIGREE WORK is a decorative piping technique, also known as scribbling, where royal icing is piped in close lines, changing direction constantly so the beginning and end of the line cannot be found. Very close in appearance to cornelli work.

FIRM PEAK is a term used to describe royal icing once it has been beaten and stiffened. It means the peaks stand firmly without dropping over at their tips. Royal icing is beaten or thinned to different consistencies depending on the firmness needed for each technique. Firm peak is used for outlines or other piping that needs to hold its shape.

FLAT ICING is covering the top and sides of a cake with a smooth coat of royal icing.

Flower, petal and leaf cutters make professional-looking sugar flowers.

Edible food colourings are available as paste, liquid or chalks.

11

Veiners are used to imprint realistic leaves.

Piping tubes are also known as tips and nozzles.

Glass-headed pins have brightly coloured tops.

FLOODING is another name for runout, used because the thinned icing is 'flooded' over the design.

FLORIST'S TAPE is used for taping the stems of sugar flowers, either to strengthen and colour them or to secure them together.

FLOWER PASTE is used primarily for hand-modelled flowers, but can also be used for other decorations that are delicate or which require the strength of this hard-setting paste. Most recipes will include gum tragacanth. This gum strengthens the paste and enables it to be rolled out so thinly it is translucent. Flower paste can be home-made or bought from cake decorating suppliers, either in small blocks or as a powder to be mixed with water.

FONDANT ICING or ready-rolled fondant, or soft fondant is another name for sugarpaste.

GANACHE is a mixture of chocolate and cream, most often used as an icing for cakes.

GARRETT FRILL is a paste frill that can be applied to a cake, often around the side or to edge a plaque but sometimes as part of a modelling design. It can be made using a garrett frill cutter or a large fluted cutter with a smaller plain cutter to remove the centre.

GLASS-HEAD PINS are used in cake decorating because they have large coloured tops which cannot easily get lost in the icing.

GUM ARABIC is a pale-coloured powder from the acacia tree. It is sold by specialist suppliers and is used as a glaze or an edible glue.

GUM TRAGACANTH is a gum extracted from a small tree or bush found in Mediterranean countries. It is used to stiffen pastes such as modelling or flower paste and is available as a cream-coloured powder that expands when moistened. It is expensive but only a small amount is needed. CMC (carboxymethyl cellulose) is a cheaper alternative and is often used to replace some or all of gum tragacanth in pastillage.

HEAT LAMP is used for the initial drying of royal icing runouts. It gives a sheen to the finished decorations. An ordinary angle-poise lamp with a flexible arm can be used.

ICING RULER is a metal ruler with straight edges for dragging across soft royal icing to give a smooth finish when icing the tops of cakes.

INLAY is a technique carried out on soft sugarpaste. One portion of the paste is cut and lifted away. It is replaced with another piece of sugarpaste of the same shape but a different colour. The join is then smoothed over.

LEAF CUTTERS are available in different sizes and shapes and cover many varieties of plant, from rose or ivy leaves to oak or holly. They are worth investing in but you could cut out freehand or use templates.

LEAF VEINER is pressed onto a paste leaf to leave the impression of veins.

LIQUID GLUCOSE is another name for corn syrup or clear corn syrup. It is used in pastes such as modelling paste and sugarpaste to keep them pliable.

MARBLING is a method of colouring sugarpaste or marzipan. Colour is added and only partially kneaded in, so that the effect is streaky or marbled.

MARZIPAN is a paste made from icing sugar, ground almonds and egg. There are recipes for marzipan dating back many centuries. Marzipan is most usually known as a covering for fruit cakes before they are then covered with royal icing or sugarpaste. Home-made marzipan is superior to ready-made, and the paler variety of ready-made is of higher quality than the bright yellow. Do not overwork marzipan by kneading too long or the oil will be released from the almonds and the marzipan will become greasy. Also known as almond paste.

MODELLING PASTE is used primarily for hand modelling figures. It sets hard and contains gum tragacanth for strengthening and stiffening.

NON-STICK BAKING PAPER, also known as baking parchment, is paper with a waxed coating, which prevents absorption of moisture so that cake mixture or icing decorations will not stick. Greaseproof paper is not suitable for piping runouts although it is used for lining cake tins.

NOZZLE is another name for a piping tube.

PASTILLAGE is a stiff white paste used for making flowers and models. When cold, the paste sets hard but it will quickly become pliable once warmed and kneaded by hand. It can be rolled out extremely thinly, until it is transparent, and then it can be cut and modelled into flowers. Once dry, the paste resembles thin china—firm, yet brittle and easily broken.

PETAL DUSTS are fine powders in varying colours, used for dusting on sugar flowers or dry surfaces to give a background tint or variation in shades of colour. They are also useful for dusting the edges of frills. Use when liquid colours would inhibit the drying of icing. Also known as blossom tints or dusting powder.

PIPING GEL is a clear sticky gel that becomes fluid when warmed. It can be coloured for piping on dry sugarpaste or royal icing. It maintains a shiny, wet look when set. Also known as piping jelly.

PLAQUES are rolled and cut out pieces of sugarpaste or pastillage, prepared and decorated in advance, then secured to the cake.

PRESSURE PIPING is a piping technique where varying pressure is applied to the piping bag to create a three-dimensional effect to the icing.

QUILTING is a decorative technique inherited from needlework. Small and large stitching (tailor's) wheels are used to create the effect of stitched lines on an image.

RIBBED BOARD is a working board with thin ribbed lines in it for imprinting on soft paste. It is useful for techniques such as smocking.

RIBBED ROLLING PIN is a rolling pin with ribbed lines in it for imprinting on soft paste. It is useful for techniques such as smocking.

RIBBON INSERTION is another decorating technique inherited from needlework. Soft paste is cut at intervals, using a template, and small lengths of ribbon are inserted into the cuts to look as if the ribbon has been threaded through the icing. A ribbon insertion tool makes the cuts and inserts the ribbon, but this can be done freehand with a sharp scalpel and tweezers.

ROYAL ICING is a soft mixture of egg whites or albumen and icing sugar, which then dries extremely hard. It can be spread over cakes and boards or used for piping. The prefix 'royal' is thought to have been added after this icing was used on Queen Victoria's wedding cake, although this type of icing undoubtedly was in existence long before then.

RUNOUTS are royal icing pieces piped onto non-stick baking paper or acetate. An outline is piped onto the paper and this is filled in with thinned icing. Once dry, the runout is removed from the paper and secured to the cake. Three-dimensional models can also be created. Also known as floodwork, flooding or runins.

SCRIBERS are used for transferring outlines onto soft paste without leaving pencil marks. It is like tracing but leaves an indented impression. The scriber is rather like a ball-point pen without the nib.

SMOCKING is a technique inherited from needlework. Fine lines are impressed in soft sugarpaste, either with a ribbed rolling pin or board. These are pinched together at intervals with tweezers and lines of coloured royal icing are piped over the top in a pattern to represent thread.

SMOOTHER is a flat plastic tool for rubbing over the surface of freshly sugarpasted cakes or plaques to give a smooth surface. It removes any folds or wrinkles in the icing. Ideally, work with two smoothers, one on each side of the cake, for a good finish.

SNAIL TRAIL is a piped edging for cakes or boards, created by piping a series of small teardrops touching each other and slightly overlapping.

SOFT PEAK is a term used to describe royal icing once it has been beaten and stiffened. It means the peaks stand up but droop over at their tips. Royal icing is beaten or thinned to different consistencies depending on the firmness needed for each piping technique.

STAMENS are the central parts of flowers. When making sugar flowers you can buy realistic-looking stamens in a wide variety of colours and sizes. Stamens with stiff threads can be placed into the throat of the flower easily. Those with soft threads can be stiffened with egg white or sugar syrup. Buy white stamens and colour them with food colouring. Curve them over your finger to make them more lifelike.

SUGAR SYRUP is a mixture of sugar and water, heated until the sugar dissolves. It is useful as a glue or stiffener.

SUGARPASTE is a soft pliable paste that is extremely versatile. It can be rolled out to cover cakes, made into plaques or modelled flowers and frills or impressed with patterns. It is easily coloured. Also known as fondant icing or rolled fondant.

TIP is another name for a piping tube.

TURNTABLE is a useful tool for coating cakes with royal icing as it allows you to approach the cake from all sides. If you are not intending to do much royal icing, you can use an upturned cake tin instead.

VEINING TOOLS are stick-like tool with lines that are rolled over icing or paste to give the impression of veins. To make your own, glue a piece of corn husk securely onto a skewer or cake dowel.

Stamens are the delicate central sections of flowers.

Ribbons are useful for trimming board edges.

Piping bags can be bought or made from paper.

EQUIPMENT

Cake decorating is easier and quicker, and you will achieve more professional results, if you have the right tools for the job. All are available from specialist decorating suppliers.

METAL RULER
Used to spread royal icing smoothly and give a perfect surface.

ICING SMOOTHER
Used to smooth the surface of marizpan- or sugarpaste-covered cakes. For best results, have two and use one in each hand.

MODELLING TOOLS
These are bought singly or in kits and are used to draw on, shape, frill or hollow out soft surfaces such as sugarpaste, modelling paste, flower paste or marzipan. From left: anger tool, bone-end tool, Dresden tool and scalpel.

RIBBED ROLLING PIN
Used to create a regular grooved imprint on soft icings. Necessary for smocking on sugarpaste.

CELSTICKS
Available in different sizes for fine modelling work and making sugar flowers. The pointed end is used to open up centres of flowers, while the rounded end is used to soften or frill petal edges.

MINI ROLLING PIN
Available in plastic or wood and used to roll out small amounts of icing or paste for modelling or making sugar flowers.

TURNTABLE
Enables the cake to be turned easily during royal icing or intricate side piping, but a round cake tin can be used instead. Different heights and sizes are available. A tilting turntable is a good investment if you enjoy extension work.

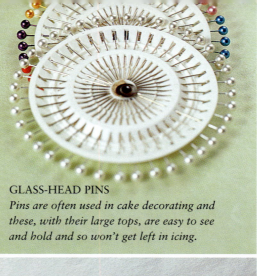

GLASS-HEAD PINS
Pins are often used in cake decorating and these, with their large tops, are easy to see and hold and so won't get left in icing.

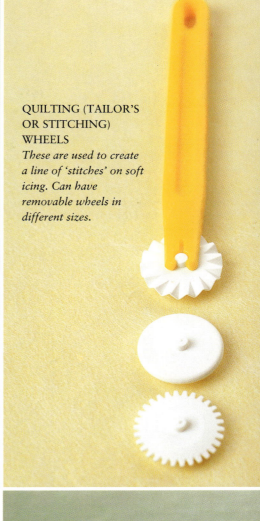

QUILTING (TAILOR'S OR STITCHING) WHEELS
These are used to create a line of 'stitches' on soft icing. Can have removable wheels in different sizes.

RIBBON INSERTION TOOL
Small tool for cutting short, straight holes in soft paste and inserting short lengths of ribbon simultaneously.

VEINING TOOL
Marks veins on leaves when rolled over soft paste or icing. Also creates a textured finish on soft icing.

PALETTE KNIVES
Indispensable equipment for cake decorating. Used to spread icing smoothly or lift small pieces of dried icing such as runouts or lace.

BALL TOOL
Used for modelling or making sugar flowers, for smoothing the edge of petals or rounding the centres.

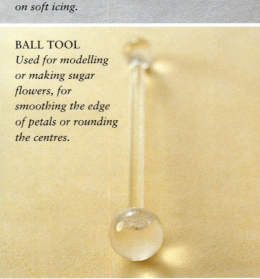

FOAM PAD (CELPAD)
Provides a soft surface for fine modelling and making sugar flowers. Ideal when using a ball tool or plunger cutters. Work over foam when assembling sprays of sugar flowers.

PIPING BAGS
Make your own from baking paper or buy jaconette, nylon, plastic or disposable bags. A screw attachment can be added to the end of a fabric bag to make changing the tube easier.

FLORIST'S WIRE
Covered flexible wire. The thickness is expressed as a gauge number—softer wire has a higher gauge number and is used for smaller pieces (so you would use 33-gauge for small flowers and 24-gauge for larger flowers).

WOODEN CAKE DOWELS
Long thin cylinders of wood with one pointed end, used to support cake tiers but also helpful for modelling.

CRIMPERS
Used to pinch together the edges of soft icing to give a decorative effect. Resemble large tweezers.

PAINT BRUSHES
Textures range from soft to hard and sizes vary. Used to paint with food colouring or dust finished pieces with powder colours.

STAMENS
Used for flower centres or to assemble tiny plunger flowers. Packets of assorted colours and sizes available.

LEAF VEINER
Plastic pads marked with realistic leaf texture for imprinting the surface of soft paste sugar leaves.

PIPING TUBES (TIPS OR NOZZLES)
The lower the number, the finer the tube (with 0000 being the finest). Star, basket weave and leaf tubes also available. Can be made from plastic or metal, with or without screw attachments.

PILLARS
Use solid pillars, or hollow pillars slipped over wooden dowels, to support tiers. A huge variety of shapes and sizes available, mainly in plastic, although these can easily be covered.

LACE MOULD
Leaves a decorative lace impression when rolled or pressed over soft icing.

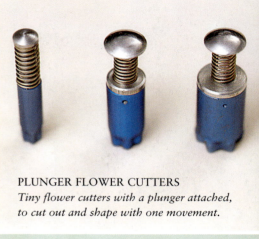

PLUNGER FLOWER CUTTERS
Tiny flower cutters with a plunger attached, to cut out and shape with one movement.

PETAL CUTTERS
Can be bought with one side for cutting petals and the other for cutting leaves (as shown). Available in metal or plastic.

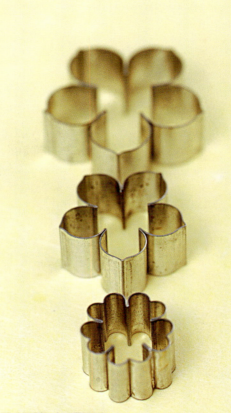

FLOWER CUTTERS
For cutting whole small flower shapes. Available in many different varieties. Graduating in size and available in metal or plastic.

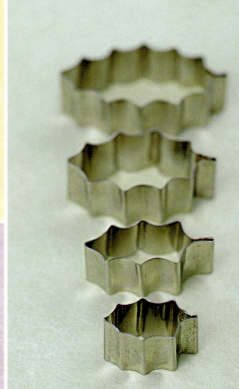

LEAF CUTTERS
Available in many different shapes and variety of leaf. Graduating in size and available in metal or plastic.

DUSTING CHALKS
Non-toxic chalks for colouring dried icing. Scrape the chalk off the sticks and dust over with a brush. Soften the colour by mixing with a little cornflour.

CAKE BASICS

There is no getting away from the fact that, however gorgeous the decorations, your cake will be a disappointment if it doesn't taste as wonderful as it should. Your fruit cake should be moist and grow even better with age, your sponge be light as a tin of feathers and your chocolate mud cake talked about for months to come. This chapter will tell you all you need to know about baking cakes, covering them with sugarpaste or royal icing, putting them on boards and even building them up into layers. The following basic cakes and icings are then suitable for use in any of the recipes in the book, although high-quality sugarpaste, pastillage and flower paste are all available commercially.

BEFORE YOU START

Cake decorating is not difficult, but it is something that requires patience, time and attention to detail.
Like most skills, your results will get better with practice, but, before you attempt to make the recipes
in this book, read the following hints, tips and instructions.

Tins need to be lined
before the cake mixture
is poured in.

Cover plain cake boards
with paper or fabric.

Always read through the recipe from start to finish before you begin. In fact, before you even start to prepare and shop for your ingredients. This is important whatever you are cooking but in cake decorating, which can be time-consuming and require specialist equipment, it is absolutely vital.

HOW TO USE THIS BOOK

The first five chapters in this book will lead you through the basics and techniques of cake decorating. The following five chapters feature decorating ideas for cakes that you can make once you have baked your basic cake, made the basic icings and understood the initial techniques. Because these initial techniques are the same for almost every recipe, we simply state in the method 'cover the cake with marzipan and leave to dry', 'cover the cake with sugarpaste' or 'cover the cake board' etc. You will need to turn back to the specific pages showing these techniques (pages 38–49) if you are just starting off and need fuller instructions. So, when you are covering a cake with royal icing, don't forget that you will need all the equipment associated with that technique, such as an icing ruler and side scraper, as well as the equipment listed in the actual recipe.

On pages 10–13 of this book you will have seen a glossary of cake decorating terms. Do not forget to refer to this whenever you are unsure of an ingredient or instruction.

The cakes in each chapter appear in general order of difficulty, so those at the start of the chapter are easy and suitable for beginners, while those at the end are harder and often employ more advanced techniques. This, of course, is subjective, in that you may have a talent for piping with royal icing but not be able to cover a cake neatly with sugarpaste. If you are a complete beginner it is probably best to start by making some of the gateaux, using cream, chocolate and fruit, before you move on to the iced cakes. Cakes covered with buttercream are also easy for beginners—if you make any mistakes you can simply smooth them over and start again. You can even put buttercream in a piping bag and use to practise your icing techniques.

KITCHEN CUPBOARD

At the beginning of each recipe you will find a list of ingredients (food-stuffs required) and equipment necessary to make the cake photographed. We assume you will have the basics in your kitchen cupboard and so, for reasons of space and practicality, these are not stated in the ingredients or equipment lists. These include icing sugar and cornflour for rolling out icings or modelling or flower paste. (A hint for using these: make a bag from muslin, or even a clean stocking, and fill with icing sugar or cornflour, then use it as a sort of 'powder puff' for dusting surfaces.) You will obviously need a rolling pin and a selection of greaseproof, non-stick baking and parchment papers for lining and tracing templates and plastic wrap for preventing icing drying out. You will need mixing bowls, cake tins, sharp knives and, if you are going to do much decorating, you will probably also want to buy a scalpel and a kit of tools. If there is any equipment with which you are unfamiliar, turn to the equipment pictures on pages 14–17. You may find that the particular item is sold under a different name where you live.

For many recipes you will need paper piping bags. Instructions on how to make these are given on page 63. Often you can just snip the end off the paper piping bag but for more intricate piping with royal icing you will require piping tubes (also called tips or nozzles). You will find these tubes listed in the equipment list for each recipe, after the ingredients, and you will probably need to buy a few in graduating sizes.

Also listed are food colourings. For many cakes the colouring will be completely subjective and the colours we have listed are merely a guide for making the cake as pictured. For other cakes, such as the Christmas painted cakes, you may need to follow the colourings more exactly and perhaps have several shades of each colour available for giving a natural result. This is why the ingredients list may state 'greens and browns' under food colourings—you may need a couple of shades of each. Once again, read through the recipe first and see what is required.

TIMING

It cannot be stressed too often that good cake decorators need to be organised people. They need to have read the recipe from start to finish and checked they have all the equipment needed. If several cake tins are needed, these could be borrowed and special shaped tins can be hired from decorating shops. Provision needs to be made for baking several cakes that may not all fit in the oven at the same time. And remember, while sponge cakes are fairly quick to prepare and bake, fruit cakes or large chocolate cakes can take quite a bit of time both in the mixing and in the baking.

Timing is crucial to cake decorating. The basic cake is usually baked, allowed to cool and then covered with both marzipan and sugarpaste or royal icing. It may then need to be left to dry for three days before the next stage of decorating. If a cake is then to be royal iced, it has to be left to dry between each coat. So, as you can see, the whole process can take several days and a lot of organisation.

THE BASIC CAKE

You will find the cake size required for the recipe listed first on the ingredients list. This will say 'two 30 cm round cakes' or '18 cm square cake' but will not specify what type of cake to use because for most recipes you can use any of the basic cakes you like. The recipes for the basic cakes will tell you how to make all the cakes in all the sizes listed in the recipes. However, even if you would like to have chocolate mud cake every time, you do need to think about a few factors before you choose the basic cake.

Most wedding cakes are traditionally fruit cakes. This is for historical reasons (the dark fruit cake was originally known as the 'groom's cake' and was cut up and sent home with the guests, while the 'bride's cake' would be lighter and crumbled over her head to ensure fertility and good luck) but there are also practical reasons. Fruit cakes store well (in fact, their flavour matures with age) and this is important for wedding cakes for several reasons. Firstly, wedding cakes can take a long time to decorate and so need to be baked well in advance and left to sit for a long time while icings dry. Secondly, some people still like to save the top tier of the cake to celebrate the christening of a first child or their first wedding anniversary. Thirdly, if you are making a tiered cake using dowels and pillars you will find it needs to be fairly dense and heavy and this usually means a fruit cake is best. If you love chocolate cake and want to make it the base for your wedding cake, you need to decorate it much closer to the time of the wedding and you won't be able to store it for as long. A compromise is to make the top tier fruit cake and the other tiers in your other choice.

It is traditional to make Christmas cakes from fruit cakes but christening and birthday cakes can be just about anything you want, as long as you're not intending to store them for too long. Storage times can be found at the end of all the basic cake recipes.

Some of the modelled and sculpted cakes (like the piano on page 172 or the dream castle on page 171) do have to be made from Madeira cakes as they need to be firm and stand up well. Many of the children's cakes are not suitable for fruit cakes... fruit cake and buttercream is a clash of flavours. The introductory notes to the recipes will guide you if any specific cake should be used.

If you are using an unusual shaped tin and aren't sure what quantity of the basic cake mixture to make, you can measure the volume of the tin using water. Fill a 20 cm (8 inch) round tin with water and then pour into the shaped tin until filled. That way you can calculate how many quantities of the basic 20 cm mixture are needed to fill the tin.

SERVING QUANTITIES

We haven't put serving quantities on our cake recipes because these can be so subjective. Obviously, the richer the cake, the smaller the slice that will be wanted. But as a rough guide, a fruit cake is usually cut into small fingers, about 2.5 cm (1 inch). So a basic 23 cm (9 inch) cake will serve around 10 people, one 18 x 25 cm (7 x 10 inch) oval cake will serve 20–30 people and a two-tiered cake (one 30 cm and one 15 cm round cake) will serve 70–80 people as a wedding cake. If you're feeding small children, you will hopefully be able to serve more with that size cake.

If you particularly like one of the smaller cakes, or are running on a tight budget for either finances or time, you can make the 'real' cake and also make a 'kitchen' cake. This is a larger cake that is simply covered with marzipan and sugarpaste or royal icing (to match the 'real' cake) and can be cut behind the scenes and brought out on plates after the 'real' cake is cut. This is useful for large gatherings.

ADAPTING THE RECIPES

Cake decorating is an art, a talent and a passion and those who are passionate about their topic will have the experience and equipment to adapt most of these recipes in any way they choose. So, cakes that are royal iced can be covered with sugarpaste if you find it easier, colours of icings can change and modelling figures can change their features and clothes and be personalised. In fact, you will probably find that the more personal you can make your cakes, the better.

Marzipan is used underneath both royal icing and sugarpaste.

Piping tubes come in a wide variety of sizes. The smaller the tube, the finer the piping work will be.

Sugar flowers and leaves are not difficult to make.

BASIC CAKE RECIPES

RICH FRUIT CAKE

1   Mix together the dried fruit, chopped glacé cherries and brandy, cover and leave for several hours or until absorbed. Preheat the oven to 140°C (275°F/Gas 1). Lightly grease the tin and line the base and side, following the instructions on page 38.

2   Beat the butter and sugar until combined. Gradually add the eggs, beating well after each addition. Transfer to a large bowl and stir in the soaked fruit alternately with the sifted flour, mixed spice and chopped almonds. Spoon into the tin and smooth the surface. Tap the tin on the work surface to remove any air bubbles in the mixture.

3   Following the instructions on page 39, wrap a folded piece of newspaper around the outside of the tin and tie securely with string. Place the tin on several sheets of neatly folded newspaper and bake for the time stated below. Using the chart as a guide, test the cake towards the end of the cooking time. A skewer inserted into the centre of the cake should come out clean. After baking, you can drizzle the cake with a little extra brandy if you like. Cover the cake with non-stick baking paper and foil and leave to cool in the tin.

STORAGE When cold, remove from the tin and wrap tightly in plastic wrap. Keep in a cool, dry place or fridge for 6 months, or freeze for 3 years.

| Round tin | 15 cm/6 in | 18 cm/7 in | 20 cm/8 in | 22 cm/9 in | 25 cm/10 in | 28 cm/11 in | 30 cm/12 in | |
Square tin	12 cm/5 in	15 cm/6 in	18 cm/7 in	20 cm/8 in	22 cm/9 in	25 cm/10 in	28 cm/11 in	30 cm/12 in
Mixed dried fruit	440 g/14 oz	625 g/1¼ lb	875 g/1¾ lb	1.1 kg/2¼ lb	1.5 kg/3 lb	1.8 kg/3¾ lb	2.2 kg/4½ lb	2.6 kg/5¼ lb
Glacé cherries	45 g/1½ oz	60 g/2 oz	90 g/3 oz	100 g/3½ oz	150 g/5 oz	200 g/6½ oz	250 g/8 oz	280 g/9 oz
Brandy	40 ml/1½ fl oz	40 ml/1½ fl oz	40 ml/1½ fl oz	60 ml/2 fl oz	60 ml/2 fl oz	80 ml/2¾ fl oz	120 ml/4 fl oz	160 ml/5 fl oz
Butter, softened	100 g/3½ oz	150 g/5 oz	200 g/6½ oz	280 g/9 oz	410 g/13 oz	470 g/15 oz	560 g/1 lb 2 oz	690 g/1 lb 6 oz
Muscovado sugar	100 g/3½ oz	150 g/5 oz	200 g/6½ oz	280 g/9 oz	410 g/13 oz	470 g/15 oz	560 g/1 lb 2 oz	690 g/1 lb 6 oz
Eggs	2	3	3	4	6	8	8	10
Plain flour	125 g/4 oz	185 g/6 oz	250 g/8 oz	375 g/12 oz	500 g/1 lb	625 g/1¼ lb	750 g/1½ lb	875 g/1 lb 13 oz
Mixed spice	¾ tsp	1 tsp	1½ tsp	2 tsp	3 tsp	4 tsp	4 tsp	5 tsp
Blanched almonds	25 g/¾ oz	30 g/1 oz	45 g/1½ oz	60 g/2 oz	90 g/3 oz	125 g/4 oz	160 g/5 oz	200 g/6½ oz
Baking time	2 hrs	2–2¼ hrs	3–3¼ hrs	3½–3¾ hrs	4 hrs	4½–4¾ hrs	5–5¼ hrs	5¼–5½ hrs

LIGHT FRUIT CAKE

1   Mix together the dried fruit, mixed peel, apricots and brandy, cover and leave for several hours or until absorbed. Preheat the oven to 140°C (275°F/Gas 1). Lightly grease the tin and line the base and side, following the instructions on page 38.

2   Beat the butter and sugar until combined. Gradually add the eggs, beating well after each addition. The mixture may look curdled at this stage. Transfer to a large bowl and stir in the sifted flour and spice. Stir in the soaked fruit. Spoon into the tin and smooth the surface. Tap the tin on the work surface to remove any air bubbles in the mixture.

3   Following the instructions on page 39, wrap a folded piece of newspaper around the outside of the tin and tie securely with string. Place the tin on several sheets of neatly folded newspaper and bake for the time stated below. Using the chart as a guide, test the cake towards the end of the cooking time. A skewer inserted into the centre of the cake should come out clean. After baking you can drizzle the cake with a little extra brandy if you like. Cover the cake with non-stick baking paper and foil and leave to cool in the tin.

STORAGE When cold, remove from the tin, wrap in plastic and store in an airtight container in the fridge for 2 weeks, or freeze for a year.

Round tin	15 cm/6 in	18 cm/7 in	20 cm/8 in	22 cm/9 in	25 cm/10 in	28 cm/11 in	30 cm/12 in	
Square tin	12 cm/5 in	15 cm/6 in	18 cm/7 in	20 cm/8 in	22 cm/9 in	25 cm/10 in	28 cm/11 in	30 cm/12 in
Mixed dried fruit	250 g/8 oz	440 g/14 oz	500 g/1 lb	750 g/1$^{1}/_{2}$ lb	1 kg/2 lb	1.25 kg/2$^{1}/_{2}$ lb	1.5 kg/3 lb	1.75 kg/3$^{1}/_{2}$ lb
Mixed peel	15 g/$^{1}/_{2}$ oz	30 g/1 oz	30 g/1 oz	60 g/2 oz	90 g/3 oz	125 g/4 oz	140 g/4$^{1}/_{2}$ oz	150 g/5 oz
Dried apricots, chopped	60 g/2 oz	60 g/2 oz	125 g/4 oz	185 g/6 oz	250 g/8 oz	315 g/10 oz	370 g/12 oz	435 g/14 oz
Brandy	40 ml/1$^{1}/_{2}$ fl oz	40 ml/1$^{1}/_{2}$ fl oz	40 ml/1$^{1}/_{2}$ fl oz	60 ml/2 fl oz	60 ml/2 fl oz	80 ml/2$^{3}/_{4}$ fl oz	120 ml/4 fl oz	160 ml/5 fl oz
Butter, softened	160 g/5$^{1}/_{2}$ oz	250 g/8 oz	315 g/10 oz	440 g/14 oz	525 g/1lb 1oz	625 g/1$^{1}/_{4}$ lb	880 g/1 lb 13 oz	1 kg/2 lb
Light brown or muscovado sugar	160 g/5$^{1}/_{2}$ oz	250 g/8 oz	315 g/10 oz	440 g/14 oz	525 g/1lb 1oz	625 g/1$^{1}/_{4}$ lb	880 g/1 lb 13 oz	1 kg/2 lb
Eggs	2	4	4	5	6	7	10	11
Plain flour	185 g/6 oz	315 g/10 oz	375 g/12 oz	500 g/1 lb	625 g/1$^{1}/_{4}$ lb	750 g/1$^{1}/_{4}$ lb	1 kg/2 lb	1.12 kg/2 lb 4 oz
Mixed spice	1 tsp	1$^{1}/_{2}$ tsp	2 tsp	3 tsp	4 tsp	5 tsp	6 tsp	7 tsp
Baking time	2 hrs 5 mins	2–2$^{1}/_{4}$ hrs	3–3$^{1}/_{2}$ hrs	3$^{1}/_{2}$–3$^{3}/_{4}$ hrs	4 hrs	4$^{1}/_{2}$–4$^{3}/_{4}$ hrs	5–5$^{1}/_{4}$ hrs	5$^{1}/_{4}$ hrs–5$^{1}/_{2}$ hrs

BASIC CAKE RECIPES

MADEIRA CAKE

1 Preheat the oven to 160°C (315°F/Gas 2–3). Grease the tin and line the base, following the instructions on page 38. Beat the butter and sugar until light and fluffy. Add the eggs one at a time, beating well after each addition. Transfer to a large bowl and fold in the sifted flours. Stir in the milk.

2 Spoon into the tin and smooth the surface. Bake for the time stated below. Using the chart as a guide, test the cake towards the end of the cooking time. A skewer inserted into the centre of the cake should come out clean. After baking, leave to cool in the tin for at least 5 minutes, before turning out onto a wire rack to cool.

STORAGE Can be kept in an airtight container in the fridge for 2 weeks, or frozen for 2 months.

| Round tin | 15 cm/6 in | 18 cm/7 in | 20 cm/8 in | 22 cm/9 in | 25 cm/10 in | 28 cm/11 in | 30 cm/12 in | |
Square tin	12 cm/5 in	15 cm/6 in	18 cm/7 in	20 cm/8 in	22 cm/9 in	25 cm/10 in	28 cm/11 in	30 cm/12 in
Butter, softened	135 g/4½ oz	200 g/6½ oz	250 g/8 oz	310 g/11 oz	400 g/13 oz	610 g/1¼ lb	715 g/1 lb 7 oz	810 g/1 lb 10 oz
Caster sugar	135 g/4½ oz	200 g/6½ oz	250 g/8 oz	310 g/11 oz	400 g/13 oz	610 g/1¼ lb	715 g/1 lb 7 oz	810 g/1 lb 10 oz
Eggs	2	4	5	6	8	9	10	11
Plain flour	110 g/3½ oz	150 g/5 oz	185 g/6 oz	230 g/7 oz	300 g/10 oz	460 g/14 oz	535 g/1 lb 1 oz	610 g/1¼ lb
Self-raising flour	35 g/1 oz	50 g/1½ oz	60 g/2 oz	75 g/2½ oz	95 g/3 oz	150 g/5 oz	175 g/6 oz	200 g/6½ oz
Milk	2 tsp	3 tsp	1 tab	6 tsp	2 tabs	2½ tabs	3½ tabs	4½ tabs
Baking time	1 hr	1¼ hrs	1 hr 25 mins	1 hr 35 mins	1 hr 40 mins	1 hr 55 mins	2 hrs 10 mins	2 hrs 20 mins

GLACE FRUIT CAKE

1   Preheat the oven to 180°C (350°F/Gas 4). Lightly grease and line the tin, following the instructions on page 38.

2   Mix the glacé fruits (use light fruit, such as oranges, pears, apricots and pineapple), mixed peel and chopped almonds and toss with 30 g (1 oz) of the flour, to keep the fruit separate. Sift together the remaining flours. Beat the butter, orange rind, lemon rind and sugar until light and fluffy. Gradually add the eggs, beating well after each addition.

3   Transfer to a large bowl and stir in the flour alternately with the fruit mixture and the sherry. Spoon into the tin and smooth the surface. Tap the tin on the work surface to remove any air bubbles in the mixture. Bake for 30 minutes, then reduce the heat to 160°C (315°F/Gas 2–3) and bake for the time stated in the chart below. Using the chart as a guide, test the cake towards the end of the cooking time. A skewer inserted into the centre of the cake should come out clean. Leave the cake to cool in the tin.

STORAGE Refrigerate the cold cake in an airtight container for 2 weeks, or freeze for 2 months.

Round tin	15 cm/6 in	18 cm/7 in	20 cm/8 in	22 cm/9 in	25 cm/10 in	28 cm/11 in	30 cm/12 in
Square tin	12 cm/5 in	15 cm/6 in	18 cm/7 in	20 cm/8 in	22 cm/9 in	25 cm/10 in	28 cm/11 in
Light-coloured glacé fruit	340 g/11 oz	540 g/1 lb 1 oz	600 g/1¼ lb	675 g/1 lb 6 oz	840 g/1¾ lb	1.05 kg/2 lb 1 oz	1.4 kg/2 lb 13 oz
Mixed peel	30 g/1 oz	45 g/1½ oz	50 g/1½ oz	55 g/2 oz	70 g/2½ oz	100 g/3½ oz	135 g/4½ oz
Blanched almonds	40 g/1½ oz	60 g/2 oz	70 g/2½ oz	80 g/3 oz	100 g/3½ oz	160 g/5½ oz	200 g/6½ oz
Plain flour	115 g/4 oz	185 g/6 oz	200 g/6½ oz	225 g/7 oz	280 g/9 oz	550 g/1 lb 2 oz	670 g/1 lb 6 oz
Self-raising flour	40 g/1½ oz	60 g/2 oz	70 g/2½ oz	80 g/3 oz	100 g/3½ oz	160 g/5½ oz	200 g/6½ oz
Butter, softened	125 g/4 oz	190 g/6 oz	220 g/7 oz	250 g/8 oz	310 g/11 oz	500 g/1 lb	625 g/1¼ lb
Grated orange rind	1½ tsp	2 tsp	3 tsp	3 tsp	4 tsp	6 tsp	7½ tsp
Grated lemon rind	1½ tsp	2 tsp	3 tsp	3 tsp	4 tsp	6 tsp	7½ tsp
Caster sugar	125 g/4 oz	190 g/6 oz	220 g/7 oz	250 g/8 oz	310 g/11 oz	500 g/1 lb	625 g/1¼ lb
Eggs	2	3	4	5	6	8	10
Sweet sherry	30 ml/1 fl oz	40 ml/1½ fl oz	50 ml/1½ fl oz	60 ml/2 fl oz	80 ml/2¾ fl oz	110 ml/3½ fl oz	140 ml/5 fl oz
Baking time after reducing heat	1 hr 20 mins	1½ hrs	1 hr 40 mins	1¾ hrs	1 hr 50 mins	1 hr 55 mins	2 hrs

BASIC CAKE RECIPES

CLASSIC SPONGE

1   Preheat the oven to 180°C (350°F/Gas 4). Brush two tins with melted butter (the recipe makes enough for two sponges). Line the bases with non-stick baking paper, then grease the paper. Dust the tins lightly with a little extra flour, shaking off the excess. Sift the flours three times onto paper.

2   Beat the eggs in a large bowl with electric beaters for 7 minutes or until thick and pale. Gradually add the sugar, beating well after each addition. Using a metal spoon, fold in the sifted flour and boiling water. Spread evenly into the tins and bake for 25 minutes or until the sponge is lightly golden and shrinks slightly from the side of the tin. Leave the cakes in their tins for 5 minutes before turning onto wire cake racks to cool.

STORAGE A classic sponge should always be eaten on the day it is baked. It will not store.

2 x round tins	22 cm/9 in
2 x square tins	20 cm/8 in
Plain flour	75 g/2½ oz
Self-raising flour	150 g/5 oz
Eggs	6
Caster sugar	220 g/7 oz
Boiling water	8 tsp
Baking time	25 mins

GENOISE SPONGE

1   Preheat the oven to 180°C (350°F/Gas 4). Brush two tins with melted butter. Line the bases with non-stick baking paper, then grease the paper. Dust the tins lightly with a little extra flour, shaking off the excess. Sift the flour three times onto paper.

2   Mix the eggs and sugar in a large heatproof bowl. Place the bowl over a pan of simmering water and beat with electric beaters for 8 minutes or until the mixture is thick and fluffy and the beaters will leave a ribbon that doesn't sink immediately. Remove from the heat and beat for 3 minutes or until slightly cooled.

3   Add the cooled butter and sifted flour and, using a large metal spoon, fold in quickly and lightly until just combined. Spread into the two tins and bake for the time stated below or until the sponge is lightly golden and shrinks slightly from the side of the tin. Leave the cakes in their tins for 5 minutes before turning out onto wire cake racks to cool.

STORAGE Store in an airtight container in the fridge for 1 day.

VARIATIONS For a chocolate sponge, remove 40 g of the flour and use 40 g cocoa powder instead. For mocha, add 1 tablespoon instant coffee and 2 teaspoons boiling water with the melted butter.

| 2 x round tins | 20 cm/8 in | 22 cm/9 in |
2 x square tins	18 cm/7 in	20 cm/8 in
Plain flour	225 g/7 oz	300 g/10 oz
Eggs.	6	8
Caster sugar	165 g/5½ oz	220 g/7 oz
Butter, melted	75 g/2½ oz	100 g/3½ oz
Baking time	15–20 mins	25 mins

BASIC CAKE RECIPES

COCONUT CAKE

1   Preheat the oven to 180°C (350°F/Gas 4). Lightly grease the tin and line the base with non-stick baking paper, following the instructions on page 38. Beat the butter, sugar and coconut essence until light and fluffy. Add the eggs one at a time, beating well after each addition. Transfer to large bowl and fold in the combined coconut and sifted flour alternately with spoonfuls of buttermilk.

2   Spoon the mixture into the tin and smooth the surface. Bake for the time stated below. Using the chart as a guide, test the cake towards the end of the cooking time. A skewer inserted into the centre of the cake should come out clean. Leave the cake in the tin for at least 5 minutes before turning out onto a wire rack to cool.

STORAGE Keep in an airtight container in the fridge for a week or freeze for 2 months.

| Round tin | 15 cm/6 in | 18 cm/7 in | 20 cm/8 in | 22 cm/9 in | 25 cm/10 in | 28 cm/11 in | 30 cm/12 in | |
Square tin	12 cm/5 in	15 cm/6 in	18 cm/7 in	20 cm/8 in	22 cm/9 in	25 cm/10 in	28 cm/11 in	30 cm/12 in
Butter, softened	75 g/2¹/₂ oz	125 g/4 oz	200 g/6¹/₂ oz	220 g/7 oz	250 g/8 oz	375 g/12 oz	440 g/14 oz	515 g/1 lb
Caster sugar	110 g/3¹/₂ oz	180 g/6 oz	300 g/10 oz	325 g/11 oz	365 g/12 oz	550 g/1 lb 2 oz	650 g/1 lb 5 oz	760 g/1¹/₂ lb
Coconut essence	¹/₂ tsp	³/₄ tsp	³/₄ tsp	1 tsp	1 tsp	2¹/₂ tsp	3 tsp	3¹/₂ tsp
Eggs	1	2	2	3	4	6	6	7
Desiccated coconut	45 g/1¹/₂ oz	75 g/2¹/₂ oz	120 g/4 oz	130 g/4 oz	150 g/5 oz	225 g/7 oz	260 g/9 oz	300 g/10 oz
Self-raising flour	125 g/4 oz	210 g/7 oz	335 g/11 oz	360 g/12 oz	415 g/13 oz	625 g/1 lb 5 oz	720 g/1¹/₂ lb	850 g/1³/₄ lb
Buttermilk	125 ml/4 fl oz	210 ml/7 fl oz	335 ml/11 fl oz	360 ml/12 fl oz	415 ml/13 fl oz	625 ml/21 fl oz	720 ml/23 fl oz	850 ml/27 fl oz
Baking time	50 mins	1 hr	1 hr 10 mins	1¹/₄ hrs	1 hr 20 mins	1 hr 25 mins	1 hr 35 mins	1³/₄ hrs

CARROT CAKE

1   Preheat the oven to 170°C (325°F/Gas 3). Grease the tin and line the base, following the instructions on page 38. Sift together the flours, spices and bicarbonate of soda into a large bowl and make a well in the centre. Whisk together the oil, sugar, eggs and golden syrup. Gradually pour into the well, stirring until combined. Stir in the carrot and chopped nuts.

2   Spoon the mixture into the tin and smooth the surface. Bake for the time stated below. Using the chart as a guide, test the cake towards the end of the cooking time. A skewer inserted into the centre should come out clean. Leave the cake to cool in the tin for at least 15 minutes before turning onto a wire cake rack to cool.

STORAGE Keep in an airtight container in the fridge for a week or freeze for 2 months.

| Round tin | 15 cm/6 in | 18 cm/7 in | 20 cm/8 in | 22 cm/9 in | 25 cm/10 in | 28 cm/11 in | 30 cm/12 in | |
Square tin	12 cm/5 in	15 cm/6 in	18 cm/7 in	20 cm/8 in	22 cm/9 in	25 cm/10 in	28 cm/11 in	30 cm/12 in
Self-raising flour	90 g/3 oz	125 g/4 oz	150 g/5 oz	170 g/5½ oz	250 g/8 oz	350 g/11 oz	400 g/13 oz	450 g/14 oz
Plain flour	90 g/3 oz	125 g/4 oz	150 g/5 oz	170 g/5½ oz	250 g/8 oz	350 g/11 oz	400 g/13 oz	450 g/14 oz
Ground cinnamon	1 tsp	1 tsp	1¾ tsp	2 tsp	2¼ tsp	3 tsp	4 tsp	4¼ tsp
Ground ginger	½ tsp	¾ tsp	¾ tsp	1 tsp	1¼ tsp	2 tsp	2¼ tsp	2¾ tsp
Ground nutmeg	¼ tsp	¼ tsp	½ tsp	½ tsp	¾ tsp	1 tsp	1¼ tsp	1½ tsp
Bicarbonate of soda	½ tsp	½ tsp	¾ tsp	1 tsp	1 tsp	1½ tsp	2 tsp	2 tsp
Vegetable oil	100 ml/3½ fl oz	120 ml/4 fl oz	175 ml/6 fl oz	200 ml/6½ fl oz	250 ml/8 fl oz	400 ml/13 fl oz	485 ml/15 fl oz	520 ml/17 fl oz
Brown sugar	115 g/4 oz	140 g/4½ oz	200 g/6½ oz	225 g/7 oz	280 g/9 oz	460 g/15 oz	500 g/1 lb	600 g/1¼ lb
Eggs	2	3	4	4	5	6	8	8
Golden syrup	60 ml/2 fl oz	70 ml/2½ fl oz	100 ml/3½ fl oz	125 ml/4 fl oz	140 ml/5 fl oz	250 ml/8 fl oz	265 ml/8½ fl oz	320 ml/10 fl oz
Grated carrot	250 g/8 oz	315 g/10 oz	450 g/14 oz	500 g/1 lb	620 g/1¼ lb	1 kg/2 lb	1.1 kg/2 lb 3 oz	1.3 kg/2 lb 10 oz
Pecans or walnuts	30 g/1 oz	50 g/1½ oz	50 g/1½ oz	60 g/2 oz	70 g/2½ oz	90 g/3 oz	110 g/3½ oz	125 g/4 oz
Baking time	1 hr 20 mins	1½ hrs	1 hr 35 mins	1¾ hrs	1 hr 55 mins	2 hrs 10 mins	2 hrs 20 mins	2½ hrs

BASIC CAKE RECIPES

CHOCOLATE CAKE

1   Preheat the oven to 180°C (350°F/Gas 4). Lightly grease the tin and line the base, following the instructions on page 38. Beat the butter, sugar and vanilla extract with electric beaters until light and fluffy. Add the eggs one at a time, beating well after each addition. Transfer to large bowl and fold in the combined sifted flours, bicarbonate of soda and cocoa powder alternately with the buttermilk.

2   Spoon into the tin and smooth the surface. Bake for the time stated below. Using the chart as a guide, test the cake towards the end of the cooking time. A skewer inserted into the centre should come out clean. Leave the cake to cool in the tin for at least 5 minutes before turning onto a wire cake rack to cool completely.

STORAGE Keep in an airtight container in the fridge for a week or freeze for 2 months.

Round tin	15 cm/6 in	18 cm/7 in	20 cm/8 in	22 cm/9 in	25 cm/10 in	28 cm/11 in	30 cm/12 in	
Square tin	12 cm/5 in	15 cm/6 in	18 cm/7 in	20 cm/8 in	22 cm/9 in	25 cm/10 in	28 cm/11 in	30 cm/12 in
Butter, softened	90 g/3 oz	140 g/5 oz	165 g/5^1/2 oz	185 g/6 oz	225 g/7 oz	325 g/11 oz	465 g/15 oz	560 g/1 lb 2 oz
Caster sugar	165 g/5^1/2 oz	250 g/8 oz	300 g/10 oz	330 g/11 oz	410 g/13 oz	570 g/1 lb 2 oz	660 g/1 lb 5 oz	825 g/1 lb 11 oz
Vanilla extract	1 tsp	1^1/2 tsp	2 tsp	2^1/2 tsp	3 tsp	4 tsp	5 tsp	6 tsp
Eggs	2	2	3	3	4	5	6	7
Self-raising flour	40 g/1^1/2 oz	55 g/2 oz	65 g/2 oz	75 g/2^1/2 oz	95 g/3 oz	125 g/4 oz	150 g/5 oz	190 g/6 oz
Plain flour	115 g/4 oz	165 g/5^1/2 oz	200 g/6^1/2 oz	225 g/7 oz	280 g/9 oz	350 g/11 oz	445 g/14 oz	560 g/1 lb 2 oz
Bicarbonate of soda	^{1}/2 tsp	^{3}/4 tsp	1 tsp	1^1/2 tsp	1^3/4 tsp	2^1/4 tsp	2^1/2 tsp	2^3/4 tsp
Cocoa powder	40 g/1^1/2 oz	60 g/2 oz	70 g/2^1/2 oz	80 g/2^3/4 oz	90 g/3 oz	110 g/3^1/2 oz	120 g/4 oz	160 g/5 oz
Buttermilk	140 ml/5 fl oz	210 ml/7 fl oz	250 ml/8 fl oz	280 ml/9 fl oz	350 ml/11 fl oz	500 ml/16 fl oz	560 ml/18 fl oz	700 ml/22 fl oz
Baking time	50 mins	1 hr	1 hr 10 mins	1^1/4 hrs	1 hr 20 mins	1^1/2 hrs	1 hr 40 mins	1 hr 50 mins

CHOCOLATE MUD CAKE

1   Preheat the oven to 160°C (315°F/Gas 2–3). Grease the tin and line with a collar that extends 2 cm (3/4 inch) above the height of the tin, following the instructions on page 38. Put the butter, chocolate and coffee in a pan with the water and stir over low heat until melted, then remove from the heat.

2   Sift the flours, cocoa and bicarbonate of soda into a large bowl. Stir in the sugar and make a well in the centre. Add the combined eggs, oil and buttermilk and the chocolate mixture, stirring with a large spoon until completely combined.

3   Pour the mixture into the tin and bake for the time stated below. Using the chart as a guide, test the cake towards the end of the cooking time. A skewer inserted into the centre should come out clean, though it may be a little sticky. Leave the cake in the tin until cold.

STORAGE Keep in an airtight container in the fridge for up to 3 weeks or freeze for 2 months.

| Round tin | 15 cm/6 in | 18 cm/7 in | 20 cm/8 in | 22 cm/9 in | 25 cm/10 in | 28 cm/11 in | 30 cm/12 in | |
Square tin	12 cm/5 in	15 cm/6 in	18 cm/7 in	20 cm/8 in	22 cm/9 in	25 cm/10 in	28 cm/11 in	30 cm/12 in
Butter	110 g/3½ oz	130 g/4 oz	190 g/6 oz	220 g/7 oz	250 g/8 oz	400 g/13 oz	440 g/14 oz	525 g/1 lb 1 oz
Dark chocolate	110 g/3½ oz	130 g/4 oz	190 g/6 oz	220 g/7 oz	250 g/8 oz	400 g/13 oz	440 g/14 oz	525 g/1 lb 1 oz
Instant coffee	2 tsp	3 tsp	4 tsp	6 tsp	8 tsp	12 tsp	2½ tabs	2½ tabs
Water	80 ml/2¾ fl oz	95 ml/3 fl oz	140 ml/5 fl oz	160 ml/5½ fl oz	180 ml/6 fl oz	290 ml/10 fl oz	320 ml/11 fl oz	385 ml/12 fl oz
Self-raising flour	65 g/2 oz	75 g/2½ oz	110 g/3½ oz	125 g/4 oz	150 g/5 oz	250 g/8 oz	280 g/9 oz	330 g/11 oz
Plain flour	65 g/2 oz	75 g/2½ oz	110 g/3½ oz	125 g/4 oz	150 g/5 oz	250 g/8 oz	280 g/9 oz	330 g/11 oz
Cocoa powder	25 g/1 oz	30 g/1 oz	40 g/1½ oz	50 g/1½ oz	60 g/2 oz	90 g/3 oz	110 g/3½ oz	125 g/4 oz
Bicarbonate of soda	¼ tsp	¼ tsp	¼ tsp	½ tsp	½ tsp	¾ tsp	1 tsp	1 tsp
Caster sugar	240 g/8 oz	300 g/10 oz	420 g/14 oz	480 g/15 oz	550 g/1 lb 2 oz	860 g/1¾ lb	960 g/2 lb	1.2 kg/2 lb 6 oz
Eggs	2	2	3	4	4	7	8	9
Vegetable oil	4 tsp	5 tsp	6 tsp	7 tsp	8 tsp	2½ tabs	3 tabs	3½ tabs
Buttermilk	60 ml/2 fl oz	70 ml/2½ fl oz	95 ml/3 fl oz	110 ml/3½ fl oz	125 ml/4 fl oz	200 ml/6½ fl oz	220 ml/7 fl oz	270 ml/9 fl oz
Baking time	1 hr 10 mins	1½ hrs	1 hr 40 mins	1¾ hrs	1 hr 50 mins	2 hrs 25 mins	2 hrs 40 mins	2 hrs 55 mins

BASIC ICING RECIPES

MARZIPAN

750 g (1¹/2 lb) icing sugar
200 g (6¹/2 oz) ground almonds
2 egg yolks
2 tablespoons sweet sherry
2 teaspoons glycerine
1 tablespoon lemon juice
few drops almond essence

1   Sift the icing sugar into a large bowl, then remove a cupful for use when kneading. Stir the almonds into the icing sugar and make a well in the centre. Mix together the egg yolks, sherry, glycerine, lemon juice and almond essence and pour into the well. Stir with a knife until stiff.

2   Use the reserved icing sugar to dust a work surface and knead the marzipan for 3–5 minutes, adding more icing sugar as necessary to prevent sticking. Knead until the marzipan is smooth and pliable.

3   Use immediately or wrap in plastic and store in an airtight container in a cool place (not the fridge) for up to 3 days. Roll out on a surface dusted with icing sugar to use.

Makes 1 kg (2 lb)

ROYAL ICING

7 egg whites, or 45 g (1¹/2 oz) albumen powder
    dissolved in 315 ml (10 fl oz) water and strained
1.75 kg (3¹/2 lb) icing sugar, sifted

1   Put the egg white or albumen in the bowl of an electric mixer (see Note). Stir in the sugar. Beat on slow speed for 4 minutes for 'soft peak' or 5 minutes for 'firm peak'.

2   'Soft peak' will be the first consistency reached and is used for coating cakes and piping with tubes. When lifted from the bowl with a spatula the peak will stand up but droop over slightly at the tip.

3   For 'firm peak' icing, continue beating until the icing has a definite peak that will not fall when shaken.

Makes enough to cover a 22 cm (9 inch) cake, make decorations and cover a board.

NOTE For large quantities, use a mixer. To make royal icing by hand, prepare a smaller quantity: use 2 egg whites or dissolve 30 g (1 oz) albumen powder in 4 tablespoons water, then strain. Place in a large bowl and add 500 g (1 lb) icing sugar, a tablespoon at a time, beating constantly. It will take about 20 minutes to reach soft-peak consistency.

SUGARPASTE

5 teaspoons gelatine
125 ml (4 fl oz) liquid glucose
1 tablespoon glycerine
1 kg (2 lb) icing sugar

1   Sprinkle the gelatine over 3 table-spoons water in a small bowl. Leave until the gelatine is spongy. Place the bowl in a pan of hot water and stir until the gelatine has dissolved. Add the glucose and the glycerine and stir until melted. Cool for 1 minute.

2   Sift the icing sugar into a large bowl, then remove a cupful for use when kneading. Make a well in the centre of the icing sugar and pour in the gelatine mixture. Combine with a wooden spoon, then use a dry hand to knead until the icing has a dough-like texture, adding a little of the reserved icing sugar if necessary. Turn out onto a work surface dusted with icing sugar and knead until smooth and pliable, adding more icing sugar as necessary to prevent sticking.

3   Use immediately, or wrap in plastic and store in an airtight container in a cool place (not the fridge) for up to 3 days. Roll out on a surface dusted with icing sugar to use.

Makes 1 kg (2 lb)

CHOCOLATE SUGARPASTE

500 g (1 lb) good-quality chocolate, chopped
150 ml (5 fl oz) liquid glucose
50 ml (1³/4 fl oz) sugar syrup (see Note)
about 600 g (1¹/4 lb) sugarpaste

1   Put the chocolate in a heatproof bowl and place over a pan of hot water—don't let the base of the bowl touch the water. Stir occasionally until the chocolate has melted.

2   Combine the glucose and sugar syrup in a bowl and place this in another bowl of hot water. Stir until just warm, then add to the chocolate. Stir with a wooden spoon. Cover or transfer to a plastic bag and store at room temperature for 24 hours before using. Do not refrigerate. Before using, knead lightly to make pliable. Knead the chocolate paste with an equal weight of sugarpaste on a surface dusted with icing sugar and it is now ready to use. Roll out between sheets of plastic thicker than plastic wrap.

Makes 1.5 kg (3 lb)

NOTE For sugar syrup, mix 6 tablespoons sugar in 5 tablespoons water, bring to the boil and boil for 3 minutes. Cool to room temperature and store in a glass container with a tight lid. Store at room temperature.

BASIC ICING RECIPES

MODELLING PASTE

280 g (9 oz) icing sugar
3 teaspoons gum tragacanth
1 teaspoon liquid glucose
315 g (10 oz) sugarpaste

1   Sift together the icing sugar and gum tragacanth. Add the glucose and 6 teaspoons cold water and mix well. Knead to form a soft dough, then combine with an equal weight of sugarpaste.

2   If the paste is too dry, knead in a little white vegetable fat (vegetable shortening or 'Copha') or egg white. If the paste is too sticky, knead in a little cornflour. Roll out on a surface dusted with cornflour and do fine work with a tiny smear of white vegetable fat on your fingers.

Makes about 325 g (11 oz)

MODELLING CHOCOLATE

125 g (4 oz) dark, milk or white chocolate
2 tablespoons liquid glucose, warmed

1   Melt the chocolate in a heatproof bowl over a pan of hot water (don't let the base of the bowl sit in the water). Remove from the heat and stir in the glucose until the mixture is just combined.

2   Put the paste in a plastic bag and chill for about 1 hour, until firm but pliable. Can be kept, tightly wrapped in the bag, in a cool place for several weeks. Break off pieces as required and knead until pliable. Roll out on a surface dusted with cornflour.

Makes about 180 g (6 oz)

FLOWER PASTE

2 teaspoons gelatine
2 teaspoons liquid glucose
3 teaspoons white vegetable fat (shortening)
500 g (1 lb) icing sugar
3 teaspoons gum tragacanth
1 egg white

1   Mix the gelatine and 5 teaspoons water in a bowl and leave for 1 hour. Stand over a pan of hot water and stir until dissolved. Add the glucose and white fat and continue to stir over heat until melted and combined.

2   Sift the sugar and gum tragacanth into a mixer bowl. Add the gelatine mix and egg white and beat at low speed until combined. Increase to high and beat for 5 minutes until white and stringy. Put in a plastic bag and then an airtight container. Refrigerate for 24 hours. Knead well before use with hands lightly greased with white vegetable fat. If the paste is dry, knead in a little egg white. If too sticky, add a little icing sugar. This paste can be cut into small pieces and frozen.

Makes about 500 g (1 lb)

PASTILLAGE

1 teaspoon gum tragacanth
500 g (1 lb) sugarpaste

1   Knead the gum tragacanth into the sugarpaste. Store in a plastic bag in an airtight container for 24 hours before using. Roll out on a work surface dusted with a little cornflour.

Makes 500 g (1 lb)

NOTE Just a few of the recipes in this book require pastillage—a hard-setting paste used for modelling. In many cases it is probably not worth making your own. Buy an instant dry-mix type that you simply mix with water.

BASIC ICING RECIPES

BUTTERCREAM

125 g (4 oz) unsalted butter, softened
250 g (8 oz) icing sugar
2 teaspoons boiling water

1   Beat the butter with electric beaters until light and fluffy. Gradually add the icing sugar, beating well after each addition. Add the water and beat well. Can be frozen for up to 3 months. Defrost in the fridge for a day before using.

Makes enough to cover and fill a 22 cm (9 inch) round cake

VARIATIONS

■ **Citrus buttercream** Beat in 2 teaspoons finely grated lemon, orange or lime rind.

■ **Coffee buttercream** Dissolve 4 teaspoons instant coffee in the 2 teaspoons of boiling water before adding.

■ **Almond** Beat 1 teaspoon almond essence into the buttercream.

■ **Chocolate** Beat in 30 g (1 oz) sifted cocoa powder.

CHOCOLATE FROSTING

60 g (2 oz) dark chocolate, chopped
185 g (6 oz) caster sugar
1 egg white
pinch of cream of tartar

1   Put the chocolate in a heatproof bowl over a pan of barely simmering water (don't let the base of the bowl sit in the water) and stir occasionally until melted.

2   Put the sugar, egg white and cream of tartar in a large heatproof bowl and place over another pan of barely simmering water. Using electric beaters, beat thoroughly for 6–8 minutes, or until soft peaks form, then remove from the heat. Whisk in the melted chocolate and then spread over the cake immediately with a palette knife.

Makes enough to cover a 20 cm (8 inch) round cake

GLACE ICING

185 g (6 oz) icing sugar
1 teaspoon unsalted butter, softened
4–8 teaspoons milk or water
food colouring

1   Sift the icing sugar into a bowl and stir in the butter and enough milk or water to make a thick paste. Colour the icing at this stage if necessary. Warm slightly in a microwave or by standing the bowl in a pan of hot water, until thick and pourable. Use immediately to prevent a crust forming and pour over the cake while warm.

Makes enough to cover a 22 cm (9 inch) round cake

VARIATIONS

■ **Citrus icing** Use lemon or orange juice in place of the milk.

■ **Chocolate icing** Stir in 4 teaspoons sifted cocoa powder

■ **Strawberry icing** Stir in a little pink food colouring and strawberry essence.

■ **Passionfruit icing** Use passionfruit pulp in place of the milk.

CHOCOLATE GANACHE

155 g (5 oz) dark chocolate, chopped
155 ml (5 fl oz) cream

1   Put the chocolate and cream in a heatproof bowl over a pan of barely simmering water (don't let the base of the bowl sit in the water). Stir gently with a wooden spoon until smooth.

2   Remove from the heat and leave until thickened enough to coat the back of the spoon very thickly. The ganache is now ready to pour over a cake. Alternatively, leave until cool, then beat lightly until thick enough to spread or pipe.

Makes enough to cover a 22 cm (9 inch) round cake

LINING CAKE TINS

Cake tins are lined to prevent cakes sticking to them during baking and to give the cake protection from the heat of the oven. The following method of lining tins is suitable for most simple tin shapes. Lightly grease the cake tin with melted unsalted butter or a mild-flavoured vegetable oil (do not use olive oil—the flavour is too strong). This helps to keep the lining paper in place. You can use either greaseproof or non-stick baking paper for lining tins and some cake-makers like to use a layer of brown paper underneath for extra protection.

TO LINE A ROUND TIN Cut a strip of paper long enough to go around the outside of the tin and 2.5 cm (1 inch) taller than the height of the tin. Fold down a cuff about 2 cm (3/4 inch) deep along the length of the strip. Cut the folded cuff diagonally at 1 cm (1/2 inch) intervals. Fit the paper strip around the inside of the tin, with the cuts on the base of the tin, pressing the cuts out at right angles so they sit flat on the base. Place the cake tin on a double piece of paper and draw around it. Cut out the circle and place it in the base of the tin, over the cuts in the paper.

TO LINE A SQUARE TIN Use the same method as for a round tin, above, or if you are in a hurry, place the tin on a sheet of paper and draw around it to make a square the same size as the base of the tin. Place this in the tin and press it onto the base. Cut a strip of paper long enough to fit around the edge of the tin and 2.5 cm (1 inch) taller than the height of the tin. Place this around the inside edge of the tin. This is a quick method that may leave a small gap around the bottom edge of the tin. In most cases this won't matter, but if you're making a sticky cake, use the foolproof method.

TO LINE AN ODD-SHAPED TIN Cut a strip to fit around the inside of the tin as for a round cake tin. When placing the strip into the tin you will need to snip into the points or curves of the shape, so the paper sits flat. Draw around the outside of the tin, as before, to make a lining for the base and place this on top of the cuts.

Left to right: Brushing and lining a round tin with non-stick baking paper; Quick-lining a square tin; Extra-thickness newspaper lining outside the tin for slow cooking; Making a collar for a high cake.

MADEIRA CAKES Many bakers only line the base of the tin for Madeira cakes and this will be enough to prevent sticking in most cases. However, if you have the time, it is safer to line the side as well to be sure the cake doesn't stick.

SPONGE CAKES To prevent sticking, the tins must be greased and the bases lined, then the whole tin dusted with flour.

EXTRA-THICKNESS LININGS Average-sized cakes or lighter-style fruit cakes that are not in the oven for extended cooking times only require a single layer of lining paper in the tin. However, larger cakes or those that require longer cooking times (such as most fruit cakes and mud cakes cooked in very large tins) need extra protection from the heat to prevent them drying out. This extra protection is given by lining both the inside and outside of the tin. The inside of the tin is lined with brown paper and then greaseproof or non-stick baking paper and then a thick layer of newspaper is wrapped around the outside. Tie the newspaper around the tin securely with string and then sit the tin on several layers of folded newspaper on the oven shelf (because the oven temperature is low, it is quite safe to have the paper in the oven). After baking, leave the cake to cool completely in the newspaper wrapping, then turn it out of the tin and peel away the lining paper.

TO MAKE A COLLAR A collar extends the height of a cake and gives extra protection during cooking. Lightly grease the tin, then cut a strip of non-stick baking paper long enough to fit around the edge and tall enough to extend 5 cm (2 inches) above the top. Fold down a cuff, 2 cm (3/4 inch) deep, along the length. Make diagonal cuts up to the fold line, 1 cm (1/2 inch) apart. Fit the collar around the inside edge of the tin with the cuts in the base, pressing them out so they sit flat. Cut a piece of paper to fit the base, drawing around the tin as a guide. A single layer of paper is usually enough for a collar on a normal-sized cake. Large cakes and slow-cooking fruit cakes will need two layers for the collar and base.

COVERING CAKES WITH MARZIPAN

Marzipan is used under icing to give a good flavour. You will need about 1 kg (2 lb) marzipan for a 22 cm (9 inch) cake. Keep marzipan covered with plastic wrap until you are ready to use it, to prevent it drying out, then briefly knead until smooth and pliable on a work surface lightly dusted with icing sugar. Trim the dome from the top of the cake with a large sharp knife to make a flat surface. Don't use a serrated knife on a fruit cake—the fruit may drag and tear the cake. Turn the cake over so that the smooth base now becomes the top. Use small pieces of marzipan to plug any holes in the cake.

SUGARPASTE-COVERED CAKES This method creates a cake with soft rounded edges, suitable for then covering with sugarpaste. Put the cake on a board or sheet of non-stick baking paper. Heat a couple of tablespoons of apricot jam with 1 tablespoon water until it boils (to kill bacteria), then sieve to remove any lumps. This is called an 'apricot glaze' and is used as a glue to hold the icing in place. Brush the cake lightly all over with apricot glaze, using a pastry brush. This method is suitable for both round cakes and those with corners. Roll out the marzipan to about 5 mm (1/4 inch) thick and

about 7.5 cm (3 inches) wider than the diameter or width of the cake. Don't make it too big or you'll find it difficult to remove the folds in the marzipan. To give more control and prevent tearing the marzipan as you lift it, roll it over the rolling pin, then carefully move it across onto the cake, unrolling and smoothing it over the base and side. Dust your hands with icing sugar and smooth firmly over the cake to remove any folds or wrinkles. Trim off the excess icing with a sharp knife. Pierce any air bubbles with a large glass-head or pearl pin. Smooth the icing again with the palm of your hands

Left to right: Trimming the dome from the top of the cake to make it flat; Plugging any holes with pieces of marzipan; Placing the rolled-out marzipan over a cake that is going to be covered with sugarpaste; Cutting pieces of marzipan to cover a round cake that is going to be royal-iced; Covering a square cake with marzipan, giving sharp edges to be royal-iced.

or an icing smoother, keeping your hands dusted with icing sugar to prevent sticking. Leave the marzipan to dry for at least 24 hours before covering with sugarpaste.

ROYAL-ICING COVERED CAKES This method creates a cake with strong sharp edges suitable for then coating with royal icing. Roll out the marzipan 5 mm (¹/4 inch) thick and slightly larger than the top of the cake. Brush the top of the cake lightly with apricot glaze. Invert the cake onto the marzipan and trim with a sharp knife to the same size as the cake. Invert the cake again

onto a sheet of non-stick baking paper.
Round cakes: Measure the circumference of the cake. Brush the side of the cake with apricot glaze. Roll out the marzipan into a long strip. Trim this neatly so it is as long as the circumference of the cake but slightly larger in height. Dust lightly with icing sugar and gently roll up, then unroll it around the side of the cake. Trim and seal the marzipan by cutting in towards the centre with a sharp knife. Dust your hands lightly with icing sugar and smooth the marzipan all over, or use an icing smoother. Dry for at least 24 hours before covering with royal icing.

Cakes with corners: Roll out the marzipan to 5 mm (¹/4 inch) thick and cut into rectangles that are slightly larger than the sides of the cake. Brush one of the sides of the cake lightly with apricot glaze. Position a matching piece of marzipan on the side of the cake and press it against the side of the cake. Trim and seal it by cutting the edge in towards the centre. Trim at the corners to fit. Repeat on the remaining sides. Dust your hands lightly with icing sugar and smooth the marzipan all over, or use an icing smoother. Leave to dry for at least 24 hours before covering with royal icing.

COVERING CAKES WITH SUGARPASTE

Covering a cake with sugarpaste gives soft edges, in keeping with modern delicate designs (royal icing sets much harder and gives firm sharp edges). Sugarpaste is also known as soft icing and rolled fondant and is available in packets from the supermarket, or you can make your own using the recipe on page 33. You will need about 1 kg (2 lb) ready-made sugarpaste for a 20 cm (8 inch) cake. Keep sugarpaste covered with plastic wrap until you are ready to use it, to prevent it drying out. Unused packet sugarpaste can be wrapped in plastic and stored in the fridge for several weeks.

PREPARING THE CAKE Cover the cake with marzipan as described on page 40 and dry completely. (If you don't like marzipan you can cover the cake with two layers of sugarpaste, following the same method.) Brush the marzipan lightly with clear alcohol such as gin, vodka or kirsch, or, for children, use a sugar syrup (equal quantities of sugar and water, stirred over low heat until dissolved, then left to cool). Don't use too much liquid, just enough to make the marzipan 'tacky'. Brush the cake thoroughly: if there are any unbrushed areas the icing won't stick and may cause air bubbles.

ROLLING OUT THE SUGARPASTE This method is suitable for covering both round cakes and cakes with corners. Put the cake on a large piece of non-stick baking paper, securing it to the paper with royal icing. Knead the sugarpaste until pliable on a work surface lightly dusted with icing sugar. If you are going to colour the sugarpaste, do it at this stage (see page 52). Roll out the sugarpaste to about 5 mm (1/4 inch) thick and about 7.5 cm (3 inches) wider than the diameter of the cake. Move the sugarpaste often to prevent sticking—if you need to add more icing sugar, rub it into the surface.

Left to right: The cake is covered with marzipan and brushed with clear alcohol or sugar syrup so the sugarpaste will stick; Knead and roll out the sugarpaste until slightly larger than the cake, then use the rolling pin to lower it over the cake; Using a special smoother will give a neat finish; Trim away the excess sugarpaste and secure the cake to the board with royal icing.

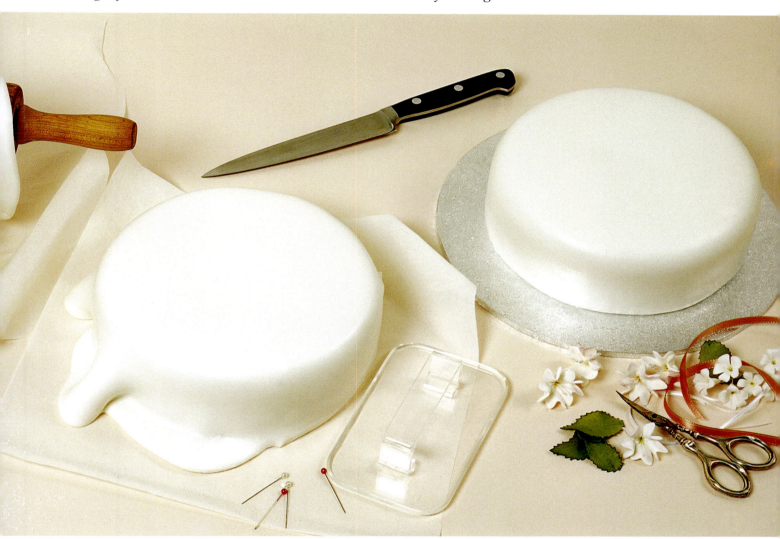

COVERING THE CAKE To give more control and prevent tearing the sugarpaste as you lift it, roll it over the rolling pin, then carefully lift it and move it across onto the cake, unrolling and smoothing it over the base and side. Dust your hands with icing sugar and smooth firmly down and over the cake to remove any folds or wrinkles in the sugarpaste. Once the icing is smooth, trim off the excess sugarpaste with a sharp knife. (Wrap the trimmings and any leftover icing in plastic wrap and store in a cool dry place for making models and other decorations.)

Pierce any air bubbles in the sugarpaste with a large glass-head or pearl pin (if the pin hole is still visible when the sugarpaste is dry, use a little royal icing in the same colour to plug the hole, then wipe away the excess to leave a smooth finish). Smooth over the sugarpaste again with the palm of your hands or an icing smoother, keeping your hands lightly dusted with icing sugar to prevent them sticking. If a fold or crease occurs in the icing, carefully lift it out from the side of the cake and then gently ease it in again, smoothing as you go. Leave the sugarpaste to dry for at least 24 hours before continuing.

MOVING THE COVERED CAKE TO A CAKE BOARD Once the sugarpaste is completely dry, use the non-stick baking paper as a sling to lift it onto a board. Secure the paper under the cake to the board with a few dabs of royal icing and then trim away the paper from around the cake with a scalpel so that it can't be seen. (This makes it easy to transfer the cake to the board without putting fingerprints in the icing and also protects the cake from contact with the board—some foil-covered boards can react badly with fruit cakes or the colour from the board can stain the edge of the icing.)

COVERING CAKES WITH ROYAL ICING

Royal icing sets hard and is normally used only on fruit cakes as it needs a strong base for support. If you are making a layered cake, remember dowels and pillars will crack the icing: you need to use stands. Royal-icing a cake is more time-consuming than covering with sugarpaste: three or four thin layers are spread over the cake and each coat is left to dry for 8 hours. You will need about 1.25 kg (2¹/₂ lb) royal icing to cover a 22 cm (9 inch) cake with three coats. Cover the icing with a damp cloth while you are working to prevent a crust forming. Store in an airtight container with plastic wrap on the surface. It is not necessary to keep the icing

refrigerated. Re-beat the icing to its original consistency (preferably in a mixer) at least every two days. A turntable is useful for covering the cake but, if you don't have one, use an upturned round cake tin.

The consistency of the royal icing for the first and second coats should be 'soft peak' (peaks of icing should stand up and droop over at the tips). Stir in a few drops of water or egg white to soften the icing if necessary. Stir gently before use to blend it and remove air bubbles (the icing changes texture when left to sit). Cover the cake with marzipan, giving sharp edges as shown on page 41, and let the marzipan dry completely.

ICING ROUND CAKES

Top of the cake: Put the turntable on a damp cloth and place the cake on the turntable. Place a large spoonful of icing in the centre of the cake and, with a palette knife, using a motion like spreading butter on bread, smooth the icing over the surface of the cake, keeping the knife quite flat to eliminate any air bubbles. Continue until the top of the cake is completely covered. To smooth the surface, hold the tip of the palette knife in the centre of the cake at a slight angle, while turning the turntable. Wipe an icing ruler with a damp cloth and place on the far edge of the cake, holding it at either

Left to right: Spreading royal icing over the top of a cake with a palette knife; Spread the first coat of royal icing around the side of the cake by turning the turntable; Wait until the first coat of icing is dry before applying the second coat in the same way; Apply three or four coats if necessary to give a beautiful smooth finish.

end, thumbs uppermost. Angle the ruler slightly to the surface of the cake and drag it towards you, then pull it off. Wipe clean and repeat if necessary. Remove the excess icing from the top edge of the cake by holding a palette knife parallel with the side and pushing down with a cutting motion. Leave to dry before coating the side of the cake.

Side of the cake: Using the same 'buttering' action, apply royal icing with a palette knife held parallel with the side of the cake, then wipe a side scraper with a damp cloth. Hold the side scraper by spreading your fingers over the back of it and use the pad of your little finger to lift the scraper away from the

cake board slightly. Place the scraper at a slight angle to the side of the cake and, touching the icing, turn the cake on the turntable, keeping the scraper in the same spot. Use the palette knife to remove excess icing from the top edge of the cake: keep the knife flat and cut inwards as you move around the top. Leave the icing to dry for 8 hours, then remove the rough edges with a sharp knife. Dust off the sugar dust with a large soft brush. Repeat to apply a second coat and leave to dry. For the third coat, thin the icing down a little. If you are still not happy with the smooth finish, apply a fourth coat, also of thinned icing.

SQUARE CAKES
For a square cake, apply the icing to the top as for the round cake, then 'butter' the icing onto one of the sides of the cake, holding the palette knife vertically and positioning your finger down the back of the blade to apply pressure to the icing and disperse air bubbles. Move the scraper along the side and, at the end of the side, pull it off towards yourself. Start the second side by bringing the 'take off' mark made by the scraper on the first side around to the second side. Repeat until you have coated all four sides. Always ensure that all the edges are neat before drying and applying the next coat.

COVERING CAKE BOARDS

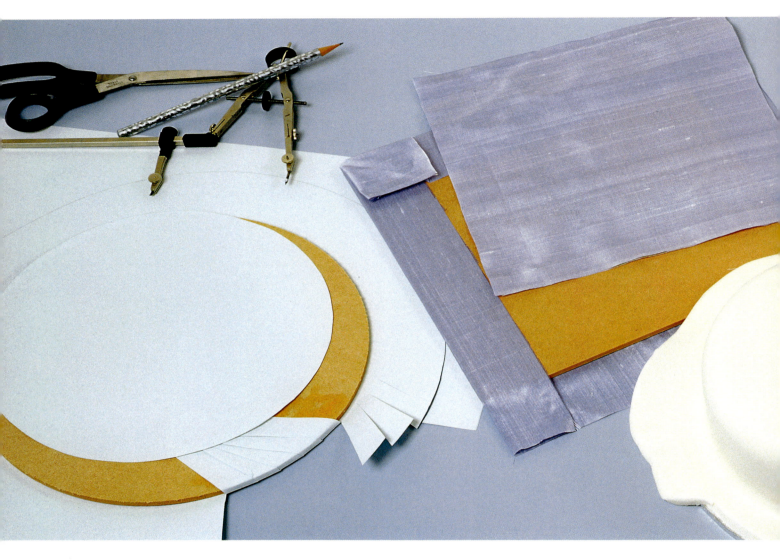

Cake boards are used to support and transport cakes. You can buy boards or cut them to size from heavy-duty cardboard (for light cakes) or thin sheets of chipboard. Cakes with several tiers need a thick board under the bottom layer. Cover boards with coloured paper, fabric, or sugarpaste or royal icing. Some papers, being porous, will absorb oils from the cake and stain. If you're worried about this, cover the paper with clear plastic or place a layer of non-stick baking paper between the cake and board.

COVERING WITH PAPER OR FABRIC

To cover a round board, place the board on an upside-down sheet of paper. Draw around it, then draw an outline 5 cm (2 inches) outside this line and cut out the larger outline. Make diagonal cuts 1 cm (1/2 inch) apart around the edge, cutting in as far as the smaller outline. Brush the board with glue and put onto the paper, pressing out any air bubbles. Fold the cut edges over and secure with glue. Cut another round of paper slightly smaller than the board and stick over the top to hide the cut edge. On some tiered cakes the underneath of the board will be visible, so cover it neatly.

To cover a board with corners with paper or fabric, place the board on an upside-down sheet of paper. Draw around the board, then draw an outline 5 cm (2 inches) larger than the board and cut this out. Brush the board with glue and put onto the paper, pressing out any air bubbles. Fold in the sides and secure with tape or glue, folding the corners in neatly as you go. Cut another piece of paper slightly smaller than the board and glue over the top to hide the folded edge. **To cover unusual-shaped boards**, use the same methods, taking care with the corners. These can tear easily, especially if you're using glue, which will soften the paper.

COVERING WITH SUGARPASTE

Strip method: Place the cake on the board. Cut a strip of sugarpaste to fit around the board. Brush the board with water, position the strip with the cut edge against the cake, then trim the outer edge. If it is a large cake, use two strips. Overlap any joins, cut

Left to right: Covering a round board with paper; Covering a square board with fabric; Covering a board with sugarpaste using the 'all-in-one' and template methods; Covering a board with royal icing.

through the two thicknesses and remove the excess. Pinch the two edges of sugarpaste together and smooth over the surface. For a square cake, cut four lengths the same measurement as the board, overlap at the corners and cut through from the corner point of the board to the corner of the cake, then smooth the join.

'All-in-one' method: This gives a good clean line. Place the cake on the board. Brush the cake and board lightly with clear alcohol or sugar syrup. Roll out the icing large enough to cover the cake and board in one go. Lift the sugarpaste, positioning it on the edge of the board and then onto the cake. Smooth over the top and sides, gently pressing the sugarpaste into the side of the cake, the edge

where the cake meets the board and then over the board. Smooth over and trim off the excess icing, using a cutting motion away from the edge of the board.

Template method: Cover the cake with sugarpaste and leave to dry for 24 hours. Cut a paper template the size of the cake. Brush the edge of the board with clear alcohol, roll out the sugarpaste large enough to cover the whole board, cover the board and trim the edge. Put the template on the board where the cake will sit and cut around the edge. Remove the template and lift out the piece of sugarpaste. Place a dab of royal icing into the hole and then place the cake into the hole. Smooth the sugarpaste on the board into the join.

COVERING WITH ROYAL ICING

Small boards can be coated completely, large boards can be coated with an 8 cm (3 inch) band round the edge. Spread the board with slightly thinned-down icing, with the same 'buttering' motion used to coat the cake. A turntable will help with a neat finish. Clean the edge of the board with the palette knife using a downward cutting motion. Wipe the knife regularly with a damp cloth. When finished, wipe the edge of the board with a damp cloth and leave to dry. Coat the cake on a temporary board, placing a thin cake card, the same size and shape as the cake, underneath. Keep this under the cake when it is put on the real board, to prevent the colour on the cake staining the board icing.

TIERS AND LAYERS

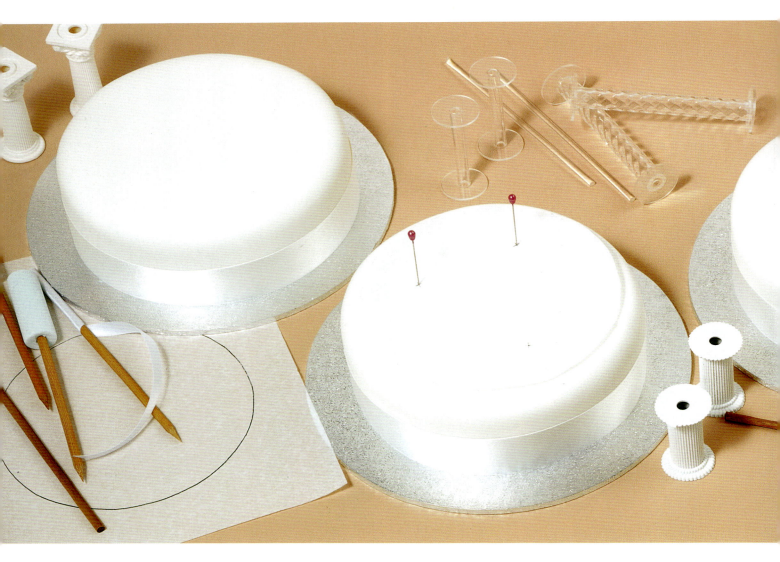

Light cakes that have just two or three layers can be placed directly on top of each other. But cakes that are made up of many layers, especially heavy fruit cakes, need to be supported by pillars so they don't collapse. As a general rule most tiered cakes are wedding cakes, but you can certainly make other cakes in tiers too. Make sure the cakes are well balanced and visually appealing, either perfectly centred above each other or obviously off-centre. You don't have to have the cakes the same height apart—the top layer could be raised up high. The following method, using dowels and pillars, is suitable for cakes covered with sugarpaste. You cannot insert dowels into royal icing and need to support the layers with ring stands.

CAKE BOARDS Each of the cakes needs to be on a cake board. You can make the cake boards invisible by making them slightly smaller than the cakes or, if you want the boards to be visible, cover them in paper or icing. Remember that if you are using tall pillars you will be able to see the underside of the cake boards, so make sure they are neatly covered. It is important to remember that the bottom tier of the cake has to support the weight of all the other layers.

CAKE DOWELS Thick wooden dowels with a point at one end are used to support the cake. These are hidden from view by covering them with pillars or decorating with ribbon or sugarpaste to match the cake.

POSITIONING THE DOWELS Trace the outline of the top cake onto paper. Place the paper over the lower cake and make pin pricks through it where you will put the pillars. Make the pricks 3 cm (1¼ inches) in from the outer edge of the top cake and take care that they are evenly spaced. Use four pillars for a square cake and three or four for a round cake (work out the spacing by folding the paper into quarters, then open it out over the cake). For odd-shaped cakes, or cakes with the top tier off-centre, it doesn't matter how many supports you use, as long as you space them evenly to hold the weight. Continue down the layers until you have made a template of each cake and marked the pillar positions onto the cake beneath it.

Left to right: Trace the outline of the cake onto paper to make a template for the dowels; Make pin pricks through the paper; Pushing in and cutting off the dowels; Covering dowels with hollow pillars.

PUTTING IN THE DOWELS Push the dowels into the pin prick marks on the cake, pointed ends first, as far as they will go (they will probably go down until they touch the board unless you are using a particularly dense fruit cake). Then remove the dowels and reposition point-up so that they are sitting on their flat ends and are more stable. If the cake is to sit directly on top of the cake below, without being raised above it, mark the dowel level with the icing, then take it out and cut the dowel off at the mark. Re-insert the dowel into the same hole. Repeat with the other dowels so that they all sit level with the icing on the cake. Sit the smaller cake on the top so that it completely covers the dowels.

For cakes with tiers that are to be separated, there are two different types of pillars that you can use: hollow and solid. If you are using solid pillars, insert the dowels as above, cutting them off level with the icing, and simply sit the pillars on top, securing with royal icing. If you are using hollow pillars, insert the dowels as above but, before marking, put one of the pillars over the dowel. Now mark the dowel level with the top of the pillar, remove the pillar and dowel and cut the dowel off at the mark. Re-insert the dowel into the same hole. If you're using clear perspex pillars, you can paint the top of the dowel with a non-toxic paint so that it is the same colour as the icing and can't be seen through the pillar.

OTHER IDEAS A wide variety of stands and pillars are available, such as tilting cake stands and perspex or glass tubes. If you glue ribbon or paper onto the dowels, remember to allow for the height of the cake and icing and leave this portion undecorated. Light cakes can be layered with upturned glasses.

TRANSPORTING Layered cakes need to be transported carefully to avoid accidents. Firstly separate the cake into layers, leaving the pillars and dowels in place. Then cut a piece of thin foam the size of each layer. Put this in the base of a box about the same size as the cake to minimise movement. Use a folded strip of baking paper as a 'sling' to lift each cake layer into its own box.

49

WORKING WITH SUGARPASTE

Sugarpaste is a good starting place for beginners to cake decorating. It is soft and pliable, easily coloured and shaped and very exciting to work with... and if things do go wrong, you can simply roll it out again. You can even buy ready-coloured sugarpaste, although it is fun to tint your own. Sugarpaste dries softer than royal icing and is perfect for a variety of techniques. Now that you've covered your cake, the following pages will show you the basics in decorating, such as how to emboss, inlay different coloured pieces into a design and finish edges neatly.

ADDING COLOUR

CHOOSING A COLOUR SCHEME

Firstly, choose a base colour for the icing: for wedding cakes this is often white and for children a bright primary colour, and there is a whole colour spectrum inbetween. A monochromatic colour scheme uses shades of only one colour: so if the base colour is pale yellow the decorations will be darker tones of yellow. A complementary scheme uses colours that are opposite each other on the colour spectrum, such as yellow and violet, red and green, orange and blue. Use the colours in different shades and just small touches so that they do not look garish. A harmonious colour scheme uses several colours that are next to each other on the colour spectrum, such as pinks and purples.

COLOURING SUGARPASTE Both sugarpaste and royal icing can be coloured any shade of the colour spectrum and mixing and experimenting with colours can be very rewarding. You can buy ready-coloured sugarpaste, colour your own while it is still soft or paint it once the icing is dry. The easiest way to change the overall colour of sugarpaste (or marzipan) is by adding paste or liquid food colouring (paste is usually better quality, will give a stronger colour and is more manageable to use). When using any liquid colourings, never pour them directly from the bottle: use a dropper or pour a little into a small container (an ice-cube tray or the insert from a box of chocolates) and use sparingly. Knead the sugarpaste lightly on a

surface dusted with icing sugar, then dip the end of a cocktail stick into the food colouring and wipe it onto the sugarpaste (remember that a little colour can go a long way, so add a tiny dab at a time, especially if you want soft colours). Knead gently again until the colour is evenly distributed. Check by cutting the sugarpaste in half, kneading again if necessary. Once you've reached the right colour, wrap the sugarpaste in plastic until you're ready to use it. Royal icing can be coloured by using liquid food colourings.

MARBLING Marbling is achieved by partially blending two different colours of sugarpaste to create streaks. Do this either by rolling coloured strips of sugarpaste

From left: Use the spectrum to create a colour scheme; Add colour sparingly with a cocktail stick; Sugarpaste can be coloured by marbling, sponging or painting with a fine brush and liquid colour.

together, working with your fingers until marbled. Or knead the white sugarpaste until pliable and add random drops of paste or liquid colouring. Fold and twist the sugarpaste until the colour starts to streak. The more you knead the icing, the less obvious the marbling, so don't overwork it.

SPONGING Sponging can give your cake a mottled effect. Use a sponge and some food colouring diluted with a little clear alcohol (alcohol dries faster than water). Dip a small piece of sponge in the colour: don't saturate with liquid, it needs to be just damp. Practise on a spare piece of icing first to get the right effect, then work directly on the cake. If you like, mask off any areas of the cake that you

don't want to colour by using a paper template. Sponge the cake, then lift off the template and let the colouring dry. This can give you a quick stencilled look, using a bought or home-made stencil. You can use more than one colour but, to avoid smudging, wait until one colour is completely dry before applying the next. To create a mottled textured effect, use the same method to sponge with diluted royal icing.

HAND-PAINTING Painting is good for adding details such as eyes and mouths to figures, or free-painting scenes onto plain iced cakes or plaques to be attached to cakes. Use paste or powder colourings, mixed with clear alcohol. Before applying any colour,

ensure the icing is completely dry and firm to the touch. Use a very fine brush and don't overload the brush or the icing will be too wet and make the colour streaky. Dip your brush lightly in the colour then dab off any excess onto a sheet of paper towel.

Food colouring pens are excellent for marking features and fine details on modelling figures. To transfer a picture freehand onto a cake, lightly draw it with a sharp instrument. Alternatively, 'trace' the design onto the surface of the cake, by tracing from the original onto tracing paper, then placing the paper over the cake. Go over the design with a scriber or prick lightly with a pin so that it is transferred to the cake and ready to paint.

DECORATIVE DESIGNS

These decorative designs are easy methods to tidy up areas on your cake that can look 'unfinished', such as the edge where the cake and board meet or a plaque is attached. As you become more experienced you can use them to hide the top of extension work. Embossing is a leatherwork technique that requires no special tools—use patterned buttons, jewellery or decorative spoon handles. Garrett frills are flared frills that are attached to the top, side or corners of cakes or used in modelling. Broderie anglaise gives a lace finish. All of these designs are carried out on soft sugarpaste (however, if you find your paste is too soft, knead in a little flower paste to firm it up).

EDGING

ROPE Twist thin rolls of sugarpaste together and secure to the side of the cake with water or edible glue. Use one or two colours of sugarpaste, and different sizes.

PLAIT Plait three thin rolls of sugarpaste and secure to the side of the cake with water or edible glue. Use one, two or three different colours.

CRIMPING An old technique originally called 'pinching'. Crimp a thin roll of sugarpaste around the base of a cake or use a pair of crimpers (overweight tweezers) to crimp the top edge of a cake or board.

EMBOSSING

You can make your own embossing tool with a clean button or piece of jewellery. Press the embossing tool gently but evenly into soft sugarpaste or marzipan, spacing the pattern evenly as you work.

To cover a large area, simply repeat the embossing. Don't press too hard: the indentations should be all the same depth.

Paint the design with paste, liquid or powder colouring, mixed with water or clear alcohol. Add lettering with royal icing.

GARRETT FRILLS

Mark a line on the cake where the frill will be attached. Roll out sugarpaste on a board lightly dusted with cornflour.

Cut out a frill with a Garrett frill cutter. Alternatively use a fluted cutter and cut out the centre with a plain cutter.

Working with the paste close to the edge of your board, frill with the side of a cocktail stick. Hold the stick with one hand and press lightly with the forefinger of your other hand, turning the frill as you go.

Cut through the frill to make one long strip and turn it over. Brush a little water or egg white along the flat edge. Lift up with both hands and press gently onto the marked line.

Tuck the cut ends under slightly to neaten and ease out the frill with the cocktail stick. Dust the frilled edge with colour. For layered frills, apply the bottom layer first. You could make the layers different colours.

To finish the top edge of the frill, you could pipe a small snail trail or fine design along the top, or attach small icing flowers with a little royal icing or roll a quilting wheel on the soft edge for a stitched look.

BRODERIE ANGLAISE

Trace the pattern onto non-stick baking paper and position over the sugarpaste. Mark the main points of the pattern through to the icing with a pin.

Lift off the paper and cut out the holes with a number 2 or 3 piping tube. To make oval holes hold the nozzle at an angle. (If making broderie anglaise directly on the cake, enlarge the holes with a modelling tool.)

Pipe around the holes with royal icing, using a number 0 or 1 piping tube. Neaten the edges of the royal icing with a damp paintbrush. Use all white or coloured icings.

INLAY, BAS-RELIEF & APPLIQUE

These easy techniques involve cutting out shapes and applying them to the cake or a plaque, either by removing a section of the icing and replacing it (inlay) or by laying the pieces on top of the existing icing (appliqué and bas-relief). Sugarpaste is mainly used, but try modelling paste for fine work. When using inlay directly on a covered cake, do not brush the marzipan with clear alcohol before applying the sugarpaste as you need to be able to remove sections easily. Appliqué and bas-relief are similar techniques—cutting out coloured pieces of icing and sticking them to the cake or a plaque, with bas-relief building the icing into three-dimensional designs.

INLAY

Trace a template onto non-stick baking paper and place over the icing (this technique is usually done on the top of the cake, but you can also make plaques). Secure with glass-head pins inside the line of the shape.

Mark through the paper all the way around the shape with a pin. Cut out the shape with a scalpel on the outside of the pin marks for a neat finish and lift out.

Roll out coloured sugarpaste to the same thickness as the piece of sugarpaste just removed. Cut out the same shape (using the template and the same method).

Put the piece of coloured icing into the space left by the removed piece of icing. Smooth over with your fingertips to ease the edges together neatly.

Make more templates to cut out and inlay the other parts of the design.

Smooth over with an icing smoother once all the pieces are inlaid.

BAS-RELIEF

Trace a template onto thin card. Roll out the sugarpaste to about 3 mm (1/8 inch) thick and cut out a piece of icing with the template and a scalpel. Moisten the back of the shape with a little water and attach to the cake.

Use small pieces of sugarpaste and roll out or mould with your fingers to build up areas of the design. Attach with a little water. (Don't build the pieces up too high.)

Cut out another shape the same as the base, moisten the back lightly and place over the built-up icing, smoothing down. Make finishing touches with royal icing or food colouring, dusting powders or chalks.

APPLIQUE

Trace a template onto thin card. Cut out separate templates for each layer or colour. Roll out each colour of sugarpaste to about 3 mm (1/8 inch) thick. Cut out the shapes with the template and wrap in plastic.

Moisten the back of each shape with a little water and attach to the cake or icing plaque in order.

Pipe decorations, names etc onto the appliqué to finish. Use letter cutters to create names on a plaque or cake. Attach with a little water.

NEEDLEWORK DESIGNS

These decorative features, taken from needlework, are worked onto soft paste. Quilting gives the impression of a padded image with stitch marks joining the pieces—you will need small and large quilting wheels. Smocking is a form of embroidery, with the soft icing gathered into tiny pleats—you will need a ridged rolling pin for making thin parallel lines in the icing and a pair of tweezers or special smocking tweezers. Ribbons of fabric or icing can be 'woven' into sugarpaste using the ribbon insertion technique. A ribbon insertion tool is useful, but you can manage with a scalpel and tweezers. The iced cake should be left until the sugarpaste has firmed a little on the surface.

QUILTING

Choose a cutter or trace your design onto paper. Transfer the design to the cake by pressing the cutter firmly into the icing or pin-pricking through the paper.

Use the small quilting wheel to make any marks on the background, such as grass, strings for balloons etc. You can then dust around this area with colour.

Use white firm-peak royal icing to pipe the padding into your design. Pad in the central areas to give three dimensions to the design. Leave to dry.

Cut out quilting pieces from coloured sugarpaste, using your original cutter. Smooth down and moisten all the edges and place over the padded areas. Mark all around the design with your small wheel.

Cut out small pieces of different coloured sugarpaste to add the detail to your design (teddy's muzzle, feet etc). Indent holes for noses and eyes and fill with dark sugarpaste.

Use the small quilting wheel to stitch over the design, defining the outline of heads and bodies.

SMOCKING

Cut a cardboard template to the shape of the piece of smocking. Roll out the sugarpaste to about 3 mm ($^1/8$ inch) thick and then roll again with a ribbed rolling pin to about 1.75 mm ($^1/16$ inch) thick.

Place the template on the sugarpaste and cut out with a sharp knife (always cut panels with an even number of ribs). Moisten the back of the sugarpaste with water and attach to the cake.

Using ordinary or smocking tweezers, gently squeeze together pairs of ridges to make the smocking (because you have an even number of ribs, there won't be a spare rib left at the end).

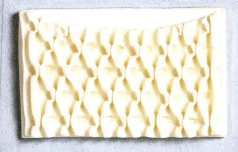

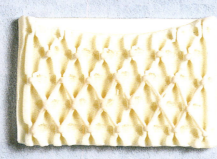

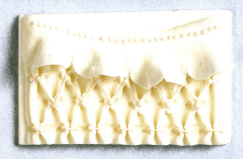

If you are applying several panels next to each other, ensure the crimping pattern continues from one panel to the next.

Colour a small amount of royal icing and, using a piping bag with a small plain tube, pipe a line or dot (to represent a stitch) over the top of the icing where the pleats are pinched together.

Pipe threads from the pinched pleat on the upper row to the pinched pleat on the next row down, to represent the loose embroidery thread. Neaten the cut edge with a line of piping or a frill.

RIBBON INSERTION

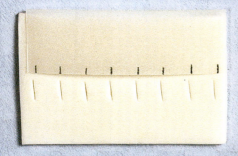

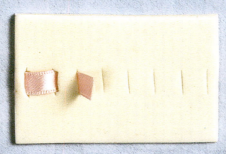

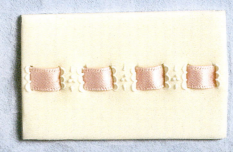

Make evenly spaced pencil marks along the edge of a piece of paper to show the lengths of ribbon and gaps. Hold the paper on your sugarpaste and cut evenly spaced slits with a scalpel, using the paper as a guide.

Cut the ribbon into lengths a little longer than the gaps between the slits and hold one end with tweezers. Insert the other end into the slit with a scalpel.

Insert the loose end of the ribbon into the other slit with a scalpel. (You could use a ribbon insertion tool, which will make the slits in the icing and insert the ribbon at the same time.)

WORKING WITH ROYAL ICING

Royal icing is a little bit more tricky to work with than sugarpaste. It starts off runny and sets to a very hard finish, making it ideal for piping intricate lines, shapes and even figures that then set hard. The following pages will lead you through the basics of royal icing, from how to make and fill your piping bag and how to hold it and squeeze out the icing, to the different shapes you can produce and then the most intricate embroidery work.

PIPING WITH ROYAL ICING

While sugarpaste decorations are moulded, cut out, draped over or stuck onto cakes, royal icing is spread over the cake or piped into delicate patterns with a bag and tube. Royal icing can be piped directly onto cakes that are covered either with sugarpaste or royal icing; it can be piped onto sugarpaste plaques, or it can be piped onto non-stick baking paper or acetate, dried under a heat lamp and then attached to the cake with royal icing.

ICING CONSISTENCIES Once the icing is made, it is beaten, by hand or electric beaters, until it reaches a thicker consistency. The two main terms used for the consistency of royal icing are soft peak and firm peak.

Soft peak means that when you lift a spoonful of icing from the bowl, the icing below should retain its shape with a peak, which just bends over at the top.

Firm peak means that when a spoonful of icing is lifted from the bowl, the icing should easily retain a peak without bending over. Firm peak is generally used for piping shells or borders. Sometimes a technique such as pressure piping or runouts calls for a specific consistency; this is produced by making alterations such as watering down soft or firm peak icing and instructions will be given in the recipe. It is important not to have air bubbles in your royal icing: stir before use or pipe through one bag and into another. Store icing in an airtight container

for up to two days with plastic wrap pressed over the surface to eliminate any air that will make a crust. To store short term, simply cover the bowl with plastic or a damp cloth, or, if you have already put the icing into a bag, wrap the bag in plastic and then a damp cloth to prevent it drying out. Cover the ends of tubes to prevent icing drying on the tips.

COLOURING ROYAL ICING Like sugarpaste, royal icing can be coloured before use or painted when it is dry. If using paste colours, add a little at a time with a cocktail stick. If using liquid food colours, colour the icing before watering down, so it is not runny. Food colourings containing glycerine may inhibit drying.

From left: Royal icing at soft and firm peak stages; Cover with plastic wrap to prevent drying out; Colouring with paste; Making a piping bag; Tubes come in many sizes to pipe varying widths of line.

PIPING BAGS You can buy piping bags made of plastic, nylon or jaconette or use piping syringes. But for better control, make your own bags with paper. Cut a 25 cm (10 inch) square of non-stick baking paper in half diagonally to make two triangles. Holding one triangle with its longest side away from you, fold the right-hand point over to meet the bottom point, curling the paper around to make a cone. Fold the left-hand point over the cone and bring all three points together. Fold the points over twice to secure. Cut off 1 cm (1/2 inch) of the tip and fit a piping tube inside the bag. Make all the bags needed before you start: if you are using different tubes and colours of icing, you will need a different bag for each.

TUBES, TIPS AND NOZZLES These range from fine writing tubes to large tubes for stars, basketwork, leaves and petals. Shapes vary from plain round to stars. The sizes are universal measures with number 000 being the finest and 4 the largest. Generally, the smaller the tube, the thinner the icing should be. Also, the smaller the tube you are using, the finer the work and the smaller the bag should be, to give you maximum control. Tips is the American term and nozzles an alternative name.

TO START PIPING Fill the piping bag only two-thirds full—if you put too much in, icing may seep from the top—and then fold over the top of the bag. It is best to hold the icing

bag with two hands, however experienced you are. Use the index finger of one hand to support the bag underneath, with the thumb keeping the bag closed at the top and applying pressure. Rest the index finger of the other hand against the base of the bag to guide the tube and prevent your hand shaking through the application of pressure.

To pipe a line, touch the tube against the surface where you are piping and squeeze. Once the icing starts to flow and attaches itself to the surface, start to slowly pull away. If you don't pull away immediately, a bulb will form at the start of your icing. If you squeeze the bag too hard, your line will be curly, if you squeeze too softly, the line will fade and break.

BASIC PIPING

Linework is the basic piping technique, with the most popular linework being the edging or outlining of shell, bulb and scroll borders to give the cake a 'finished' appearance. Overpiping on top of an existing line will make the outline more prominent. Half-fill the bag with soft-peak royal icing and hold the bag with your index finger underneath to support it and your thumb on top, keeping the bag closed and applying pressure. Use the index finger of your other hand to steady the tube. Touch the tip of the tube on the surface and, as soon as you feel the icing attached, slowly pull away. If you squeeze too hard your lines will be curly; not enough pressure and they will break.

ZIGZAG

Holding the bag at a 60° angle, using constant pressure and with the tube touching the surface, pipe a zigzag line. Work from side to side, making the zigzag wider in the centre.

BULB

Hold the bag at a 90° angle, with the tube just above the surface. Squeeze with even pressure to form a circle of icing. Release the pressure and take off gently. If small peaks occur, touch down with a damp paintbrush.

C SHAPE

Holding the bag at a 90° angle, pipe a curved 'C' shape, using constant even pressure. Release the pressure and remove the tube with a backward motion to help prevent a peak forming.

SNAIL TRAIL

Hold the bag at a 60° angle, just touching the tube on the surface. Make a bulb of icing, then ease off the pressure sideways to make a tail. Pipe the next teardrop over the tail of the previous one to make a line.

TEARDROP

Hold the bag at a 60° angle, just touching the tube on the surface. Make a bulb of icing, then ease off the pressure sideways to make a tail.

LINE

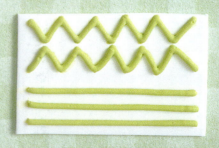

Hold the bag at a 60° angle, just touching the tube on the surface, squeeze with even pressure and slowly pull away. For zigzags, pipe short lines, releasing the pressure and lifting off at the end of each line.

TWISTED ROPE

Hold the bag at a 45° angle. Using constant pressure, gradually rotate the bag across the icing surface to create a coil effect.

BASKETWEAVE

Using a basketweave tube, hold the bag at a 45° angle. Apply even pressure to the bag and pipe horizontal lines, spaced a little apart. Pipe vertical lines alternately over the rows, following the pattern shown.

STAR

Use small or large star tubes. Hold the bag upright, squeeze out the icing and then pull up into a point. These can be piped in a border or used to cover a large area on the top or side of the cake.

C SCROLL

Hold the bag at a 90° angle and pipe a bulb. Applying gentle pressure, twist your wrist to make a 'C'. To create texture, agitate the tube up and down while releasing the pressure on the bag.

ALTERNATING SHELLS

Make a bulb, then sweep the tube down to the surface to make a tail, angling it slightly. Pipe another shell, slightly lower than the first and just touching, bringing the tail up to the same line. Continue to the right.

ROSETTE

Tubes for rosettes have finer indentaions than star tubes. Hold the bag almost upright and squeeze, moving the bag in a circular motion and lifting slightly. To finish, bring the tube to the centre and pull off.

SHELL BORDER

Hold the bag at a 45° angle and squeeze to make a bulb. Reducing the pressure, sweep the tube down towards the surface to form the tail. Make the next shell over the tail of the previous to form a border.

FLEUR-DE-LYS

Pipe a central elongated shell, then pipe a curved shell on the left, bringing the tail to the same point as the first shell. Pipe a curved shell from the right, bringing the tail to the same point.

S SCROLL

Hold the bag at a 90° angle and pipe a bulb. Apply more pressure while agitating the bag up and down to make the beginnning of the scroll. Releasing the pressure, turn your wrist anti-clockwise, then clockwise.

PRESSURE PIPING

Pressure piping means increasing and decreasing the pressure on the bag to produce shapes that are more three-dimensional than the basic shapes. It is an excellent technique for decorative flowers and figures. The icing must be soft enough to pipe into shapes but not so runny that it won't hold the shape. Gradually water down soft-peak royal icing until it will hold its shape but goes smooth when a knife is agitated on the surface. You can pipe directly onto the top or around the side of an iced cake, or pipe onto non-stick baking paper and dry under a lamp. Remove the piece from the paper with a palette knife when dry and attach to the cake with a dab of wet royal icing.

ROSE

Attach a cone of marzipan to a cocktail stick. Use firm-peak royal icing and a large petal tube. Hold the bag so the thin end of the tube is facing upwards at a 45° angle and the curved side faces the cone.

Pipe icing onto the tip of the cone. For the centre, pipe while rotating the stick, release the pressure and pull away the tube. For petals, turn the tube so the curve faces away from the cone with the thin edge uppermost.

Pipe just below the rose centre with even pressure, turning the stick and lifting the tube to form a horseshoe shaped petal. Add petals in odd numbers. Dry, then slide off the stick and trim the base to sit flat.

RABBIT

If you need, draw out a template to guide you. Using a number 2 piping tube and pale brown icing, pipe two small elongated bulbs to make feet.

Pipe two circular bulbs for the head and body, one on top of the other with the body larger than the head.

Pipe elongated teardrops for the ears, flopping one over. Pipe a bulb of white on the body for the tail. Paint whiskers and other detail directly onto the cake.

REINDEER

If you need, draw out a template to guide you. Pipe antlers, using brown royal icing and a number 2 tube. Pipe ears in white royal icing, flopping them over.

Pipe the head in a large teardrop shape, applying more pressure to increase the height at the muzzle. Pipe white elongated teardrops for the eyes, meeting in the centre.

Pipe a red bulb over the base of the eyes for the nose. When dry, paint in black eyes and more features.

TEDDY BEAR

If you need, draw out a template to guide you. Using a number 2 tube and cream icing, pipe ears and a body, creating a smooth surface on the icing by moving the piping tube around in the icing while piping.

Pipe the head in the same way as the body. Pipe a bulb for each leg, then a second layer of overlapping bulbs for the feet. Pipe bulbs for the muzzle and arms, adding small bulbs for the paws.

Pipe on a small dot for the nose. Dust the bear or paint with food colouring and paint in features with a fine paintbrush.

DUCK

If you need, draw out a template to guide you. Using white icing and a number 1 tube, pipe two overlapping layers of shells to make a teardrop shape for the wing. Leave to dry.

With a number 1 tube, pipe yellow royal icing to make the beak and feet. With a number 2 tube, pipe an 's' scroll to make the head and neck.

Squeeze very hard on the bag to make the body. Set the wing into the body while the body is still wet. Pipe a blue dot for the duck's eye.

RUNOUTS

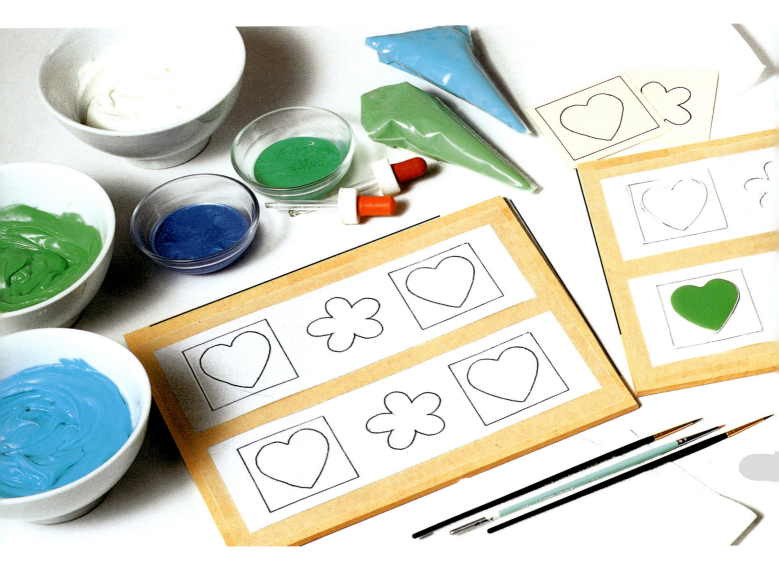

Runouts are made by piping an outline onto non-stick baking paper or acetate (a material that will not absorb liquid and stick to the icing) and then filling in the outline with thinner icing, like colouring in a picture. The design is left to dry and then gently lifted off the paper and attached to the cake. The technique is used to create a picture or make small intricate pieces to be incorporated into other designs or techniques, such as making doors or shutters for a gingerbread house. The simplest form of runout is the picture plaque, but you can create two-sided or three-dimensional runouts that stand up on the cake. The technique is sometimes known as flooding, because the area within the outline is 'flooded' with icing.

THE CONSISTENCY OF THE ICING

For runouts, it is important to use freshly beaten royal icing. Fit a piping bag with a number 1 or 0 tube and fill with firm-peak icing for piping the outline. Then begin to 'let down' the icing for flooding, by stirring in water a drop at a time until the icing has the consistency of thick (double) cream (do not beat in the water or your icing may contain a lot of air bubbles). Gently paddle out air bubbles with a palette knife. If you are going to colour the icing, do this before letting down, so that it does not become too runny, and use a colouring that does not contain glycerine, which would inhibit the drying of the runout. To test the consistency, draw a line across the surface of the icing with a knife; the mark should disappear by the count of 10. Half-fill an icing bag with the icing—you do not need a tube.

MAKING THE OUTLINE Trace your design onto paper and secure this to a flat work surface. Lay a sheet of non-stick baking paper or acetate over the top and secure with masking tape. Make sure both pieces of paper are smooth and flat. Pipe over the outline of the pattern with the firm-peak icing, making sure all the joins are neat. Leave to dry until 'crusted' over under a hot lamp before filling in the design. More experienced decorators can colour in or 'flood' the icing directly without piping an outline first.

From left: Draw the designs on paper and secure to a flat surface; Pipe the outlines with firm peak icing; Flood the designs, pushing the icing into corners; Remove the dry runouts with a palette knife.

FILLING IN THE OUTLINE Cut a small hole, the size of a number 1 tube for small sections or a number 2 tube for large sections, in the bag with the runout icing and begin to colour in the design by flooding. Hold the point of the bag close to the outline. Move the bag slowly backwards and forwards, using a little pressure to ease the icing out, as if you were colouring in a shape with a pen. Once the first area is flooded, release the pressure on the bag and remove, from the side of the area and over the piped outline, so that you do not get a mark in the smooth icing. Beginners may find it easier to mark on the paper with pencil the order in which to flood the areas.

Place under a heat lamp for a few

minutes to allow the sugar to crust over on the top surface (the lamp will ensure the surface of the runout doesn't sink by taking too long to dry, and also gives a shiny finish).

Gradually build up the picture using the various colours, leaving the icing of each section to form a crust before starting the next. This will help define the sections. If you are using very dark colours, leave to dry for slightly longer to avoid the colours running (if you find your colours are running, your icing may be too runny).

Use a paintbrush or the tip of the piping bag to help ease the icing into the corners of the design and break any air bubbles that appear. Raised areas, such as arms or clothing, can be created by piping two layers.

DRYING When all the different sections of the runout are complete, place under a heat lamp immediately for 1 hour to ensure the runout dries with a good sheen. Then put the runout in a warm dry room and leave to dry completely. Small pieces will need about 24 hours and larger pieces 48 hours (pieces that are sunken have taken too long to dry). When dry, carefully peel off the masking tape, holding the picture in position, and pull the runout to the edge of the board. Gently peel the paper off the back. Or slide a palette knife under the runout.

Finishing touches and facial features can be painted or dusted on by hand when dry, either before you remove the runouts from the paper or after.

RUNOUT COLLARS

Runout collars are made to be attached to the top surface of cakes and extend over the edge, increasing the border and giving the cake an appearance of importance and being larger than it actually is. The design used for the runout collar is sometimes repeated around the base on the board in place of the conventional piped border. Runout collars are delicate, so it is a good idea to always make two collars in case of breakages, or make several spare pieces if your collar is made in separate parts.

PIPING THE OUTLINE For a simple collar, measure the top of the cake and draw a template of the collar design on paper, ensuring the collar extends over the edge of

the cake. Attach the paper to a flat working surface and secure a piece of non-stick baking paper or acetate over the top with masking tape.

Fit a piping bag with a number 1 or 0 tube and fill with firm-peak royal icing. Pipe over the outline. Score the non-stick paper with a scalpel, making a cross in the centre and a slit between each corner of the collar and the secured corner of the paper. This will stop the collar warping and changing its shape while it is drying.

THE CONSISTENCY OF THE ICING

For flooding the runout collar the consistency of the icing needs to be fairly thin. 'Let down' the icing by stirring in water

a drop at a time until the icing has the consistency of cream (do not beat in the water or your icing may contain a lot of air bubbles). Gently paddle out air bubbles with a palette knife. If you are going to colour the icing, do this before letting down, so that it does not become too runny, and use a colouring that does not contain glycerine, which would inhibit the drying of the runout. To test the consistency, draw a line across the surface of the icing with a knife; the mark should disappear by the count of 5. Fill a piping bag with the icing—you do not need a tube on the icing bag. Cut a number 2 size hole in the bag and squeeze the icing into a second large bag to get rid of the air bubbles.

From left: Check that the collar fits the size of the cake; Pipe the outline with firm peak icing; Flood the collar, pushing the icing into the corners; Secure the dry collar to the top of the cake.

FILLING IN THE OUTLINE Cut a number 2 hole in the piping bag containing the runout icing and start flooding the collar, working around the collar in small sections at a time, ensuring there are no joins visible. Push the icing gently into the corners of the collar with a damp paintbrush. Burst any air bubbles with the paintbrush or a pin.

Put the collar under a heat lamp to crust over the surface and give it a sheen. Remove the lamp and leave the collar in a warm dry place until hard.

ATTACHING TO THE CAKE Release the collar from the paper or acetate by easing a fine palette knife between the two, gently working your way around the collar. Attach to the top of the cake by piping soft royal icing along the top edges of the cake and carefully lifting the collar into position. Do not press the collar but allow it to settle on the soft icing. Leave to dry. If you like, finish the inside edge of the collar with piping lines, scrolls, flowers or dots.

COLLAR DESIGNS Collars do not have to be made as one whole round or square piece; they can be made in smaller sections and attached separately to the top of the cake. This is especially useful for multi-sided cakes such as hexagons or octagons. The joins can be decorated with piping or covered with a small flooded design called an overlay. Quarter or corner collars are easy for beginners as they can be adjusted to fit the cake. For square cakes you can also make four small corner collars.

Side collars are used as an alternative to corner collars. These are made in four or more pieces for square or multi-sided cakes.

The designs for collars can vary from a simple circle or square extending over the edges of a round or square cake, to elaborate curved patterns such as a collar of overlapping leaves, stars or hearts. Designs can be made more airy and delicate by leaving sections of the pattern unflooded. This section can then be left empty or decorated when the rest of the collar is dry. Advanced cake decorators can pipe filigree into the spaces in the collar.

EMBROIDERY

Embroidery is another piping technique for giving a cake a 'finished' look. Decoration can be as simple as plain white 'hailspots' or repeating flowers around the cake. There are many types of embroidery, the two most popular being tube and brush embroidery. Tube embroidery can be piped either freehand or with a template, but with brush embroidery it is best to use a template. These techniques can be used both on the cake and board. Filigree is ornamental fine lacework that can be piped directly onto a cake, or piped onto paper like a runout and removed when dry. Pieces can even be 'glued' together with wet icing to create three-dimensional decorations.

EMBROIDERY

HAIL SPOTS
Pipe soft-peak royal icing with a number 1 tube randomly in tiny dots over the cake. Use white icing or coloured for contrast and group together to create flowers.

ROSES
Pipe soft-peak royal icing with a number 1 tube, creating curved lines that spread outwards in a circular pattern. Pipe stems and leaves in a contrasting colour.

DAISIES
Pipe soft-peak royal icing with a number 1 tube to make either pointed or rounded petals. Pipe a bulb in the centre and stems and leaves in a contrasting colour.

TUBE EMBROIDERY

Trace your design onto paper. Turn the paper over and place in position on the sugarpaste.

Trace over the top of the design with a scriber and lift away the paper. (Alternatively you can prick the design onto the cake through the template with a pin.)

Using a number 1 or 0 tube, pipe over the scribed lines and dots with the icing representing neat parallel stitches. You can use white or coloured icing.

BRUSH EMBROIDERY

Trace your design onto paper. Turn the paper over and place under a sheet of perspex. Hold in position with masking tape. Pipe over the outline on the perspex with a number 1 tube and leave to dry.

Turn the perspex over and press the hard royal icing onto soft sugarpaste. Press firmly and then lift off the perspex. The outline should be indented into the sugarpaste. Alternatively, scribe the outline.

Pipe over a small area of the outline with soft-peak royal icing, using a number 1 or 2 tube. Work with a small area at a time, so the icing doesn't dry.

Using a small damp paintbrush, touch the surface of the royal icing and stroke it downwards towards the centre of the design. Large areas can be covered with a flat brush.

Create texture by using a finer brush for small details, or even piping fine lines. Extra dimension can be given by piping and brushing another layer over the first, once it is dry. Once dry, coloured dusts can be used.

Interesting effects can be created by using white brush embroidery on a cake iced with coloured sugarpaste or marzipan.

FILIGREE

Pipe directly onto the iced cake or onto non-stick baking paper. Use a number 1 or 0 tube, holding the tube lightly against the surface, and pipe a continual line of random 'm' and 'w' shapes in a long string.

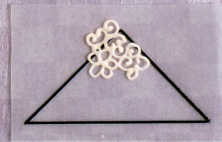
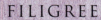

If you are piping on paper, it is useful to draw an outline to guide you. Change direction often and keep the lines close. Leave to dry for at least 24 hours, then remove from the paper with a palette knife.

Make three-dimensional filigree designs by gluing together several pieces when dry. But you will need to touch the lines together occasionally when piping, so the design is more stable when removed from the paper.

73

LACE AND EXTENSION WORK

Small pieces of lace icing, piped onto non-stick baking paper as runouts and attached to the cake when dry, are another excellent device for neatening unsightly edges. Attach them over the top edge of Garrett frills or extension work with tiny dabs of wet icing. Extension work consists of parallel lines of royal icing piped from the cake's surface to a 'bridge' of piping already constructed on the cake. There are two basic shapes of bridgework: the first is built up by piping continuous loops of the same size directly on top of each other, as we've shown here; the second starts with small loops, which are overpiped with longer loops, increasing in length.

LACE

Trace the pattern for the lace onto paper and repeat as many times as you like, leaving a little room between each piece.

Place a piece of non-stick baking paper over the pattern. Fit a piping bag with a 0 or 00 tube, fill with royal icing and pipe over the patterns, ensuring the lines touch where designed, giving strength to the lace.

When the lace is dry, colour the pieces with dusting powder or chalk colours.

Carefully lift the lace from the paper by folding back the paper and sliding a spatula under the icing pieces.

Attach the lace to the cake with a little dot or line of royal icing (this will depend on the design of the lace—you don't want to be able to see the icing 'glue' beneath), piped either onto the cake or the edge of the lace.

You can make curved lace by drying pieces draped over a piece of dowel. Remember to make plenty of extra lace as you will always break some pieces. If you are transporting the cake, take some spares with you.

EXTENSION WORK

Make a paper template for the curved shapes of the bridgework, ensuring that the pattern will fit evenly in the space allowed (eg along one side of the cake) and that all the divisions of the 'bridge' are equal.

Mark the bridgework and the top of the extension work on the cake with a scriber. Remove the template before piping.

Pipe a loop of icing over the scribed line. Then work around the cake, piping over the scribed lines so that they touch.

Pipe a second loop directly on top of the first loop to make the start of a 'bridge'.

Continue building up the loops on top of each other, until you have several layers and the bridgework seems strong and secure. (You can also strengthen these by painting with thinned icing.)

Using a number 1 or 0 tube, pipe parallel lines from the top scribed line to the bridge you have made. These lines should be straight and close enough together not to allow another line to be piped between them.

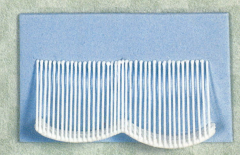

To achieve straight and even lines, tilt the top of the cake slightly towards you, allowing gravity to pull the icing line directly perpendicular. Take care not to stretch the icing or the line may vary in thickness.

When each line is complete, stop squeezing and carefully lower the tube under the bridge to break the flow of icing. Neaten the top of the work by piping a small row of loops to hide the tops. Finish off with piped dots.

Alternatively, attach pieces of sugar lace along the top edge of the extension work.

SUGAR FLOWERS

Sugar flowers range from the simplest 'filler' flowers made with plunger cutters, to fantastic creations of roses, poppies and sweet peas that are difficult to tell apart from the real thing. They are made from flower paste (see page 35 or buy the ready-made variety) that is rolled out on a surface lightly dusted with cornflour. If you are interested in making sugar flowers, this is the time when you need to start investing in equipment—some good petal cutters, a kit of tools for frilling edges, balling, cupping and shaping flowers and a wide variety of colourings and petal dusts. The flowers are made on pieces of florist's wire and can then be taped into sprays or posies in the same ways as fresh blooms.

SIMPLE FILLER FLOWERS

'Filler' flowers are simple blossoms used to fill out a spray or posy. The easiest way to make flowers is by using one of the many types of cutter available—you will need to invest in petal cutters, stamens, florist's wire and tape, and a set of tools for frilling and balling petals. Flower paste is used for all the cutter flowers. Only use a small ball of paste at a time, rolling it out thinly so that it is pliable but not sticky. Thick paste is difficult to frill or cup and the finished flowers may look clumsy. Keep your paste covered with plastic when not using to prevent it drying out. If your paste is too hard, knead in a little egg white or water. If it is too soft, knead in extra icing sugar.

DAFFODIL

Roll out a small ball of yellow flower paste quite thinly. Cut two flowers with a snowdrop cutter. Shape the edges with a ball tool and pinch at the tip to form a point.

To make the trumpet, form a tiny cone of paste, then open up and thin the narrow end with a skewer. Secure one flower on top of another with water so six petals are visible.

Moisten the trumpet with water and attach to the centre of the petals to finish the daffodil. Insert a moist hooked wire for a stem if necessary. Leave to dry.

BLOSSOM

Thinly roll out a small piece of flower paste. Cut out flowers with a blossom, daphne or primrose cutter and put on a piece of sponge. Shape by pressing a ball tool in the centre of each flower.

Use a glass-head pin to make a small hole in the middle of each flower. Leave to dry. Thread a stamen through each flower and secure in place by piping a dot of royal icing in the centre of each flower.

Cut some floristry tape into thin strips. Tape a few flowers to a piece of 28-gauge wire, keeping the flowers close together. The flowers can be made with coloured paste or brushed with dusting powder when dry.

DAISY

Roll a small ball of flower paste and flatten into a stubby cone. Insert a moist hooked piece of 26-gauge wire into the centre. Flatten and dry. Paint with yellow-tinted egg white and dip in polenta. Leave to dry.

Roll out white flower paste and cut out daisy shapes with a cutter. Cut the eight petals in half to make 16, rounding the ends with a scalpel. Use a ball tool to curl the petals, pulling gently towards the centre.

Turn over and curl one or two petals in the other direction. Moisten the centre of the petals and insert the yellow centre by poking the wire through the middle of the petals. Press lightly to secure. Dry in a stand.

STEPHANOTIS

To make buds, roll a dumb-bell shape of white paste around moist 26-gauge wire. Cut out a tiny calyx with a cutter, moisten with water and thread the calyx through the wire and up onto the bud base.

For flowers, roll paste into a small ball then press into a dumb-bell with one larger end. Hold upright and squash the larger end down on a board to flatten until large enough to roll into a circle with a dowel.

Place a stephanotis cutter over the top and cut out from the circle. Smooth the back of each petal with a ball tool. Turn over and thin the centre of each petal with a cocktail stick. Push onto wire and add a calyx.

IVY LEAVES

Roll out flower paste and use ivy cutters or templates to cut out various sized leaves.

Insert a moist 26-gauge wire through the centre of the leaf. Vein the leaf with an ivy veiner and soften the edges, curving some slightly. Leave to dry.

Dust the leaf with forest green dusting powder and the edges with brown, or paint with paste or liquid colours and leave to dry Alternatively, cut the leaves from green-tinted flower paste.

ROSES

Roses are perennial favourites, especially for wedding cakes. The rose is made around a central solid cone with the petals added in overlapping layers. Invest in many different sizes of cutters for both petals and leaves. Even if you are making white roses, tint or dust them with a hint of colour to give depth and character.

MATERIALS
white and green-tinted flower paste
18, 26 and 28-gauge wires
green florist's tape
assorted colourings and petal dust

EQUIPMENT
rose petal cutters
large rose petal veiner
rose calyx cutters
rose leaf cutters
extra large leaf cutter
large briar rose leaf veiner
apple tray or cupped former

CONE

Roll white flower paste into a cone with a sharp point and broad base. (Make it no longer than the small rose petal cutter, and smaller for buds.) Cover a half length of 18-gauge wire with tape and hook the end.

Moisten the wire with egg white and insert into the base of the cone, making sure that the hook goes almost to the tip. Pinch the base of the cone firmly onto the wire. Make as many as you need and dry overnight.

Colour a large amount of flower paste to the required colour (we've used pale melon). Start with a pale base colour and tint with petal dust when complete. For white roses, use a touch of melon for a warm glow, or bitter-lemon for a green tinge.

FIRST AND SECOND LAYERS

Roll out some coloured flower paste thinly and cut out four petals with the smaller rose petal cutter.

Place the petals on a pad and soften the edges with the rounded end of a large celstick, working half on the paste and half on the pad. Do not frill the edges of the petals, simply soften the harsh cut edge.

Moisten the central part of one of the petals and place it against a dried cone, leaving at least 5 mm (1/4 inch) of the petal above the tip of the cone.

Tuck the left-hand side of the petal in towards the cone to hide the tip of the cone completely. Wrap the other side of the petal around to form a tight spiral, leaving the end slightly open.

Moisten the bases of the remaining petals. Tuck the first underneath the open edge of the petal on the cone, the second underneath the first and the third under the second. The petals should now be fairly evenly spaced.

Moisten the petals and close them tight, pulling them down at an angle rather than wrapping straight around. There are enough petals on the cone to make a small bud but for a larger rose open up the last petal.

THIRD AND FOURTH LAYERS

Roll out some more paste and cut out another three petals with the same size cutter as before. Soften the edges, then mark with the veiner (you don't need to vein small roses). Moisten the base of each petal again.

Tuck the first petal of the third layer under the last petal of the second layer. Continue as before, this time pinching a very gentle central vein on each petal between your finger and thumb as you add it to the rose.

Cut out another three petals and repeat, this time wrapping the petals less tightly.

FIFTH LAYER

Roll out more paste and cut another three petals, using the slightly larger petal cutter. Vein and soften each of the petals as before.

Cup the centre of each petal with the rounded end of a large celstick. Moisten the base of each petal and attach them as before, making sure that the centre of each covers a join in the previous layer.

The rose should now be quite open; curl back the petal edges with your fingers or a cocktail stick. This flower is termed a 'half rose' and most bouquets use more half roses than full ones.

SIXTH LAYER

The sixth layer can either follow on as before or the petals can be wired individually. Roll out a small piece of paste, leaving a thicker ridge down the centre (this ridge should be very subtle).

Cut out the petal, using the same size cutter as before. Hook and moisten the end of a 26-gauge wire. Insert only into the base of the ridge. Soften the edges and mark with the veiner.

Stroke the centre of the petal towards yourself to stretch it and cup it slightly. Curl the edges back a little at this stage. Place into an apple tray former to dry. Repeat to make 8 to 10 petals.

ASSEMBLY AND COLOURING

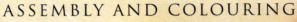

Taping the petals around the rose centre and then petal dusting gives a balanced result. Mix together primrose, lemon and white petal dust. Dust in at the base of each petal on the inside and heavier on the back.

Next, mix together the selected main colour (we used a mixture of apricot and plum petal dust). Start by dusting the centre of the rose, firmly and quite strong in colour.

Gradually dust the outer petals, starting at the edges and fading down to the base.

CALYX

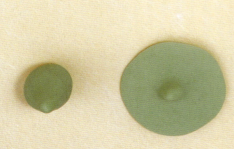

Roll a ball of mid-green flower paste into a cone and pinch out the base to form a hat shape.

Using a small cocktail stick, roll out the base to make it a little thinner. Place the calyx cutter over the top and cut out. Elongate each sepal by rolling with the cocktail stick.

Place the calyx cutter on a pad and cup the inner part of each of the sepals. Dust the inner calyx with a mixture of white and moss green to make it paler.

Make fine cuts in the edges of each sepal to give them a 'hairy' appearance.

Moisten the centre of the calyx and attach it to the back of the rose or bud, positioning each sepal so that it covers a join between two outer petals. On a full rose it would curl right back and on a bud it would be tight.

Dust the outer part of the calyx with dark green and moss. Keep the very edges of each sepal much paler. Leave to dry.

LEAVES

Roll out some mid-green paste, leaving a thick ridge down the centre (a grooved board may be used). Cut out a selection of sizes using rose leaf cutters. You need one large, two medium and two small leaves per stem.

Cut lengths of 26- or 28-gauge wire into four. Moisten one end of each wire and insert into the thick ridge of a leaf, at least half the length of the leaf. Vein the leaf with the briar rose leaf veiner.

Place the leaf on a pad and soften the edges with a large celstick. Pinch a vein down the centre of the leaf and shape the leaf between your finger and thumb to give movement.

Dust the back of each leaf with white and moss green petal dust. Overdust with plum and aubergine on the edges and bring a little of the colour down on to the veins. Turn over; dust the edges and one side darker.

Dust the upper side of the leaf with dark green and then overdust with either holly/ivy or moss green. Leave to dry.

Tape the leaves together into groups of three or five, starting with a large leaf, then the two medium, then the two small leaves.

SWEET PEAS

We've used a mass of these delicate sweet pea flowers, trailing stems and entwining tendrils, for our fairy-tale wedding cake on page 262. It is a good idea to have a real garden sweet pea next to you while you work to check the fine details and colouring. We've used cutters for the petals, but if you can't find any you could make a template.

MATERIALS
white and green-tinted flower paste
20, 24, 28 and 30-gauge wires
primrose, spring green, white, moss green,
dark green, plum and deep purple petal dust

EQUIPMENT
scalpel
rose petal cutters
nile green florist's tape
small rose calyx cutter
sweet pea cutters
ceramic silk veining tool
Dresden tool
fine pliers
fresh sweet pea foliage or peony veiners

KEEL

There are two central petals fused together at the base that contain the stamens. This section is known as the keel. Roll a ball of white flower paste into a teardrop with a slight point at the rounded end as well.

Flatten with your fingers to form a pasty shape. Moisten a hooked 24-gauge wire and insert into the base of the shape. Pinch a sharp angle to the edge of the rounded part.

Using a sharp scalpel, indent and open up the straight edge to represent the opening for the stamens. Curve the straight edge back a little. You will need to make a keel for each of the flowers and buds.

BUDS

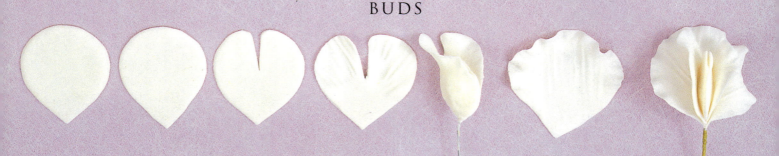

The keel for some of the smaller buds should be smaller than those for the flowers. Roll out white flower paste thinly and cut out two rose petal shapes with the rose cutters.

Using a sharp scalpel, cut out a very narrow, deep 'V' shape in one petal. Frill the edges with a cocktail stick or ball tool. Moisten the base of the petal and wrap around to the flat side of the keel.

Frill the second petal, draw down a central vein, moisten the base and wrap around the split petal. Pinch the whole piece together at the base to secure and then curl back the outer petal a little.

CALYX

Form a ball of green flower paste into a teardrop. Flatten the round end to make a base and place, point up, on the board. Thin the base with a cocktail stick.

Place the small rose calyx cutter over the top and cut out the calyx. Elongate each of the sepals by rolling them with the celstick.

Place the calyx on a pad, flat side down, and hollow out the centre of each sepal with the broad end of the Dresden tool.

Turn over and open up the centre of the calyx with the pointed end of a celstick. Moisten the centre and thread on to the back of the flower.

Position two of the sepals onto the back of the outer petal shape. Pinch and curl the tips of the calyx back slightly.

Tape over the stem with florist's tape. To bend the stem, hold the point of the stem directly behind the calyx with fine pliers. Hold the wire at the end and bend this end over to give a neat curve. Colour the bud.

WING PETALS

To make wing petals, roll out a piece of white flower paste, leaving a slightly thicker area running halfway down the centre of the petal. Cut out a petal with the wing petal cutter.

Hook and moisten the end of a 30-gauge wire and insert it into the base of the thick area on the petal. Pinch the base to secure. Place the petal, ridge side up, on the board.

Vein with the silk veining tool, keeping the point of the tool to the point of the petal, working in a fan shape. Soften the frill by rolling over with a cocktail stick. Repeat so that you have left and right wing petals.

STANDARD PETALS

Roll out some more paste, again leaving a thicker ridge. Cut out the petal with the cutter. Insert a hooked 28-gauge white wire into the base of the petal (do not insert the wire too far).

Vein the petal and frill with the silk veining tool. Place the petal on a pad and draw down a central vein on the upper side. Turn the petal over.

With the broad end of the Dresden tool, hollow out two small indents, one either side of the central vein at the base of the petal (this will make two raised areas on the front of the petal). Allow to firm up with a curl.

ASSEMBLY AND COLOURING

Tape the two wing petals on to either side of the keel, using florist's tape. The long side of each petal should be uppermost.

As the petals are still wet, you can now re-shape them to give a good natural appearance. Tape the standard petal tightly onto the back of the flower with florist's tape.

Squeeze the base of the petals together to form a tight, neat join, then curl the standard petal back a little (the more mature the flower is, the further back this petal will be). Leave to dry before dusting.

Mix a small amount of the primrose and spring green together with a touch of white petal dust. Dust the tip of the keel gently and in at the base of each of the petals.

Dust the petals to colour, starting at the edges and working inwards and down. Use plum and white for pale pink flowers, plum and deep purple for darker pink and deep purple with plum dust for the purple flowers.

Dust the back of the standard petals with a little green mixture. Attach the calyx as for the bud. Dust the calyx with spring and moss green with a touch of white petal dust. Bend the stem as for the bud, but not so much.

LEAVES, BRACTS AND TENDRILS

  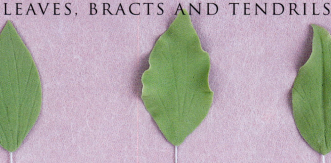  

Roll some mid-green flower paste, leaving a ridge down the centre (or use a grooved board). Place a leaf template or fresh leaf on top of the flower paste and cut out the shape (with practice you can cut these freehand).

Insert a moistened 28-gauge wire into the thick ridge of the leaf. Vein the leaf, by pressing with a fresh leaf or using a suitable veiner.

You can choose whether to give your leaves frilled or flat edges. Frill partially with the broad end of the Dresden tool and then over-frill with a cocktail stick.

Pinch the leaf to emphasise the central vein, then dry before dusting. Make the leaves in pairs. Dust in various shades of green. Where the leaf stems join the main stem there are two bracts.

Roll a small teardrop of green paste and insert a moist length of 30-gauge wire into the broad end. Flatten and pinch at the base.

The tendrils grow from the leaf stems not the flower stems. Use ¼ width tape twisted back on itself to form fine strands.

Put three tendrils together on a 24-gauge wire. Some stems have other tendrils below.

Place two leaves on either side of the tendril stem. The leaves are always in pairs. Secure with green florist's tape. Secure a pair of bracts further down the stem. Tape the flowers and buds into the stems with three or four flowers on them. Use a 20-gauge wire to form the main stem and leave a short length of each of the flower stems showing.

POPPIES

These Icelandic poppies are vibrantly coloured in scarlet and orange but, of course, you can vary the colouring. We've used a tangled bunch for our wedding cake on page 260, but they are also perfect for use in a spray of summer flowers. The flower paste is rolled paper-thin on a grooved board to make the delicate poppy petals. You can steam the flowers very quickly over hot water when they are finished to remove the dry appearance of the dust.

MATERIALS

pale green and white-tinted flower paste
small seed-head stamens
green, primrose, lemon and
aubergine petal dust
yellow polenta
orange and scarlet craft dust
20 and 28-gauge wires

EQUIPMENT

tiny 8-petal daisy cutter
angled tweezers
non-toxic craft glue
glue gun and non-toxic glue sticks
poppy cutters
orchid veiner
ceramic silk veining tool
leaf texturing tool
green florist's tape

OVARY

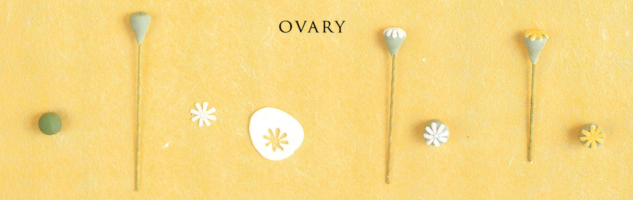

Roll a small ball of green flower paste into a cone shape. Tape over a length of 20-gauge wire, moisten the end with egg white and insert into the point of the cone. Pinch into place and flatten the top. Cover with plastic.

Roll out a small amount of white paste thinly and cut out a daisy shape with the cutter. Secure the daisy to the top of the cone. As the paste is still soft, the daisy will stick (if not, use a little water).

Dust the green part of the ovary with moss green and the daisy shape with a mixture of primrose and lemon. Use a pair of angled tweezers to emphasise the shape of the daisy if necessary. Leave to dry completely.

STAMENS

You will need half a bunch of seed-head stamens for each flower. Spread the stamens open a little. Apply glue in a strip across the stamens at the length required. Squeeze the stamens together and leave to dry.

Cut the stamens to the required length, apply glue to the base of the ovary and wrap the stamens quickly around. Dry, then dust the lengths with moss green and primrose dust and the tips with primrose and lemon dust.

To make more mature stamens, paint the tips with egg white and dip into polenta. For a flower not fully open, leave the stamens tight around the ovary. Otherwise, bend the stamens open with tweezers.

PETALS

Roll out a small amount of white flower paste very thinly on a grooved board. Cut a petal with a cutter or template. Remove from the board and insert a moistened 28-gauge white wire into the central ridge.

Press the back of the petal onto the orchid veiner. Turn over and vein the upper side. Thin out and frill the top edge with the veining tool, then a cocktail stick. Cup the centre and dry slightly over bubble wrap.

Repeat to make at least one more petal of that size. Cut at least two petals with the larger template or cutter. After veining and frilling, pinch a ridge on the upper surface of each petal. Cup the centres and leave to dry.

COLOURING AND ASSEMBLY

For vibrant colours, dust the petals while fresh. Dust a patch at the base of each petal on both sides with a mixture of primrose and lemon, then add a small amount of moss green to the very base.

For orange/red poppies, rub the orange craft dust into the paste with a brush, leaving the back a touch paler, and then overdust the edge with scarlet craft dust.

Tape the two small petals tightly behind the stamens. Tape the two larger petals behind the small petals to fill in the gaps. Leave to dry. Steam the flower to remove the dry appearance left by the dusting.

BUDS AND BRACTS

Tape over 20-gauge wire several times. Bend an open hook in the end, moisten and insert into an egg-shaped piece of flower paste. Dry. Roll out white flower paste very thinly and cut 2–3 petals. Vein and frill as before.

Stick petals to the bud with water, crumple and dust. Roll out green flower paste and texture with a brush. Cut two bracts with the small poppy cutter and hollow out slightly. Stick to either side of the bud.

Snip with scissors to add texture and make an indent with a scalpel to divide the bracts. Dust green, leaving the open edges paler, then overdust with aubergine for the rough texture. Dust the stems and bend into shape.

MAKING A FLOWER SPRAY

Fresh flowers and sugar flowers, made on stems of florist's wire, can be taped into sprays in just the same way. Sugar flowers are more delicate than fresh flowers and can chip if they are knocked. Work on a soft surface, such as foam, in case you drop a flower, and strengthen the stems with heavier wires (or by taping several wires together) so that the flowers are stable.

RIBBON LOOPS These can fill gaps in flower sprays and provide a neat finish. They also cushion flowers to prevent them knocking each other. Choose ribbon that complements the colours and size of the flowers. Two of the most commonly used ribbon loops are 'tails' and 'overhand loops'.

For a tail, fold a length of ribbon in half, lay a length of 26-gauge wire on top of the fold and tape with florist's tape. Overhand loops are made by wrapping the ribbon around your fingers several times and threading a 28-gauge wire between your index finger and the ribbon loops. Twist the wire tightly around the ribbon. Cut the ribbon tails to the length required and tape the ribbon to the wire, pinching the ribbon at the join.

POSY This is made by taping the flowers together in a circle with a domed centre. Start with the largest flower in the centre and add to this, gradually turning the posy around, making sure that you add flowers and leaves evenly and incorporating ribbon

loops if you like. A Victorian posy is a more structured version, with the flowers in each circular row being the same, so a rose might be surrounded by a circle of primroses, then violets, then leaves, then a posy frill. Cut the ends of the wire stems to the same length and tape together securely with florist's tape.

RETURN A return is a small wired spray often used as a supplementary decoration and for building more complicated displays. Returns can be taped together or taped to posies to create a variety of sprays. The overall shape of the return should be an elongated triangle. Start with buds or small flowers at the point of the triangle (you could draw the shape on paper and arrange

From left: Ribbons can be tied into loops or cut to make tails; The most basic of arrangements is the circular posy; Flowers can be taped into a return; A posy and return can be combined to make a spray.

the flowers on top of this before taping them). Tape these smaller flowers together with florist's tape, working down the stem, adding leaves and larger flowers near the wider base. Remember that the spray is three-dimensional and needs height as well as width. Trim away any unwanted wires as you work, so that the main stem remains slender, (don't trim away too much though or you will weaken the stem). You can tape ribbon loops to the spray at any time.

TEARDROP BOUQUET This consists of a posy and a return taped together (proficient flower-makers can make this bouquet as one section). Tape the return together neatly, leaving a long taped spike at the end. Tape the posy together, leaving a gap at one side. Place the return into the gap in the posy and mark where the wires cross at the back. Bend the stem of the return to a right angle at the marked point and bind the two stems with a piece of wire. Secure with florist's tape.

HOGARTH SPRAY This consists of two returns and a posy. The returns are longer than usual and are taped to either side of the posy, then bent into an 's' shaped spray.

CRESCENT This is a teardrop bouquet with a second return taped to the other end. The returns are curved around towards each other. This is usually made with a large flower in the centre.

ATTACHING TO THE CAKE When placing sprays on cakes, take care that the wires never go into the cake or icing. Insert a posy holder into the top, side or corner of the cake for the spray to sit in. The holder should protrude slightly above the level of the icing, so that it can be removed easily before cutting. Place a small piece of sugarpaste in the holder to secure the spray. Royal-iced cakes will need a bit more care, to prevent the icing cracking. Use a sharp-pointed knife to make a hole in the icing, turning the tip gently in circles to drill through. Alternatively, sprays can be attached to a base of sugarpaste. Simply poke the stems into a cone of sugarpaste that has been left to 'crust' for 30 minutes.

MODELLING

If you are planning several figures on a cake, they need to be small enough not to overwhelm the rest of the cake. A 30 g (1 oz) piece of modelling paste will make a body about 5 cm (2 inches) long (not including the head). You will need very little equipment, just modelling paste (see page 34), a few cocktail sticks and drinking straws for marking features and scrupulously clean hands. A tiny amount of white vegetable fat on your fingers will help you achieve a smooth finish and prevent the paste sticking. You can assemble the pieces after drying or while they are still soft, whichever you find easiest. Paint on features and tiny details when the figures are dry. You'll need as many paste or powder food colourings as your imagination has room for.

BASIC FIGURES

SIMPLE BODY AND ARMS

 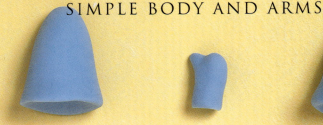 

Roll modelling paste into a smooth ball and then roll between your palms into a cone shape. Flatten the base of the cone so the figure will stand.

Stroke around the base and sides of the cone with your thumb and index finger to make a thin edge (like the hem of a garment). Make a hole for the neck with a skewer and one on either side for sleeves.

Roll two small cone shapes, half the length of the body. Pinch out a small peg at the thicker ends. Open the narrow end with the skewer to make sleeves. Brush in the body holes with edible glue and attach the arms.

T-SHAPED BODY ALTERNATIVE

Roll the ball of paste into a sausage shape, slightly thicker at one end. Pinch out the paste on either side of the thick end to make arms, rolling between your finger and thumb to lengthen.

Level the base of the body and make a hem as above. Open the sleeves and make a neck hole as above. (You can make trousers by cutting up the centre of the base. Open the trouser bottoms with a skewer to fit shoes.)

For separate trousers, use half the amount of paste for the body and roll into a sausage. Thin out the centre by rolling with one finger. Open both ends with a skewer, then fold in half, bringing the ends together.

ALL-IN-ONE BODY ALTERNATIVE

Mould flesh-coloured modelling paste into a thick sausage. Roll and thin each end to half the thickness of the middle. For the ankles, roll again to thin a short distance from each end of the sausage.

Pinch the ends of the sausage and bend to make feet. Fold the paste in the middle and bring the legs together. Squeeze the paste at the top of each leg to make knees. Roll the paste in the centre to make a thinner waist.

Mould the legs so that they are in standing or sitting positions. Use a skewer to make holes in the top and sides of the body for the head and arms. Leave to dry.

ARMS AND FEET

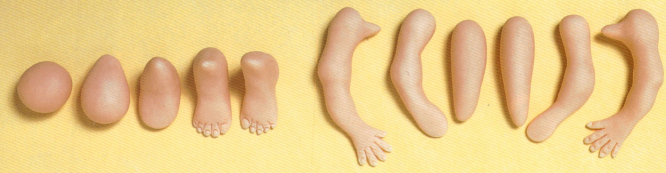

To make separate feet, roll a cone and pinch one end to flatten. Nails can be marked with a thin drinking straw cut to the shape of a nail. Mark the end of the foot and cut with a scalpel to separate the toes.

For arms, roll a small piece of flesh-coloured paste into a tapered sausage (the wide end is the shoulder). Thin at the narrow end to make a wrist and flatten the tip to an oval for the hand. Cut fingers with fine scissors.

Gently bend the arm and pinch lightly to make the elbow. On the inside of the shoulder, pinch out a piece of paste to make a small peg to fit the arm hole made in the body. Attach with edible glue when dry.

HEADS AND HANDS

Roll flesh-coloured paste into a smooth ball. Put in the palm of one hand and roll the other index finger lightly over the centre to make a fat peanut shape (with practice you can make fat chins and narrow foreheads).

Pinch the paste at the lower back of the head to make a neck. You can insert a piece of uncooked spaghetti into the neck for extra strength. Mark eyes, eyebrows and mouth with the end of a drinking straw.

Attach a small cone of paste to either side of the head for ears. Press the narrow end into the head with a paintbrush handle to hollow out the ear. Make noses with balls or cones. Mark nostrils with a pin after attaching.

Make different hairstyles by texturing rolled-out paste—a curved-blade modelling tool is useful. Use round or daisy cutters to cut out hair, shred the edge and lay over the head.

Allow heads to dry completely before painting. Use well-diluted paste colours and a very fine paintbrush. To give a blush to cheeks, use plum dusting powder mixed with cornflour.

To make separate hands, make a flattened cone of flesh-coloured paste, with a narrow end for the wrist. Cut a 'V' from one side for the thumb, then make three cuts for fingers. On large hands, mark the nails with a straw.

CHARACTERS

FATHER CHRISTMAS

Form a large flat cone of red paste for the body and make a mark down the front for the coat opening. Make holes in each side of the top of the body to insert the arms. Make two sleeve shapes and roll two sausages, pressing gently together to form the legs. Make hands, head, ears and nose from flesh-coloured paste. Form an elongated red cone and bend the tip over for the hat. Trim the coat, trousers and hat with white 'fur' and secure to the body. Add a white beard. Cut and mould small pieces of black paste for the shoes, eyes, belt and buckle and attach.

LITTLE BOY RAG DOLL

Form a large flat white cone for the body and indent where the legs will attach. Make two sausages for legs and wrap red strips around for stockings. Make two smaller flesh-coloured sausages for arms, flatten the ends to make hands and wrap in purple for sleeves. For the collar, top a purple circle with a white circle and cut out a small wedge. Wrap purple icing around the top of the body and green around the base. Add braces with stitching lines. Make a flesh-coloured head with indents for eyes. Secure arms to the body. Wrap tops of legs in green, attach to the body and add shoes. Secure collar, then head. Paint features. Pipe royal icing hair with a number 1 or 2 tube.

CHOIR BOY

Form a large elongated red cone with a hole in the top to insert the head. Make hands, a head and a nose with flesh-coloured paste. Wrap a small piece of white garrett frill around the hands for sleeves. Make a collar with rounds of frilled red and white paste. Wrap a large red garrett frill over the body, then top with a white frill. Place the collar on top of the cone, insert the head, attach arms and paint features when dry. Attach a small bow at the collar and place a small book of icing in the hands. Pipe royal icing hair with a number 1 or 2 tube.

Use coloured modelling paste or paint these characters when dry. Edible glue or royal icing will secure pieces together. Work with a tiny amount of white fat on your hands to prevent the paste sticking.

LITTLE GIRL RAG DOLL

Make a large flat cone for the body with indents to attach legs. Make two sausages for the legs and wrap red strips around for stockings. Make black shoes. Make two smaller sausages for the arms, flatten the ends and form a hand. Wrap blue garrett frill around the arms for sleeves. Make a ball of flesh-coloured icing for the head with indents for the eyes. Make a collar of blue and white garrett frills. Roll a large circle of blue paste and inlay with flowers, then frill the edges. Place over the cone to make a dress. Attach the collar, legs, arms and head. Paint or pipe on the features. Attach thin strips of rolled and twisted paste for the hair and decorate with bows.

TOY SOLDIER

Make a flat white oval for the body and mark legs and arms on the body by indenting. Roll a head from flesh-coloured paste and indent eyes and a mouth. Make a black cone for the hat. Wrap a curved strip of red paste around the body for the coat. Make epaulettes for the shoulders and small black shoes. Secure a curved strip of blue paste around the 'neck' and attach the head, then the hat. Add the epaulettes, strapping, trousers and buckle. Secure two small hands to the bottom of the sleeves and place small triangles over the hands to represent the cuffs. Paint or pipe on facial features.

FAIRY

Mould a long body and legs shape from flesh-coloured paste and form into a sitting position. Make arms and a head. Cut two wing shapes and gently frill the edges; paint on a design and leave to dry. Cut a few elongated triangles and snip in around the edges as shown. Attach these all over the body to cover like a dress. Attach the head and wings. Roll thin strips of paste around a skewer to form ringlets. Attach these and some uncurled pieces to the head. Make a small crown by cutting halfway down the side of a small cylinder of paste; trim off the corners to form points, curl back slightly and place on the hair. Paint or pipe on the facial features.

ANIMALS

MOUSE

Take a piece of paste and divide in half. Mould one half into an oval body, bent slightly into a sitting position, and use the other half for head, arms and feet. Make indents in the body to position the head, arms and feet. Roll a ball of paste for the head, moulding an elongated nose and curving it up slightly. Make circular ears, hollowing slightly with a ball tool. Secure to the head. Shape small sausages for arms, bending at the elbows, flattening the ends for hands and marking fingers. Secure small feet to the base of the body. Roll out and attach a long thin tail. Paint features when dry.

TEDDY BEAR

Roll a round ball for the body with a slightly smaller one for the head. Make indents on the body where the head, arms and legs will be attached. Shape arms and legs from sausages of paste. Cut out small circles of darker coloured paste for paws. Secure the head, arms and legs to the body and the paws to the ends of the arms and legs. Make ears from small, thickly rolled semi-circles of paste, hollowed in the centre with a ball tool, and attach to the head. Make a round muzzle and attach to the centre of the face. When dry, paint stitching on the tummy and facial features.

DOG

Make a long sausage of white paste, place small dots of black paste on it and then roll the sausage to blend them together. Stretch out the front of the sausage and cut down the middle to make legs. Open out a little and indent toes. Stretch out short hind legs and then fold around the body. Make a cone for the head, turning it up slightly at the nose. Cut the front of the head to make a mouth. Insert a small red tongue and attach black ears to the head. Attach a black spot for the nose, black circles for eyes and a small twisted roll of paste for the tail.

Use coloured modelling paste or paint these animals when dry. Edible glue or royal icing will secure pieces together. Work with a tiny amount of white fat on your hands to prevent the paste sticking.

DUCK

Make a sausage of white paste, tapered to thin at both ends. Tweak one end upwards and thin out to make a tail. Elongate the other end and mould into a neck with a head at the end. Make indents for eyes. Make a point at the front of the head where the beak will be painted. Roll a piece of paste thinly and cut out wings, freehand or using a template. Texture with feathers, using a tool or the end of a drinking straw. Roll tiny black balls for eyes. Roll out orange paste thinly and cut into webbed feet. Attach the wings and feet to the body. Press the eyes in place. Paint on the beak when dry.

PIG

Shape a large sausage into a body and make indents where the head and legs will be attached. Make small trotters from ovals with one end flattened and a cut made for trotters. Make the head from another oval, elongated at one end to form a snout. Bend the snout up slightly and make two holes for the nose and a line for the mouth. Make indents for the eyes and insert small balls of black paste. Make ears from circles of paste, cupped with a ball tool. Paint on colouring when dry.

ELEPHANT

Make a ball of paste and indent a belly button in the front centre. Make small fat sausages for legs and mark with creases and toes, using the end of a drinking straw. Make small round pink circles to represent pads. Make the elephant's head from a long oval of paste and stretch out the end to make an upturned trunk. Poke nostrils in the end of the trunk and mark lines on the top like creases. Make indents for eyes and eyebrows. Make large ears, thinning and frilling the edges slightly. Secure the legs and head to the body. Secure the pads to the legs and the ears to the side of the head. Dust when dry.

ACCESSORIES

SHOES

TIES

HATS

Colour and roll modelling paste thinly. Cut out the soles of the shoes first and then shape the tops. Join pieces with water or edible glue. Add laces and paint details when dry.

For a bow tie, pinch a rectangle of paste in the centre to narrow and wrap with a small strip of paste. For a long tie, trim both ends of a long rectangle to a point and add a small 'knot' of paste at the top. Paint when dry.

Roll out paste thinly and cut out a circle for the base. Mould the crown shape and attach to the centre of the circle. Decorate around the brim with ribbon and bows.

TOOLS

Use small pieces of coloured modelling paste, rolled into tiny strips. Dust your fingers with cornflour to prevent sticking of small pieces. Use modelling tools to flatten and hollow out pieces.

Follow real tools as a guide and paint or dust with colour when dry.

BOOKS

FLOWER POT

Form a small rectangle of paste. Trim three sides to give sharp edges, leaving one gently rounded for the spine of the book. Emboss the top and paint the top and sides of the pages when dry.

Form a piece of paste into a thimble shape and hollow out the top slightly. Attach a thin strip of icing around the top edge. Thread several small cutter flowers onto stamens.

Insert the flower stamens into the pot. Paint the pot when dry and paint inside the top rim to represent soil.

FRUIT

Roll small pieces of paste into balls. Secure small leaves to the tops of apples and pears. Break a clove in half and insert a straight piece into the top for the stalk and the remaining piece in the bottom of the fruit.

Roll lemons and oranges over a nutmeg grater to give texture. To make blackberries, roll tiny balls of paste and press together gently. Insert a green stem. Insert black stamens into red balls for the cherries.

For strawberries, roll into shape and make indents for the seeds. Add a green calyx to the tops. Paint all fruits in realistic colours when dry.

BOWS

Cut a strip of thinly rolled paste and fold in half loosely to make a loop. Gather the ends to crease. Repeat to make the other loop. Trim and gather strips to make tails. Cover the central join with a small gathered strip.

Roll a strip of paste, fold in half and moisten the ends. Repeat to make a shorter length and secure on top. Roll a small strip and fold over the central join.

Cut strips of thinly rolled paste and twist over, joining the ends. Dry, then join in the centre with royal icing. Cut ribbon tails and secure underneath with royal icing.

CHRISTMAS TRINKETS

For parcels, mould paste into cubes or rectangles and add strips of coloured paste to represent ribbon. Finish with bows or add green leaves and red balls to represent holly or poinsettias.

For the candy canes, twist red and white strips of paste together and hook over the end into a cane shape.

For the tree, cut four half Christmas trees from green paste and leave to dry. Join with royal icing, supporting until set. If you make more shapes, you can assemble the tree in a standing position.

BACKGROUNDS

SNOW

Peak royal icing and dust heavily with icing sugar.

SAND

Colour caster sugar orange-brown with liquid or paste colouring and allow to dry on a paper-lined tray. Sprinkle over soft royal icing or moistened sugarpaste.

BRICKS

Cut out rectangles of brick-coloured sugarpaste. Colour with orange and red dusting powder, then fill the joins with cement-coloured royal icing, piped with a number 2 tube.

STONE

Cut out irregular rectangles of stone-coloured sugarpaste and attach to the iced cake or board by moistening with water. Fill the joins with mortar-coloured royal icing, piping with a number 2 tube.

GRASS

Cover the cake or board with green sugarpaste and stipple with a sponge dipped in brown-green royal icing, or use a clay gun to create tufts of sugarpaste.

GRASS

Colour desiccated coconut or caster sugar with green liquid or paste colouring, then dry on a paper-lined tray. Sprinkle onto soft royal icing or moistened sugarpaste.

ROOF TILES

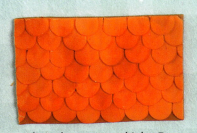

Roll out coloured sugarpaste thinly. Cut circles with a small round cutter and then lay out on the cake or board, overlapping each row. Colour with orange, red and brown dusting powders, when dry.

FLOORBOARDS

Roll together three different shades of brown sugarpaste. Flatten and cut into lengths. Make woodgrain marks with the veining end of a dresden tool. Make small holes for nails and cover with tiny pieces of grey.

EARTH

Use a clay gun to create 'crumbs' of dark brown marzipan or sugarpaste. Sprinkle over the moistened cake or board.

INLAY FLOWERS

Roll out coloured sugarpaste to the same thickness as the icing on the cake. Remove flower shapes from the cake with a cutter. Use the same cutter to insert coloured flowers in the holes left. Smooth over.

SEA

Coat the board or cake with blue sugarpaste. While still soft, push indents with your thumb to make waves. Brush on white royal icing 'surf' at the top of each wave.

POND

Blend sugarpastes tinted blue, white and green, leaving streaky. Roll into a cylinder, then into a coil. Roll out, then mark ripples on the surface with a blunt tool, following the swirls of colour.

WINDOW

Make a suitable background colour, then place a piece of leaf gelatine, cut to the same size, over the shape. Edge with strips of brown sugarpaste to make a frame. Score diamonds for leadlight windows.

MARBLE

Mix small amounts of coloured sugarpaste into larger amounts of a paler sugarpaste. Do not mix thoroughly, so the marble remains streaky. You can paint in more streaks with a fine brush.

TREE BARK

Thinly roll out brown sugarpaste. Make close parallel lines with the back of a knife. Roll a thin spiral of sugarpaste and attach, then flatten to make a wood knot. Colour with brown dusting powder.

PAVING

Paint rows of slightly uneven paving slabs directly onto sugarpaste with diluted food colourings, using a mixture of light browns, beige, green or blue.

COBBLES

Blend light brown and grey marzipan or sugarpaste, without thoroughly mixing. Cut into pieces and roll into irregular shapes. Flatten and attach to the cake or board by moistening with water.

ROCKS

Blend light brown and grey marzipan or sugarpaste, without thoroughly mixing. Cut into pieces and roll into irregular shapes.

GATEAUX

A gateau is simply a cake with its best dress on and this is the perfect starting place for beginners to cake decorating. There is no special equipment needed; in fact, the usual decorating tools are lots of whipped cream, fresh fruit and chocolate. As the chapter progresses, you will, however, learn to make tiny marzipan fruit, curls of chocolate, delicate pieces of chocolate lace and even patterned collars for fitting around the side of your cakes. Several of these recipes specify to use sponge or Madeira cakes, although many can use any of the basic cakes. But remember that fruit cakes shouldn't be combined with buttercreams and chocolate icings.

WHITE CHOCOLATE CREAM GATEAU

This gateau is richly layered with white chocolate cream and fresh berries. We've used strawberries and raspberries but you can use whatever's in season. There are no tricky techniques and this spectacular cake is simple for a beginner to make.

1 Add the melted chocolate to the mixture and beat until smooth.

2 Leave the cake to cool in the tin for 5–10 minutes before turning it out onto a wire rack to let it cool completely.

3 Heat the cream and white chocolate buttons in a bowl over simmering water—if you heat directly the chocolate may seize.

125 g (4 oz) cream cheese
60 g (2 oz) butter
185 g (6 oz) caster sugar
2 eggs, lightly beaten
100 g (3¹/₂ oz) dark chocolate, melted
250 g (8 oz) plain flour
30 g (1 oz) cocoa powder
1 teaspoon bicarbonate of soda
500 ml (16 fl oz) thick (double) cream, whipped
250 g (8 oz) strawberries or raspberries, quartered
whole strawberries, raspberries or young berries

WHITE CHOCOLATE CREAM

125 g (4 oz) white chocolate buttons (melts)
60 ml (2 fl oz) cream

EQUIPMENT

20 cm (8 inch) round cake tin

BAKING THE CAKE

1 Preheat the oven to 180°C (350°F/Gas 4). Brush the cake tin with melted butter or oil. Line the base and side with non-stick baking paper. Using electric beaters, beat the cream cheese, butter and sugar in a small bowl until light and creamy. Add the eggs gradually, beating thoroughly after each addition. Add the melted chocolate and beat until the mixture is smooth.

2 Transfer the mixture to a large bowl. Using a metal spoon, fold in the sifted flour, cocoa and soda alternately with 185 ml (6 fl oz) water. Stir until the mixture is smooth. Pour evenly into the tin and smooth the surface. Bake for 45–50 minutes or until a skewer inserted into the centre of the cake comes out clean. Leave the cake in the tin for 5–10 minutes, then turn out onto a wire rack to cool.

WHITE CHOCOLATE CREAM

3 To make the white chocolate cream, combine the white chocolate buttons and cream in a small heatproof bowl. Bring a small pan of water to a simmer, remove from the heat and place the bowl over the pan (don't let the bottom of the bowl sit in the water). Stir over the hot water until melted and the mixture is smooth. Cool in the refrigerator until spreadable, stirring occasionally.

DECORATING THE CAKE

4 Cut the cake horizontally into three even layers. Place the base layer on a serving plate. Spread with half of the white chocolate cream, top with one-fifth of the whipped cream, then half of the quartered berries. Top with the second layer of cake and repeat the layering with the remaining white chocolate cream, a quarter of the whipped cream and the rest of the quartered berries. Top with the last layer of cake. Spread the cake side and top evenly with the remaining whipped cream. If you have a piping bag you can pipe swirls of cream on top of the cake. Decorate the top of the cake with the whole or halved berries.

NOTE   The basic cake can be made several days in advance and stored in the refrigerator.

ALMOND AND APPLE GATEAU

Marzipan fruit are an easy starting place for beginners to sugar modelling and this cake is very simple. Grated apple is stirred into the basic Madeira mixture before baking, and you could do exactly the same thing with pears.

4

Press the flaked almonds into the side of the cake, then use the back of a knife to mark the cake into 16 portions.

1 quantity Madeira cake mixture for
20 cm (8 inch) round cake

2 apples
125 g (4 oz) ground almonds
1/2 teaspoon mixed spice
500 g (1 lb) marzipan
icing sugar
4 tablespoons apricot jam
315 ml (10 fl oz) thick (double) cream
1 tablespoon icing sugar
125 g (4 oz) toasted flaked almonds
whole cloves
red and green food colourings
mixed spice, to dust

EQUIPMENT

23 cm (9 inch) round cake tin
fine paintbrush

BAKING THE CAKE

1 Preheat the oven to 160°C (315°F/Gas 2–3). Grease and line the base and side of the cake tin with non-stick baking paper. Peel, core and grate the apples and stir into the cake mixture with 60 g (2 oz) of the ground almonds and the mixed spice. Spread into the tin, level the surface and bake in the oven for about 1 1/4 hours or until firm and a skewer inserted into the centre of the cake comes out clean. Leave in the tin for 5–10 minutes before turning out onto a wire rack to cool completely.

LAYERING THE CAKE

2 Halve the marzipan and set one half aside. Halve the remainder and roll out each piece, on a surface dusted with icing sugar, to a 20 cm (8 inch) circle. Split the cake horizontally into three layers.

3 Spread the bottom layer of the cake with 2 tablespoons of the jam, then cover with a round of marzipan. Place a second cake layer on top and cover with the remaining jam and the second marzipan circle. Top with the remaining layer of cake.

4 Put the cream in a bowl with the remaining ground almonds and the tablespoon of icing sugar, and whip until soft peaks form. Spread the cake with the cream mixture, using a palette knife. Press the flaked almonds around the side of the cake. Mark the top of the cake into 16 portions with the back of a knife.

MARZIPAN APPLES

5 Divide the remaining marzipan into 16 portions and form each one into a ball measuring about 2 cm (3/4 inch) in diameter. Remove the round centres of some of the cloves and press the stem end of a clove into each marzipan ball. Cut the wide ends off more cloves and press the stems into the opposite sides of the balls to make stalks. Paint the apples with diluted red and green food colourings. Arrange around the top edge of the cake and then sprinkle the whole cake top with a little mixed spice.

NOTE This cake freezes well. You can ice and decorate with the almonds, but don't add the marzipan apples until the cake has thawed.

2   Pipe even rows of pink icing over the top of the white, when still wet.

2   Drag the skewer over the lines of wet pink icing, in both directions.

PINK LAZY DAISY

We chose delicate pink daisies and pink feathered icing for our lazy daisy, but you could try simple yellow and white flowers, and tint your icing lemon yellow. Don't use fruit cake for this recipe—the combination of fruit cake and cream cheese frosting isn't good.

two 22 cm (9 inch) round cakes

CREAM CHEESE FROSTING

375 g (13 oz) cream cheese, softened
75 g (2¹/2 oz) butter, softened
90 g (3 oz) icing sugar, sifted
1 teaspoon vanilla essence

GLACE ICING

185 g (6 oz) icing sugar
1 teaspoon soft butter
1–2 tablespoons milk or water
pink food colouring

140 g (4¹/2 oz) roasted hazelnuts, roughly chopped
silk, sugar or fresh pink daisies

COVERING THE CAKE

1   To make the cream cheese frosting, beat the cream cheese and butter with electric beaters until smooth and creamy. Gradually beat in the icing sugar and the vanilla and beat until thick and creamy. Set aside half a cupful of the frosting. Slice both cakes in half horizontally and place one half on a serving plate. Spread the cake layer with a layer of frosting and top with another layer of cake. Repeat the layering with the remaining frosting and cake (the top layer of cake will not be spread with frosting). Spread the reserved frosting over the side of the cake and press the hazelnuts firmly all around the side.

ICING THE CAKE TOP

2   To make the glacé icing, sift the icing sugar into a bowl, add the butter and enough milk or water to make a thick pourable paste. Tint 2 tablespoons of the icing pink with food colouring and spoon into a paper piping bag. Pour the white icing over the cake and quickly spread to the edges. (Any drips can be trimmed off later when the icing has set.) Snip the end off the piping bag and pipe even rows of pink icing across the top of the white icing. Before it sets, gently drag a skewer across the pink lines. Then drag the skewer over the pink lines in the other direction—this will give a feathered effect. (The pink icing must be piped over the white icing while they are both wet. If the icing sets there is no alternative but to lift it off the cake and start again.) Leave the icing to set.

3   Trim off any icing that has drizzled down the side of the cake. Trim the stems from the pink daisies and place around the base, saving a couple for the centre.

NOTE   The cake can be iced a day in advance and kept in a cool dark place. Don't add the daisies until you are ready to serve or they will wilt.

GATEAU TIRAMISU

Tiramisu means 'pick-me-up' in Italian and that's certainly what this cake will do. You can make the cake up to two days in advance and store it in the fridge, but don't put the chocolate wafers around the edge until you are ready to serve or they will soften.

Beat the egg yolks and sugar in a heatproof bowl over a pan of barely simmering water.

Build up the layers of cake brushed with coffee syrup and mascarpone cream.

Trim the chocolate wafers to stand just higher than the top of the cake and arrange them around the edge of the cake.

---

two 22 cm (9 inch) genoise sponges

1 tablespoon instant coffee powder or granules
190 g (6$^{1}/_{2}$ oz) caster sugar
80 ml (2$^{3}/_{4}$ fl oz) Kahlua
4 egg yolks
500 g (1 lb) mascarpone cheese
300 ml (10 fl oz) thick (double) cream
cocoa powder
500 g (1 lb) chocolate cream wafers
(long thin cigar shaped wafers)
wide brown ribbon

MASCARPONE CREAM

1   Put the coffee powder and 110 g (3$^{1}/_{2}$ oz) of the sugar in a small pan with 250 ml (8 fl oz) water. Stir over low heat until dissolved. Remove from the heat and cool slightly, then stir in the Kahlua.

2   Beat the egg yolks and the remaining sugar in a heatproof bowl and place the bowl over a pan of barely simmering water. Beat for 3 minutes with electric beaters, or until the mixture is thick and fluffy and leaves a trail on the surface. Transfer to a cool clean bowl. Beat for 3 minutes, or until cool.

3   Gently stir the mascarpone in a large bowl to soften it. Add the egg yolk mixture, then the cream, beating slightly until thick.

ASSEMBLING THE CAKE

4   Slice the cakes in half horizontally. Place a layer of cake on a plate and brush with the coffee syrup. Spread with about a fifth of the mascarpone cream. Top with another round of cake and continue layering with the syrup, mascarpone cream and cake, finishing with mascarpone cream. Refrigerate the cake and remaining portion of filling for 1 hour.

5   Dredge the top of the cake with cocoa and spread the remaining mascarpone cream around the side. Trim the wafers to stand a little higher than the cake and press gently into the side of the cake. Tie the ribbon around the cake and fasten with a bow.

MOCHA GATEAU

This cake uses a mocha-flavoured genoise cake base but any sponge or moist rich chocolate cake could be used instead. The chocolate ganache is also flavoured with coffee, which is added just after the cream, when making the ganache recipe on page 37.

two 22 cm (9 inch) round mocha-flavoured genoise sponge cakes

150 ml (5 fl oz) thick (double) cream
1 tablespoon icing sugar
$1/4$ teaspoon vanilla essence
1 tablespoon instant coffee powder
300 g (10 oz) chocolate ganache
60 g (2 oz) dark chocolate

EQUIPMENT

number 1 piping tube
wide cream ribbon
wide brown ribbon

1   In a mixing bowl, whip the cream to soft peaks, then continue whipping while gradually adding the icing sugar and vanilla. Use to sandwich the cakes together. Place on a plate or board.

MOCHA GANACHE

2   Dissolve the coffee powder in 2 teaspoons of boiling water in a cup. Make up the chocolate ganache mixture, adding the coffee with the cream. Leave until the mixture is thickened but remains level in the bowl.

3   Pour the ganache over the cake and smooth down the side with a palette knife. Leave in a cool place to set.

CHOCOLATE LACE

4   To make the chocolate lace motifs, make several tracings of the template, right, on the same piece of paper. You will need about 35 motifs, allowing for a few breakages. Secure the tracings to a flat surface and cover with a piece of acetate or non-stick baking paper. Secure in place with tape. Melt the chocolate and put it in a paper piping bag fitted with a number 1 piping tube. Quickly pipe over the lace motif outlines and then leave to dry.

POSITIONING THE LACE

5   Using an upturned bowl, cutter or cake tin about 18 cm (7 inches) in diameter and with a very fine rim, carefully mark a central circle on top of the cake. Carefully peel the paper away from the chocolate lace. Gently press the lace pieces into the marked circle, tilting each backwards and spacing them slightly apart. Chill until set.

6   Just before serving, wrap a double layer of ribbon around the cake.

N O T E   The coffee flavouring added to both sponge and ganache can be omitted to make a plain dark chocolate gateau.

Use a bowl, large cutter or cake tin to mark a circle on top of the gateau. Position the pieces of lace spaced slightly apart and tilted a little backwards.

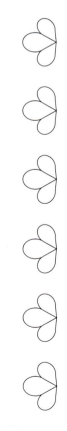

template actual size

PASSIONFRUIT AND LEMON CURD SPONGE

The sponge is layered with creamy lemon curd and then drizzled with a passionfuit topping that runs irresistibly down the side of the cake. The delicate pieces of chocolate lattice are piped onto non-stick baking paper and are easy for beginners to make.

2 Spoon the melted white chocolate buttons into a piping bag and pipe lattice patterns on the paper.

3 Stir the lemon curd over the heat until it thickens enough to coat the spoon.

4 Finish the layers with lemon cream, and roughen the surface with a fork.

5 Once the chocolate lattices have set, gently peel away the paper.

two 22 cm (9 inch) classic sponge cakes

50 g (1³/4 oz) white chocolate buttons (melts)

PASSIONFRUIT TOPPING

185 g (6 oz) passionfruit pulp (you will need 6–8 fresh passionfruit)
3 tablespoons orange juice
2 tablespoons caster sugar
1 tablespoon cornflour

LEMON CREAM

3 egg yolks
75 g (2¹/2 oz) caster sugar
2 teaspoons finely grated lemon rind
90 ml (3 fl oz) lemon juice
180 g (6 oz) unsalted butter, chopped
300 ml (10 fl oz) thick (double) cream

PASSIONFRUIT TOPPING

1 For the passionfruit topping, strain the passionfruit to separate the juice and seeds—you will need 125 ml (4 fl oz) passionfruit juice and 1¹/2 tablespoons of seeds. Put the passionfruit juice, seeds, orange juice and sugar in a small pan. Mix the cornflour with 3 tablespoons water until smooth, then add to the pan. Stir over medium heat until the mixture boils and thickens, then pour into a small bowl, lay a sheet of plastic wrap directly on the surface to prevent a skin forming and refrigerate until cold.

CHOCOLATE LATTICES

2 Bring a pan containing a little water to a simmer, then remove from the heat. Place the chocolate buttons in a heatproof bowl, then place the bowl over the pan. Don't let the base of the bowl sit in the water. Stir the chocolate over the heat until it has completely melted. Spoon the chocolate into a paper piping bag, snip off the end and pipe lattice patterns onto a sheet of non-stick baking paper. Leave to set.

LEMON CREAM

3 To make the lemon cream, put the yolks and sugar in a jug and beat well. Strain into a heatproof bowl and add the lemon rind, juice and butter. Place the bowl over a pan of gently simmering water and stir constantly for 20 minutes, or until the mixture thickens enough to coat the back of a wooden spoon. Cool completely (this is lemon curd). Fold the lemon curd into the thick cream and beat until it has the texture of thick sour cream.

ASSEMBLING THE CAKE

4 Slice each cake in half horizontally. Place one layer of cake onto a serving plate. Spread with a quarter of the lemon cream, then top with another layer of cake. Repeat with the remaining lemon cream and cake, finishing with a layer of lemon cream. Roughen the lemon cream with a fork.

5 Stir the passionfruit topping slightly to make it pourable (thin with a little orange juice if necessary), then pour evenly over the cake, allowing some to run down the side. Peel the chocolate lattices from the paper and arrange on top of the cake.

NOTE The lemon curd and passionfruit topping can be stored for up to three days. Assemble the cake an hour before serving and don't pour over the topping until ready to serve.

CHOCOLATE DECORATIONS

MELTING CHOCOLATE The following decorations can be made using melted dark, milk or white chocolate, or couverture (see below). You need to take a little care when melting chocolate as it can overheat and seize. Break into small pieces and place in a heatproof bowl over a pan of just simmered water, without letting the base of the bowl sit in the water. Once melted, stir lightly. Or melt in short bursts in the microwave.

COUVERTURE Used by professionals because it melts and coats well, giving a glossy finish and good flavour. But it must be tempered before use to make it stable. To temper couverture, break it into small pieces and melt in a heatproof bowl over a pan of simmering water until it reaches 46°C (115°F) on a sugar thermometer. Remove from the heat and stir until cooled to 27°C (80°F). Return to the heat and heat to 31°C (88°F). It is now tempered and ready to use.

COVERING A CAKE For a 20 cm (8 inch) cake you will need 250 g (8 oz) melted chocolate. Place the cake on a wire rack and pour the chocolate over it. Spread evenly with a palette knife to cover the cake completely. Leave to set. (Cut the cake with a hot dry knife to prevent cracking.)

CARAQUE CURLS Pour melted chocolate onto a marble slab or smooth surface. Spread quite thinly and leave until just set.

Draw the blade of a large knife, held at an angle of 45°, across the surface of the chocolate to shave off a thin layer that will roll into curls. Transfer the curls to a large plate until ready to use. Make striped curls by pouring melted chocolate onto the marble and making ridges through it with a fork. Leave to set and then pour a different coloured chocolate over the top. Leave until just set and then scrape off curls. You could also pour the different coloured chocolates side by side to make striped curls.

LEAVES Wash the underside of non-toxic leaves (rose or camellia) and dry well. Brush with a thin layer of melted chocolate. Set, then peel away the leaf.

Left to right: Melting chocolate over a pan of hot water; Caraque curls in two colours; Leaves painted with chocolate; Cut outs, boxes and cases for truffles; Chocolate lace runouts; Dipped fruit.

CUT OUTS Spread melted chocolate thinly over non-stick baking paper or acetate and leave to set. Cut out shapes with biscuit cutters and stick to the cake with melted chocolate. Use dark chocolate on a light cake and white chocolate on a dark cake.

BOXES Spread melted chocolate in a thin even layer over non-stick baking paper. When it has begun to set, cut it into even squares with a sharp knife (heat the knife if the chocolate has set too much). Use melted chocolate to glue the sides together.

CASES Small foil *petit four* cases make perfect moulds for shaping chocolate cases. Use the back of a teaspoon to thickly coat the inside base and side of the paper case with melted chocolate. Scoop out the excess and then turn the case upside down to set. Peel away the paper case. For a less formal look, spread a circle of melted chocolate onto a piece of plastic wrap and drape it over the base of an upturned small glass or tin. Peel away the plastic wrap when the chocolate has set completely. Cases can be filled with ganache or whipped cream, scattered over a cake or filled with truffles.

RUNOUTS Trace a design onto paper (use designs from greeting cards, letters from books or make up your own picture). Secure the paper to a flat surface and place non-stick baking paper or acetate on top. Put a little melted chocolate in a paper piping bag and pipe over the outlines. Leave to set. Place more melted chocolate (either of the same or a different colour) into another bag, fitted with a clean tube. Fill in the outline, easing chocolate into the corners with a cocktail stick if necessary. When set, carefully pull away the paper.

DIPPED FRUITS Wash and dry the fruit (grapes, cherries, strawberries). Line a tray with paper. Keep the melted chocolate in a bowl over hot water to keep it liquid. Hold each fruit by its stalk end and half-dip in the chocolate, twisting slightly. Let the excess drip back into the bowl, then lay on the paper to dry. Use on the same day.

CAPPUCCINO TRUFFLE CAKE

Once you've learnt how to make your own cappuccino truffles, you might never come out of the kitchen again. Of course, if you don't have time to make your own you can always use bought chocolates. Fruit cakes are not suitable for this recipe.

two 23 cm (9 inch) square cakes

COFFEE BUTTERCREAM

170 ml (5¹/2 fl oz) cream
300 g (10 oz) white chocolate buttons (melts)
400 g (13 oz) unsalted butter
160 g (5¹/2 oz) icing sugar
1 tablespoon instant coffee powder

200 g (6¹/2 oz) hazelnuts, roasted and
roughly chopped
16 Ferrero Rocher chocolates
cocoa powder, to dust

CAPPUCCINO TRUFFLES

80 ml (2³/4 fl oz) cream
250 g (8 oz) dark chocolate, finely chopped
3 teaspoons Kahlua
2 teaspoons instant coffee powder
200 g (6¹/2 oz) white chocolate buttons (melts)

COFFEE BUTTERCREAM

1   To make the coffee buttercream, put the cream and chocolate in a small heatproof bowl. Bring a small pan of water to a simmer, remove from the heat and place the bowl over the pan (don't let the bottom of the bowl sit in the water). Stir over the hot water until melted. Beat the butter until light and creamy, then gradually beat in the sugar until thick and white. Beat in the cooled melted chocolate until thick and fluffy. Dissolve the instant coffee in a tablespoon of hot water, allow to cool, then beat into the buttercream.

2   Cut the domes off the tops of the cakes to give level surfaces. Put one cake on a serving plate or board. Spread with a quarter of the buttercream and sandwich with the other cake. Cover with the remaining buttercream. Press the hazelnuts onto the side of the cake.

CAPPUCCINO TRUFFLES

3   To make the truffles, bring the cream to the boil in a small pan, then remove from the heat. Add the dark chocolate and stir until melted. Stir in the Kahlua and coffee. Transfer to a small bowl, cover and refrigerate until cold and thick.

4   Roll rounded teaspoons of the mixture into balls (you should be able to make 25 truffles). Place on a baking tray lined with baking paper and chill until firm. If the mixture is too soft to roll, drop rounded teaspoons of mixture onto the tray and refrigerate for 15 minutes to firm up before rolling into balls.

5   Melt the chocolate buttons in a heatproof bowl, cool slightly, then use a spoon and fork to dip and coat the truffles in the chocolate. Place on a clean piece of baking paper and refrigerate for about 15 minutes to set the chocolate.

6   Pile the truffles and chocolates on top of the cake, using any remaining melted chocolate to hold them in place. Dust with cocoa.

NOTE   The truffles can be made up to a week in advance and stored in an airtight container in the fridge. The cake can be assembled up to three days in advance and kept in an airtight container in the fridge—let it come back to room temperature before serving.

Beat in the cream and melted chocolate until the mixture is thick and fluffy.

Cover the cake with buttercream and stick the hazelnuts to the sides.

Roll rounded teaspoons of truffle mixture into balls and place on the tray.

Use a fork and a spoon to dip and coat the truffles in melted chocolate.

CHERRY MILLEFEUILLE

A millefeuille is a traditional French pastry, meaning 'thousand leaves' and referring to the many buttery layers of puff pastry. We've adapted the idea to use layers of cake and pastry, with cherries and a creamy filling.

3

Spread a third of the cherry filling over the first sheet of puff pastry and then top with a layer of cake.

3

An electric knife is ideal for trimming the edges of the cake cleanly. If you don't have one, use a large serrated knife.

4

Hold the end of the skewer with a tea towel and drag it over the icing sugar. The sugar will caramelise and create a dark line.

one 23 cm (9 inch) square coconut cake

2 sheets ready-rolled puff pastry
six 425 g (14 oz) cans stoneless black cherries
40 g (1 1/4 oz) cornflour
1.25 litres thick (double) cream
125 ml (4 fl oz) Kirsch
icing sugar

MILLEFEUILLE

1   Preheat the oven to hot 210°C (415°F/ Gas 6–7). Place one sheet of the puff pastry on a tray lined with non-stick baking paper and prick all over with a fork (this will be easier if the pastry is slightly thawed). Bake for 10 minutes, or until golden. Repeat with the second sheet of pastry. Leave to cool.

CHERRY FILLING

2   Drain the cherries, keeping 500 ml (16 fl oz) of the syrup. Mix a little of the syrup with the cornflour to make a smooth paste. Put the remaining syrup and cherries in a large pan and add the paste. Cook over medium heat, stirring until the mixture boils and thickens. Pour onto a large tray or dish to cool completely, stirring occasionally.

ASSEMBLING THE CAKE

3   Whisk the cream gently until lightly whipped. Use a large serrated knife to slice the cake into three layers. Place one sheet of cooked pastry on a board and spread with a third of the cherry mixture. Top with one layer of cake, brush the cake with some Kirsch and top with a third of the cream. Repeat these layers twice more and top with the remaining sheet of pastry. Use an electric knife or a large serrated knife to trim the edges of the layered cake so they are even. Transfer carefully to a serving plate or cake board.

CRISSCROSS TOPPING

4   Dust the top of the cake heavily with icing sugar. Hold the end of a thick metal skewer with a tea towel and heat over a flame until red hot. Press the skewer over the icing sugar to caramelise the top in a crisscross pattern—you will need to reheat the skewer several times, wiping off any icing sugar.

NOTE   This cake is best made a few hours in advance to give the layers time to settle. Dust with sugar and pattern the top with the skewer close to serving time.

PEACH AND ORANGE MOUSSE CAKE

We've used peaches for this cake but you could use other stone fruits that are in season, or even well-drained canned fruit. Fruit cakes aren't suitable for this recipe. You can buy the clear plastic (contact) for making the collar from art or cake decorating shops.

one 20 cm (8 inch) round cake

WHITE CHOCOLATE MOUSSE

150 g (5 oz) white chocolate, chopped
150 g (5 oz) cream cheese
60 g (2 oz) caster sugar
80 ml (2 3/4 fl oz) orange juice
3 teaspoons gelatine
300 ml (10 fl oz) cream, whipped
2 egg whites, whipped to soft peaks

TOPPING

125 ml (4 fl oz) fresh orange juice, strained
1 tablespoon caster sugar
3/4 teaspoon gelatine
1 large peach, cut into wedges

EQUIPMENT

deep 20 cm (8 inch) springform tin
clear plastic (shiny contact)

1   Slice the cake in half horizontally. Lightly grease a deep 20 cm (8 inch) springform tin. Cut a piece of clear plastic about 2 cm (3/4 inch) higher than the tin and wrap around the inside of the tin as a collar. Put half of the cake in the tin (you won't need the other half, so freeze for next time or make truffles). Pull the plastic tight and secure with a paper clip and tape.

WHITE CHOCOLATE MOUSSE

2   To make the mousse, bring a pan with a little water to a simmer, then remove from the heat. Place the chocolate in a heatproof bowl, then place the bowl over the pan. Don't let the bowl sit in the water. Stir the chocolate until melted. Beat the cream cheese and sugar until smooth and creamy, then beat in the cooled melted chocolate. Heat the orange juice in a small pan and remove from the heat. Sprinkle with the gelatine and stir until dissolved. Cool slightly before beating into the cream cheese mixture. Fold in the cream, then the softly whipped egg whites. Pour the mousse over the cake base and gently tap the tin on the bench to level the surface. Chill for several hours or until firm.

ORANGE TOPPING

3   To make the topping, put the orange juice and sugar in a small pan. Stir over low heat until the sugar has dissolved. Sprinkle with the gelatine and continue stirring until it has dissolved. Remove from the heat and leave to cool. Arrange the sliced peach on top of the mousse. Carefully pour the topping over the cake. Refrigerate for several hours, or until the topping has completely set, before removing the cake from the tin. Carefully pull away the plastic.

Pull the clear plastic tight and fix in position, so that the mousse will set in line with the cake.

Fold the softly whipped egg whites into the mousse mixture with a large metal spoon, keeping in as much air as possible.

Arrange the peach slices on top of the cake and then pour the orange topping over them. Leave to set before removing the plastic collar.

SWEET FIG AND CHOCOLATE CAKE

This glamorously understated cake is perfect for a sophisticated occasion where style and taste are the most important items on the menu. Use any cake except a fruit cake—the combination of flavours would not be good.

2
Slice the cake into three layers and sandwich together with liqueur, jam and buttercream.

4
Spread the melted white chocolate in strips over a piece of non-stick baking paper and leave to dry.

4
Break the end off each strip of chocolate so that it has a flat base to stand on.

one 20 cm (8 inch) round cake

BUTTERCREAM
250 g (8 oz) butter
125 g (4 oz) icing sugar, sifted
1 teaspoon vanilla essence
2 teaspoons milk

Kirsch or other fruit-based liqueur
4 tablespoons raspberry jam
300 g (10 oz) white chocolate buttons (melts)
5 fresh figs, quartered

BUTTERCREAM

1   To make the buttercream, beat the butter with electric beaters until light and creamy. Gradually add the icing sugar alternately with the vanilla essence and milk, beating until smooth and fluffy.

2   Use a serrated knife to slice the cake horizontally into three even layers. Place the bottom layer on a board or plate. Brush with a little liqueur and spread with half the jam. Spread with a thin layer of buttercream. Place another cake layer on top and repeat the layers. Top with the remaining cake layer, and spread the rest of the buttercream evenly over the cake.

WHITE CHOCOLATE EDGING

3   Put the white chocolate buttons in a heatproof bowl. Bring a small pan of water to a simmer, remove from the heat and place the bowl over the pan (don't let the bottom of the bowl sit in the water). Stir the chocolate until melted. (Or melt in the microwave for 1 minute on high, stirring after 30 seconds.)

4   Spread the melted chocolate in 5 x 11 cm (2 x 5 inch) strips over a sheet of non-stick baking paper. Leave to set completely before removing from the paper—you will need about 20 of these shapes but make a few extra in case of breakages. Break one end of each strip or trim with a knife to give a flat base, then stand them upright around the edge of the cake, slightly overlapping. You can tie a ribbon around the cake or leave it plain. Arrange the fresh fig quarters around the edge.

NOTE   This cake can be decorated up to two days in advance, but add the figs just before serving. Keep in a cool dark place in an airtight container or in the fridge in warm weather.

MARBLE GLAZED CAKE

The secret to a good marbled finish is not to mix your icings together too thoroughly. Simply spoon them over the cake, then swirl together gently with a skewer. Use any cake for this recipe except a fruit cake, which wouldn't combine well with the chocolate buttercream.

two 20 cm (8 inch) round cakes

WHITE CHOCOLATE BUTTERCREAM

4 tablespoons cream
150 g (5 oz) white chocolate buttons (melts)
200 g (6 1/2 oz) unsalted butter
80 g (2 3/4 oz) icing sugar

80 g (2 3/4 oz) milk chocolate, chopped
125 ml (4 fl oz) cream
80 g (2 3/4 oz) dark chocolate, chopped
80 g (2 3/4 oz) white chocolate, chopped
200 g (6 1/2 oz) flaked almonds, toasted

WHITE CHOCOLATE BUTTERCREAM

1   To make the white chocolate buttercream, put the cream and chocolate in a small heatproof bowl. Bring a small pan of water to a simmer, remove from the heat and place the bowl over the pan (don't let the bottom of the bowl sit in the water). Stir the chocolate over the hot water until melted, then remove from the heat and leave to cool. Chop the butter and beat until light and creamy, then gradually beat in the sugar until thick and white. Beat in the melted chocolate until the mixture is thick and fluffy.

LAYERING THE CAKE

2   Trim away the domed tops from the cakes to give a flat surface. Using a serrated knife, cut each cake horizontally into three even layers. Place a layer of cake on a wire rack over a tray and spread with a sixth of the buttercream. Top with another layer of cake, spread that with buttercream and build up the layers, sandwiching the cake and filling. Finish with a layer of cake, cut-side-down to give a flat surface (keep the remaining portion of buttercream). Refrigerate the cake for 30 minutes to firm the filling, so that the layers don't slide apart.

3   Put the milk chocolate in a small heatproof bowl with 2 tablespoons of the cream. Bring a small pan of water to a simmer, remove from the heat and place the bowl over the pan (don't let the bottom of the bowl sit in the water). Stir the chocolate and cream over the hot water until melted and blended. Alternatively, melt in the microwave for 1 minute on High, stirring after 30 seconds. Do the same with the dark chocolate and white chocolate, blending each with 2 tablespoons cream so you have three separate chocolate mixtures.

MARBLING THE CHOCOLATE

4   Spoon dollops of each chocolate mixture randomly over the top of the cake and then swirl them together with the thick end of a skewer to create a marbling effect. Gently tap the tray on the bench to level the icing. Leave to set, then remove any drips of icing from down the side of the cake and spread the remaining buttercream around the side. Roughly crush the almonds and press over the buttercream. Transfer the cake to a serving plate.

NOTE   This cake can be stored in the fridge for up to three days after decorating. Bring to room temperature before serving.

Stand the cake on a rack over a tray and build up the layers of cake and buttercream to make one very high cake.

Make the three chocolate toppings separately and then dollop randomly over the top of the cake.

Gently swirl together the different chocolates with a skewer, not blending them too much.

3

Cut the chocolate sugarpaste into strips about 20 cm long and as high as the cake. Gently pleat the paste into loose folds and position around the side of the cake.

SUMMER FRUITS CAKE

Prettily pleated with a collar of white chocolate sugarpaste and piled high with soft fruits, this special-occasion cake makes a gorgeous centrepiece. Use whatever fruit is in season and make the white chocolate leaves following the instructions on page 116.

two 22 cm (9 inch) round orange-flavoured classic sponge cakes

315 ml (10 fl oz) thick (double) cream
150 g (5 oz) strawberry yoghurt
310 g (10 oz) white chocolate sugarpaste
icing sugar
500 g (1 lb) strawberries
185 g (6 oz) redcurrants
5 teaspoons redcurrant jelly
8 white chocolate leaves

EQUIPMENT
large pastry brush

STRAWBERRY CREAM

1 Put the cream in a large bowl with the strawberry yoghurt, and whip until soft peaks form.

2 Place one of the cakes on a large serving plate. Spread with a third of the strawberry cream filling and cover with the second cake. Using a palette knife, cover the top and side of the cake with the remaining strawberry cream.

SUGARPASTE PLEATS

3 Divide the sugarpaste into six pieces. Roll out one piece on a surface dusted with icing sugar and cut into a strip slightly deeper than the cake and about 20 cm (8 inches) long. Using your fingers, gently pleat the strip into loose folds. Position the strip around the side of the cake. Cut, shape and position more strips of sugarpaste until the side of the cake is completely covered.

FINISHING TOUCHES

4 Hull the strawberries and halve any large ones. Arrange over the top of the cake, then fill in the gaps with the redcurrants.

5 Melt the redcurrant jelly with 2 tablespoons water in a small saucepan. Cool slightly, then use a large pastry brush to brush the glaze over the fruits to make them shine. Finish by decorating with white chocolate leaves. Store in a cool place and serve within 2–3 hours.

NOTE The cake, with cream and chocolate pleating, can be assembled up to a day in advance, but pile up the fruits and glaze them no more than 2–3 hours before serving.

STRIPED CHOCOLATE CURLS CAKE

The smooth chocolate collar and creamy white chocolate ganache are topped off by a pile of fairground-striped chocolate curls. Use any of the basic cakes for this recipe, except the fruit cake. If you can't find clear plastic contact you can use non-stick baking paper.

20 cm (8 inch) round cake

WHITE CHOCOLATE GANACHE

150 g (5 oz) white chocolate buttons (melts)
130 g (4½ oz) white chocolate, chopped
125 ml (4 fl oz) cream
250 g (8 oz) unsalted butter

STRIPED CURLS

150 g (5 oz) each of dark and white chocolate buttons (melts)

CHOCOLATE COLLAR

60 g (2 oz) dark chocolate, chopped
60 g (2 oz) dark chocolate buttons (melts)

EQUIPMENT

cake decorating comb
clear plastic (shiny contact)

WHITE CHOCOLATE GANACHE

1   To make the ganache, put all the ingredients in a pan. Stir over low heat until melted and smooth. Transfer to a small bowl, cover the surface with plastic wrap and cool. Beat for 3–5 minutes, or until thick, pale and creamy.

STRIPED CURLS

2   To make the curls, put the dark chocolate buttons in a heatproof bowl. Bring a pan containing a little water to a simmer, remove from the heat and place the bowl over the pan (don't let the base of the bowl sit in the water). Stir until the chocolate has melted. Quickly spread fairly thinly over a marble board. Drag a cake decorating comb or a fork through the chocolate. Set at room temperature unless very warm.

3   Melt the white chocolate buttons and spread over the dark chocolate. Spread firmly to fill all the gaps. Leave until just set.

4   Using the edge of a sharp knife at a 45° angle, scrape over the top of the chocolate. The strips will curl as they come away—don't press too hard. If the chocolate has set too firmly, the curls will break: leave in a warm place and try again.

LAYERING THE CAKE

5   Cut the domed top off the cake to give a flat surface. Slice the cake horizontally into three even layers. Sandwich the layers together with the ganache, leaving enough to spread thinly over the top and side.

CHOCOLATE COLLAR

6   To make the collar, measure the height of the cake and add 5 mm (¼ inch). Cut a strip of plastic this wide and long enough to wrap around the cake with a small overlap. Melt all the chocolate and spread thinly and evenly over the shiny side of the plastic. Let it set a little, but you need to be able to bend the plastic without the chocolate cracking. Work quickly: wrap the plastic around the cake with the chocolate on the inside. Seal the ends and leave until the chocolate sets completely. Peel away the plastic and pile the chocolate curls up high in the centre of the cake.

NOTES   The chocolate curls can be stored in an airtight container for up to four days but don't put them on the cake until you are ready to serve. The cake can be covered a day in advance—keep in the fridge in warm weather, but allow to return to room temperature before serving.

A 'comb' is a flat plastic tool with teeth on each end. Combs are available from speciality kitchen or cake decorating shops.

Drag the comb through the chocolate. If you don't have a comb, use a fork.

Spread the white chocolate firmly, so that it fills in the gaps in the dark chocolate.

Use a sharp knife held at an angle to scrape the curls from the chocolate.

Wrap the collar around the cake with the chocolate on the inside. Leave to set.

Once set, carefully peel away the plastic to leave the chocolate collar.

DEVIL'S FOOD CAKE

Dark chocolate, white chocolate and whipped cream... this is an ultra 'wicked' cake for a special occasion or for sheer indulgence at teatime. It's easy to make, with a little bit of piping that doesn't need to be perfect.

1 Beat the cake mixture with electric beaters on low speed for 3 minutes, or until just moistened.

4 Drag a skewer through the white chocolate circles, from the centre of the cake to the outside edge.

CAKE

165 g (5½ oz) plain flour
90 g (3 oz) cocoa powder
1 teaspoon bicarbonate of soda
250 g (8 oz) caster sugar
2 eggs, lightly beaten
250 ml (8 fl oz) buttermilk
1 teaspoon vanilla essence
125 g (4 oz) butter, softened

CHOCOLATE ICING

60 g (2 oz) unsalted butter
60 g (2 oz) dark chocolate, melted

125 ml (4 fl oz) thick (double) cream, whipped
60 g (2 oz) white chocolate, chopped

EQUIPMENT

20 cm (8 inch) round cake tin

BAKING THE CAKE

1   Preheat the oven to 180°C (350°F/Gas 4). Brush a 20 cm (8 inch) round cake tin with melted butter or oil and line the base and side with non-stick baking paper. Sift the flour, cocoa and soda into a large mixing bowl. Add the sugar. Pour the combined eggs, buttermilk, essence and butter onto the dry ingredients. Using electric beaters, beat on low speed for 3 minutes or until just moistened.

2   Beat the mixture on high speed for 5 minutes or until free of lumps and increased in volume. Pour the mixture into the tin and smooth the surface. Bake for 40–50 minutes or until a skewer inserted into the centre of the cake comes out clean. Leave the cake in the tin for 15 minutes, then turn out onto a wire rack to cool completely.

CHOCOLATE ICING

3   To make the icing, combine the butter and dark chocolate in a small pan. Stir over low heat until melted, then remove from the heat and leave to cool. Trim the dome from the cake top to level the surface. Slice the cake in half horizontally, spread the bottom layer with the whipped cream and then sandwich back together. Spread the icing over the top with a palette knife.

PIPING THE WHITE CHOCOLATE

4   Place the white chocolate in a small heatproof bowl and place over a pan of barely simmering water until melted. Remove from the heat and leave to cool slightly. Spoon the melted chocolate into a small paper piping bag. Snip off the tip and pipe a small circle in the centre of the cake. Pipe another circle around it and then carry on until you have covered the top of the cake (you will probably pipe about eight circles). Before the chocolate sets, drag a skewer from the centre circle to the outside of the cake. Clean the skewer and repeat this process, making the lines evenly spaced and working around the cake like the hands of a clock.

NOTE   Store for three days unfilled in an airtight container or up to three months in the freezer, unfilled and un-iced. The filled cake is best assembled and eaten on the same day.

CUSTARD MERINGUE GATEAU

The meringue ovals, moulded between two spoons, are called 'quenelles'. Here they've been cleverly used to create a deliciously soft marshmallow border. Make sure you keep the spoons wet while making the quenelles, so the meringue doesn't stick.

5 Make the quenelles by moulding the meringue between two wet dessertspoons.

5 Scoop the quenelle off the spoon and arrange around the edge of the cake, facing the centre.

6 Brush the meringue quenelles with the strained apricot jam after they have been baked.

two 23 cm (9 inch) classic sponges

75 g (2¹/2 oz) caster sugar
300 g (10 oz) raspberries, plus extra to decorate
90 g (3 oz) flaked almonds, toasted
2 tablespoons apricot jam
icing sugar

CUSTARD FILLING

2 tablespoons custard powder
2 tablespoons cornflour
55 g (1³/4 oz) caster sugar
1 teaspoon vanilla essence
500 ml (16 fl oz) milk
2 eggs, beaten

MERINGUE TOPPING

4 egg whites
250 g (8 oz) caster sugar

1 Combine the sugar and 160 ml (5¹/2 fl oz) water in a small pan and stir over medium heat until the sugar has dissolved, then simmer for 2 minutes. Allow to cool.

CUSTARD FILLING

2 To make the custard filling, blend the custard powder, cornflour, sugar and vanilla in a pan with a little of the milk to make a smooth paste. Stir in the remaining milk and eggs and mix together well. Stir over the heat until the mixture boils and thickens. Pour into a large bowl and cover the surface with plastic wrap to prevent a skin forming. Stir occasionally to cool the custard.

LAYERING THE CAKES

3 Use a serrated knife to slice each sponge in half horizontally. Place one layer of sponge on a baking tray lined with non-stick baking paper. Brush liberally with the cooled sugar syrup. Beat the custard with a wooden spoon to soften slightly. Spread a third of the custard over the cake, scatter with a third of the raspberries, then top with more cake. Build up the layers, finishing with a layer of cake. Cover and chill the cake for at least 1 hour.

4 Preheat the oven to 250°C (500°F/Gas 10). Beat the egg whites in a small bowl until stiff peaks form. Gradually add the sugar, beating well after each addition until the sugar has dissolved. Spread a thin layer of meringue over the top and side of the cake. Press almonds over the side of the cake.

MERINGUE QUENELLES

5 Using two dessertspoons, make small ovals from the remaining meringue by dipping the spoons quickly into water, then scooping up a small amount of meringue. Use the second spoon to scoop the meringue from the first spoon, making an oval. Scoop the quenelle gently off the spoon onto the edge of the cake and continue until you have worked your way around the edge of the cake.

6 Bake for 2–3 minutes, or until the meringue is just brown on the edges. You may need to rotate the cake halfway through cooking to ensure even browning. Transfer to a serving plate. Heat the apricot jam in a small pan, push through a strainer and gently brush over the meringue ovals. Fill the centre of the cake with fresh raspberries and dust with icing sugar.

NOTE The cake can be stored in the fridge for up to two days without the meringue topping. Top with the meringue on the day of serving.

SPOTTED COLLAR CAKE

The chocolate collar is what makes this cake so spectacular... once you have perfected the technique, you can use it to make even more elaborately patterned collars for cakes and cheesecakes. If you can't find clear plastic or acetate you can use non-stick baking paper.

18 x 25 cm (7 x 10 inch) oval cake

COFFEE BUTTERCREAM

2 tablespoons cream
75 g (2¹/2 oz) white chocolate buttons (melts)
100 g (3¹/2 oz) unsalted butter, softened
40 g (1¹/4 oz) icing sugar
1 teaspoon instant coffee powder

SPOTTED COLLAR

30 g (1 oz) white chocolate buttons (melts)
30 g (1 oz) milk chocolate buttons (melts)
60 g (2 oz) dark chocolate buttons (melts)
60 g (2 oz) dark chocolate, chopped

cocoa powder

EQUIPMENT

clear plastic (shiny contact)

1   Cut the dome off the top of the cake to level the surface. Turn the cake upside down on a plate or board so that the flat base becomes the top. Measure the height of the cake. Cut a strip of clear plastic this wide, and long enough to wrap around the cake.

COFFEE BUTTERCREAM

2   To make the coffee buttercream, put the cream and chocolate buttons in a small heatproof bowl. Bring a small pan of water to a simmer, remove from the heat and place the bowl over the pan (don't let the bottom of the bowl sit in the water). Stir the chocolate until melted. Beat the butter until light and creamy, then gradually beat in the icing sugar until thick and white. Beat in the cooled melted chocolate until thick and fluffy. Dissolve the coffee powder in a teaspoon of hot water and beat into the buttercream.

3   Spread the buttercream evenly over the top and side of the cake. In warm weather you could refrigerate the cake for 10–15 minutes after this, to firm the buttercream a little.

SPOTTED COLLAR

4   To make the collar, put the white and milk chocolate buttons in separate heatproof bowls and melt as above. Alternatively, melt in the microwave for 1 minute on high heat, stirring after 30 seconds. Spoon into separate paper piping bags. Pipe large and small dots of chocolate over the shiny side of the plastic. Gently tap the plastic on the bench to flatten the dots and then leave them to set.

5   Melt the dark chocolate buttons and dark chocolate together, then cool slightly. Working quickly, spread evenly over the entire strip of plastic, over the top of the dots. Be careful not to press too hard or the dots may lift off the surface. Leave to set a little, but you need to be able to bend the strip without it cracking. Quickly wrap the strip around the cake with the chocolate on the inside. Seal the ends of the plastic and leave until set (in the fridge in warm weather). Peel the plastic from the collar and dust the cake with cocoa powder.

NOTE   You can decorate the cake and keep it in the fridge for several hours before serving. Don't attempt the chocolate collar on a very hot day—you may find it too soft to work with. Clear contact plastic is available from art or cake decorating shops.

Cut the plastic to the same height as the cake and long enough to wrap around it.

Pipe the melted milk and white chocolate in dots on the shiny side of the plastic.

Melt the dark chocolate and spread over the strip, over the dots.

Wrap the collar around the cake with the chocolate on the inside.

Once the chocolate has set, gently peel away the strip of plastic.

PEARS WITH A SPUN TOFFEE HALO

Choose the smallest pears you can find to make this delightful and whimsical creation, so they just poke out of the pecan-covered butter cake. Spinning the toffee can be a daunting job for beginners to decorating and needs a little care.

1 Core the pears through the base with a melon baller, then peel.

2 Arrange the poached pears around the edge of the cake mixture in the tin.

4 As the sugar in the pan melts, sprinkle with more sugar. Stir to melt any lumps that form.

5 Carefully flick the toffee backwards and forwards over the handle of the wooden spoon.

5 Lift the spun toffee off the spoon and mould into a halo shape.

1 quantity Madeira cake mixture for 20 cm
(8 inch) round cake

1 cinnamon stick
2 strips lemon rind
1 tablespoon lemon juice
440 g (14 oz) caster sugar
6 beurre bosc or packham pears
3 tablespoons apricot jam
2 tablespoons chopped pecans

EQUIPMENT

two 23 cm (9 inch) springform tins
wide gold ribbon

POACHING THE PEARS

1 Put the cinnamon, lemon rind, juice, 1 litre water and half the sugar in a pan large enough to hold the pears and stir over heat until the sugar has dissolved. Core the pears through the bases with a melon baller, then peel and place in the syrup. Simmer, partly covered, for 10 minutes, or until tender. Remove from the heat and leave to cool in the syrup. Drain and leave on paper towels to drain thoroughly.

BAKING THE CAKE

2 Preheat the oven to 180°C (350°F/Gas 4). Lightly grease the springform tins and cover the bases with non-stick baking paper. Divide the cake mixture between the tins. Arrange the pears around the edge of one cake, about 2.5 cm (1 inch) in from the edge, and gently press into the mixture. Bake for 40 minutes, or until a skewer inserted into the centre of the plain cake comes out clean. Cook the pear cake for a further 40 minutes, or until a skewer comes out clean. Leave the cakes in their tins for 5 minutes, then remove from the tins and cool on wire racks.

ASSEMBLING THE CAKE

3 Trim the dome from the top of the plain cake to give a level surface. Warm and strain the jam and spread some over the plain cake. Sit the pear cake on top and brush with a little jam. Sprinkle with the pecans.

SPUN TOFFEE

4 For the spun toffee, place a couple of sheets of newspaper on the floor where you will be spinning the toffee. Place a wooden spoon on the work surface with its handle over the edge, above the newspaper (weigh it down with a heavy object). Lightly oil the spoon handle. Put a heavy-based pan over medium heat, gradually sprinkle with some of the remaining sugar and, as it melts, sprinkle with the rest. Stir to melt any lumps and prevent burning. Meanwhile, run a little cold water into the sink. When the toffee is golden brown, remove the pan from the heat and place the base in the water to quickly cool the toffee and prevent it burning. This will also make the toffee thicken.

5 Hold two forks back to back and dip in the hot toffee. Carefully flick the toffee backwards and forwards over the handle of the spoon, re-dipping in the pan as often as necessary—you may need to do this several times. If the toffee gets too thick, warm it slightly over low heat. Lift the toffee off the spoon handle and mould into a large halo shape, about the same width as the top of the pears. Make a couple more halos and place over the pears. Trim around the cake with the wide ribbon to hide the join.

NOTE Best eaten on the day of baking. The toffee can be kept in an airtight container for several hours, but don't place on the cake until ready to serve or it will soften.

CHILDREN'S CAKES

Children's party cakes are probably the most fun of all to make. They are ideal for beginners because they don't have to be too perfectly finished—those sticky fingers will be picking at the icing before the cake's even hit the table. Buttercream is always a great favourite with children, and has the added advantage of being easy to make and colour. Modelling is also popular and if you can create figures that are recognisable as family, friends or pets, then your cake will probably be talked about for many years to come.

8
Spread chocolate buttercream down each side of the puppy's face, widening at the base to make into ears.

PATCH

Buttercream is an easy icing for beginners—any mistakes can be quickly smoothed over. This cake uses a small amount of sugarpaste for making the puppy's eyes—the quantity is so tiny that it's easier to buy a small packet than make your own. Use any cake except a fruit cake.

1 quantity cake mixture for a 15 cm (6 inch) round cake

1 tablespoon cocoa powder, sifted
500 g (1 lb) buttercream
60 g (2 oz) sugarpaste
black paste food colouring
3 liquorice 'laces'
1 gold foil-covered chocolate coin

EQUIPMENT
3.5 litre ovenproof mixing bowl
30 cm (12 inch) round gold cake board
cocktail stick
fine paintbrush
narrow tartan ribbon

BAKING THE CAKE
1   Preheat the oven to 160°C (315°F/Gas 2–3). Grease the base of the mixing bowl and line with a circle of non-stick baking paper. Spoon the cake mixture into the bowl and level the surface. Bake for about 40 minutes or until firm. Turn out onto a wire rack and leave to cool.

2   Trim the domed top off the cake and turn the cake upside down to give a flat surface. Beat the cocoa into a third of the buttercream.

COVERING THE CAKE
3   Reserve 3 tablespoons of the plain buttercream, then spread the remainder over the cake, covering it as smoothly as possible. Spread a little buttercream on the board at the bottom of the cake and build it up to form a 'neck'. Gently fluff up the surface of the buttercream with a cocktail stick.

NOSE
4   Spoon the reserved plain buttercream onto the cake in a mound just below the centre and spread it into a snout shape. Dampen a palette knife and smooth down the snout area to contrast with the fluffed-up surface of the rest of the buttercream.

EYES AND MOUTH
5   Spread a little of the chocolate buttercream over one eye area of the cake. Shape two white eyes from the sugarpaste and position on the cake, placing one over the area of chocolate buttercream.

6   Colour a small piece of sugarpaste black and shape it into a nose. Press gently into position.

7   Arrange pieces of liquorice 'lace' around the eyes, pressing them gently into the buttercream. Form a smiling mouth from a little more liquorice.

EARS
8   Spread small spoonfuls of the chocolate buttercream down each side of the dog's face. Flatten with a palette knife, widening at the base to shape ears. Fluff up lightly with a cocktail stick. Secure more liquorice around the ears to outline.

FINISHING TOUCHES
9   Paint the centres of the eyes black with food colouring and a fine paintbrush. Arrange the ribbon around the puppy's neck, securing the gold coin to it with a dot of buttercream.

SPOTTY SNAKE

This colourful snake uses a delicious truffle mixture that children will love. It is easy to mould and is made from cake crumbs that are left over when other cakes are shaped. Keep cake trimmings in bags in the freezer for occasions just like this.

90 g (3 oz) royal icing
brown, pink, yellow, green, black and
red food colourings
75 g (2¹/2 oz) light brown sugar
750 g (1¹/2 lb) cake crumbs
90 g (3 oz) apricot jam
90 ml (3 fl oz) evaporated milk
³/4 teaspoon vanilla essence
185 g (6 oz) chocolate, melted
600 g (1¹/4 lb) sugarpaste

EQUIPMENT

28 cm (11 inch) round cake board
2 small round cutters
narrow pink ribbon

DECORATING THE BOARD

1 Colour the royal icing brown with a few drops of food colouring and spread over the cake board. Sprinkle with the brown sugar and leave to dry.

TRUFFLE PASTE

2 Mix together the cake crumbs, apricot jam, evaporated milk and vanilla essence in a bowl, then slowly pour in the melted chocolate, stirring continuously, until a firm paste forms. If the truffle paste is too dry it will crumble and be difficult to mould—add a little more evaporated milk. If it is too soft it will not hold its shape—add a few more cake crumbs.

3 Roll the truffle paste into a sausage shape about 60 cm (24 inches) long. Colour 500 g (1 lb) of the sugarpaste bright pink, then roll out 375 g (12 oz) of it into a long narrow strip on a surface dusted with icing sugar and brush with water. Wrap around the truffle paste, taking care to seal the join. Arrange the body shape in a coil on the cake board with the join underneath. Shape the head from the remaining pink sugarpaste and attach to the body. Shape the end of the tail to a point.

SPOTS

4 Colour 60 g (2 oz) of the sugarpaste yellow and 30 g (1 oz) green. Roll out very thinly and use the cutters to make circles of yellow paste and slightly smaller circles of green. Attach the yellow circles to the snake with a little water and position a green circle on top of every other one.

FINISHING TOUCHES

5 Colour 7 g (¹/4 oz) of the sugarpaste black and 7 g (¹/4 oz) red. Shape eyes, nose and tongue from black, red and white paste and attach to the snake with a little water. Trim the board with pink ribbon, securing with double-sided tape.

NOTE Truffle paste can be made from any leftover cake trimmings. If you are using chocolate cake crumbs, bind the mixture with melted milk or dark chocolate. If using Madeira or other light cake crumbs, try using melted white chocolate.

3

Mould the truffle paste into a long sausage and then wrap in the strip of pink sugarpaste, sealing the join.

4

Roll out the yellow and green sugarpaste very thinly and then cut different-sized circles from each. Attach to the snake with a little water.

4
Secure the grass to the base of the cake with water, letting the cut edge fall away like grass.

BUNNY CAKE

A perfect idea for beginners with simple moulded rabbits and cut-out grass. Use any cake except fruit cake.

20 cm (8 inch) hexagonal cake (use mixture for 20 cm round cake)

7 tablespoons raspberry or strawberry jam
250 g (8 oz) buttercream
1.5 kg (3 lb) sugarpaste
yellow, green, pink and black paste food colourings
12 ready-made flower cake decorations

EQUIPMENT
23 cm (9 inch) round silver cake board
fine paintbrush
narrow pink ribbon

1   Slice the dome off the top of the cake to give a level surface, then cut the cake horizontally in half. Place one layer on the cake board and spread with 4 tablespoons of the jam. Cover with the buttercream, then position the second layer on top.

2   Sieve the remaining jam to remove any lumps. Brush the cake with the jam.

3   Colour 1.1 kg (2¼ lb) sugarpaste yellow. Cover the cake with the yellow sugarpaste.

GRASS
4   Colour 125 g (4 oz) of the sugarpaste green. Thinly roll out a little and cut out a 13 x 2.5 cm (5 x 1 inch) strip. Make cuts down one long side of the strip, through to the centre. Dampen the uncut edge of the strip with water, then lay it against the base of the cake so that the cut edge falls away from the cake to look like grass. Make more strips and attach all around the base of the cake.

PINK TRIM
5   Colour 60 g (2 oz) of the sugarpaste pale pink and roll it out thinly. Cut into 13 x 5 mm (5 x ¼ inch) strips, reserving the trimmings. Lightly dampen the points around the top edge of the cake with a little water. Gently twist a pink strip and secure it between two points on top of the cake. Repeat all around the cake. Secure small balls of white sugarpaste at the points where the strips meet.

BUNNIES
6   To shape a simple bunny, start by rolling a piece of white sugarpaste into a ball, about 2.5 cm (1 inch) in diameter, for the body. Add a head, ears and tail. Secure on the centre of the cake. Shape and secure three smaller bunnies. Add small noses and centres of ears from pink icing trimmings. Paint facial features on the bunnies, using a fine paintbrush and diluted black food colouring.

FINISHING TOUCHES
7   Make more grass as before, but cut into 2.5 cm (1 inch) lengths and roll into tufts. Secure the grass and bought flower decorations to the top of the cake with water. Trim the board with ribbon, securing with double-sided tape.

TRAVELLING TRUCKS

Simple shapes in bright colours appeal to very young boys. This theme works equally well with cars or trains. Use any flavour round cake except a fruit cake—the flavours don't combine well with jam and buttercream fillings.

20 cm (8 inch) round cake

7 tablespoons strawberry or raspberry jam
125 g (4 oz) buttercream
1.5 kg (3 lb) sugarpaste
assorted food colourings

EQUIPMENT
25 cm (10 inch) round silver cake board
fine paintbrush
candles
narrow ribbon

1   Slice the dome off the top of the cake to give a level surface, then cut the cake horizontally in half. Place one layer on the cake board and spread with 4 tablespoons of the jam. Cover with the buttercream, then position the second layer on top.

2   Sieve the remaining jam and brush over the cake. Cover the cake with 1 kg (2 lb) sugarpaste.

TRUCKS ON CAKE SIDE
3   Colour 125 g (4 oz) of the sugarpaste green. Reserve a little, then roll out the remainder to a strip as long as the circumference of the cake. Cut one edge straight and the other in a wavy line. Dampen the bottom edge of the cake with water, then wrap the strip around the base of the cake.

4   Trace the template, right, onto non-stick baking paper and cut out. Colour 185 g (6 oz) of the sugarpaste red. Thinly roll out half. Lay the template on the sugarpaste and cut around it to shape a truck. Dampen with water and secure the truck to the side of the cake above the green strip, leaving room to position the wheels. Make and secure more trucks.

TRUCK ON CAKE TOP
5   Shape the remaining red sugarpaste into a solid rectangle and cut out a wedge from one corner to shape the front of a truck.

BRIDGE AND WATER
6   Colour 125 g (4 oz) of the sugarpaste brown. Shape into a thick semi-circle, then cut out the centre with a knife or round cutter to make a bridge.

7   Colour a little more sugarpaste pale blue. Roll out and position on top of the cake. Carefully arrange the bridge over the blue 'water'. Shape a small path from brown trimmings and secure to the top of the cake with a little water. Secure the truck on top of the cake, raising it off the cake slightly on a piece of red sugarpaste trimmings.

FINISHING TOUCHES
8   Colour a little more sugarpaste black and shape into wheels. Secure to all the trucks.

9   Shape tiny balls of green sugarpaste from trimmings and arrange in rings on the top of the cake. Press candles into the centres, or fill with a dot of red icing. Shape small yellow 'headlights' and secure to the front of the truck. Trim the board with ribbon, securing with double-sided tape.

NOTE   The simple design of this cake is very effective. However, you could add more detail—for instance, windows and number plates on the trucks.

Shape a rectangle of red sugarpaste and then cut off a wedge from one corner to shape a truck. Make wheels from black sugarpaste and attach to the truck with water.

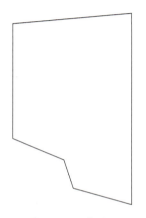

template actual size

PUSSY CAT

For any young child with a cat, this cake is going to be purrrfect. Change the colourings to match a family pet. The trickiest part of this recipe is covering the cake with sugarpaste so, once you've mastered that, it really is simple.

5

Using the red, black and off-white sugarpaste, shape the tail, eyes, nose, mouth and paws.

6

Use the template to cut out the inner and outer ears from pink and white sugarpaste. Stick the pieces together with water.

15 cm (6 inch) round cake
20 x 15 cm (8 x 6 inch) oval cake

315 g (10 oz) jam
470 g (15 oz) buttercream
2.5 kg (5 lb) sugarpaste
green, cream, pink, red and black paste food
colourings
90 g (3 oz) royal icing
liquorice 'laces'

EQUIPMENT

38 x 33 cm (15 x 13 inch) oval cake board
paintbrush
narrow brown ribbon

1   Cut the domed tops off the cakes to give a level surface. Slice both cakes in half horizontally and sandwich back together with jam.

SHAPING THE CAKE

2   The oval cake will become the cat's head and the round cake its body. To fit the two together, use the oval cake tin as a template to cut around, removing a curved section from one side of the round cake. Then fit the two cakes together neatly, securing with a little buttercream. Cover the whole cake with a thin coat of buttercream.

3   Colour 560 g (1 lb 2 oz) of the sugarpaste green and use to cover the board. Leave to dry.

4   Reserve 125 g (4 oz) of the sugarpaste and colour the remainder off-white using cream food colouring. Roll out the sugarpaste and cover the cake. Secure the cake to the board with a little royal icing.

CAT FEATURES

5   Colour 25 g (3/4oz) of the sugarpaste pink, a tiny piece red and the remainder black. Using the off-white coloured trimmings and the other colours, model the eyes, nose, mouth, tail and paws.

6   Make templates from the outline, left, for the inner and outer ears. Roll out the pink sugarpaste and white trimmings, then cut out the ears. Attach the pink inner ear to the white outer ear with a little water. Leave all these pieces to dry.

7   Using black food colouring with a small amount of royal icing added to thicken, paint on the body markings. Attach all the features, ears and tail and six liquorice whiskers with dabs of royal icing. Trim the cake board with ribbon, securing with double-sided tape.

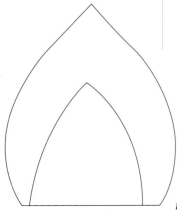

template actual size

MATCHSTICK BOYS AND GIRLS

Clear piping gel can be coloured to create bright pictures on cakes that have been covered with sugarpaste. The glossy surface of the gel retains its brightness even after drying. The outline is piped in chocolate and does not need to be perfect for this style of decoration.

15 x 23 cm (6 x 9 inch) rectangular cake (use mixture for 20 cm round cake)

500 g (1 lb) marzipan
120 g (4 oz) royal icing
500 g (1 lb) sugarpaste
60 g (2 oz) dark chocolate, melted
a few drops of glycerine
120 g (4 oz) piping gel
selection of food colourings

EQUIPMENT

20 x 30 cm (8 x 12 inch) cake board
numbers 1 and 42 or 44 piping tubes
narrow white ribbon

1   Cover the cake with marzipan and leave to dry. Secure the cake to the board with a little of the royal icing. Cover the cake and board with sugarpaste, using the all-in-one method. Leave to dry.

2   Transfer the template on page 286 onto non-stick baking paper. Transfer to the top of the cake with a scriber or by pin pricks.

PIPING THE OUTLINE

3   Mix the melted chocolate with a few drops of glycerine in a small bowl. Leave to stand for a few seconds to thicken. (The addition of the glycerine will give you greater control when piping the chocolate.) Pipe the outline of the design in chocolate using a number 1 tube.

COLOURING IN

4   Colour the piping gel by adding a few drops of food colouring. Spoon into paper piping bags (you don't need a tube) and snip off the ends. Fill in the outlines with the coloured gel.

FINISHING TOUCHES

5   Pipe a shell border with royal icing, using a number 42 or 44 tube, around the base of the cake. Trim the edge of the cake board with ribbon, securing with double-sided tape.

Mix the melted chocolate with glycerine to give you more control while piping over the outline.

Colour the gel in bright colours and then pipe into the outline, using a paper piping bag without a tube.

see template page 286

Cut out the teddy outline from the top of the cake, cutting outside the pin marks for neatness.

Cut out the teddy outline from the yellow sugarpaste and inlay into the space in the cake top.

Prick or scribe the paw and facial details onto the teddy and then inlay with brown sugarpaste.

see template page 289

CUDDLES THE BEAR

This is an easy cake for a young child's birthday or even a christening, using the inlay technique, which is simple for beginners. The number on the bear's tummy can be altered to the appropriate age.

20 cm (8 inch) round cake
500 g (1 lb) marzipan
750 g (1½ lb) sugarpaste
yellow, brown and red paste food colourings
1 tablespoon royal icing
icing sugar
brown food colour pen

EQUIPMENT

23 cm (9 inch) foil-covered cake board
scriber
narrow red ribbon

1   Cover the cake with marzipan and leave to dry for 24 hours. Trace the template from page 289 onto non-stick baking paper, then trim the paper to fit the top of the cake.

COLOURING THE SUGARPASTE

2   Colour 185 g (6 oz) of the sugarpaste yellow. Colour 15 g (½ oz) of the sugarpaste brown and 30 g (1 oz) red. Keep 15 g (½ oz) of the sugarpaste white and set aside. Brush the cake with clear alcohol, leaving an 18 cm (7 inch) wide circle in the centre unbrushed. Roll out the remaining white sugarpaste to 2.5 mm (⅛ inch) thick and cover the cake. Secure the cake to the board with a little royal icing.

INLAYING THE TEDDY OUTLINE

3   Secure the template in position on the cake top with glass-head pins just inside the outline. Use a scriber or a pin just inside the outline to transfer the outline of the teddy to the cake, then remove the tracing. Using a modelling knife or scalpel, cut the teddy shape from the white sugarpaste, cutting just outside the pin marks. Carefully lift the piece of icing from the cake top.

4   Roll out the yellow sugarpaste to 2.5 mm (⅛ inch) thick. Secure the teddy template over the yellow sugarpaste with pins and prick or scribe the design on the outside edge of the template, then remove the tracing. There will be two lines of marks on the sugarpaste—the holes that have just been made and dents from the previous transfer. Cut the section out, cutting between the two lines of marks. Lift out the section and inlay into the space in the

cake top, using your fingers to smooth over the coloured sugarpaste until the two cut edges meet and the small dents disappear.

INLAYING THE TEDDY DETAILS

5   Secure the tracing on the cake top, using the teddy outline to position it accurately. Use a scriber or pin to transfer the details of the tummy, paws, ears, eyes and nose to the teddy, then remove the tracing. Cut out the tummy and inlay with white sugarpaste as before. Cut out the facial features and inlay with brown sugarpaste. Cut out the paws and inlay with brown sugarpaste.

6   Secure the tracing on the cake top, using the teddy outline to position it accurately. Use the scriber or pin to transfer the bow and number to the cake top. Cut out the number and inlay with red sugarpaste. Cut out the bow and inlay with red sugarpaste.

7   Lightly dust the cake top with icing sugar and use a smoother to remove any dents. If the sugarpaste appears dry or cracked from the icing sugar, cover with plastic wrap for 2–3 hours until the icing sugar is absorbed. Leave the sugarpaste to dry for 48 hours or until it will not dent when pressed.

8   Use the brown food colour pen to draw in teddy's mouth. (If you are nervous about drawing freehand, use the template again, scribing the mouth onto the cake first.) Trim the cake board with ribbon, securing with double-sided tape.

NOTE   To save time when cutting out small paw sections, use the head of a pin to make small dents, then fill with small balls of brown sugarpaste.

FIRST BIRTHDAY BLOCKS

1

Leave one bar cake whole and cut the other one into three pieces.

1

Move the cake pieces into position to make a number one. You will not need the middle triangle.

3

Use a skewer to mark letters and numbers in the centre of the cubes.

4

Pipe over the skewer marks on the cubes, alternating the colours of the icing.

two 8 x 25 cm (3 x 10 inch) Madeira cakes
2 quantities buttercream from page 36
assorted food colourings

EQUIPMENT

15 x 40 cm (6 x 16 inch) cake board
skewer

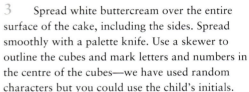

1   Trim the tops off the cakes to give a level surface. Leave one cake whole and cut the other cake in half, then slice a small triangle off one of the halves. Place the pieces on the cake board in the shape of a one—you will not need the middle triangle of the cut cake. Join the edges with a little buttercream.

2   Take out four ¼ cup portions of the buttercream and place each into a small bowl. Tint one portion red, another blue, one portion yellow and the final portion green. Spoon each colour into a small paper piping bag. Leave the largest portion of the icing white.

3   Spread white buttercream over the entire surface of the cake, including the sides. Spread smoothly with a palette knife. Use a skewer to outline the cubes and mark letters and numbers in the centre of the cubes—we have used random characters but you could use the child's initials.

4   Pipe over your skewer marks on each cube, alternating the colours of the icing so that each cube is a different colour. Then, carefully fill in the centre of the letters and numbers with the same colour you used for the outline.

SNAKES ALIVE! NUMBER TWO

Cut out the pieces of template and then secure to the tops of the cakes.

Cut around the templates and then move the cake pieces into position.

Cover the cake with green buttercream. Pipe patterns with violet buttercream.

Fill inside the piped patterns with the purple sprinkles. They will stick to the buttercream.

8 x 25 cm (3 x 10 inch) Madeira cake
20 cm (8 inch) ring Madeira cake
2 quantities buttercream from page 36
violet and green food colourings
purple sprinkles (hundreds and thousands)
2 white jellybeans
2 purple round sweets
1 red jelly snake

EQUIPMENT

skewers or toothpicks
30 cm (12 inch) square cake board

1   Do not trim the tops of the cakes—leave the cakes rounded to form the shape of a snake. Cut out the pieces of the template on page 301, and stick to the top of the cake with skewers or toothpicks. Cut the cakes to shape, then move the cake pieces into the shape of a snake. Remove the templates and toothpicks and join the pieces together with a little of the buttercream.

2   Place 2 tablespoons of the buttercream in a small bowl and tint it dark violet, similar to the colour of the sprinkles. Spoon the violet icing into a piping bag. Tint the remaining buttercream bright green.

3   Spread the green buttercream evenly over the entire cake, using a palette knife to smooth the surface. Once the snake has been completely iced with the green buttercream, pipe squiggly patches over the snake with the violet buttercream. Fill inside the patches with purple sprinkles.

4   Arrange the jellybeans in place for the eyes, pipe a little violet icing onto each of the jellybeans and stick a purple sweet to the front of it. Pipe a mouth with violet icing, then pipe two dots for the nostrils. Make a slit in the head part of the jelly snake for the tip of the tongue and trim so that it is only about 2.5 cm (1 inch) long. Insert into the mouth of the cake snake.

see template page 301

THIRD BIRD-DAY

1
Cut one ring cake in half, with one end pointed. Cut a small piece from the middle of the other cake.

1
Join the piece with the pointed end to the largest piece in the shape of a number three.

3
Arrange the jellybeans over the icing, cut-side-down and slightly over-lapping like feathers.

two 20 cm (8 inch) ring Madeira cakes
1¹/2 quantities buttercream from page 36
red and yellow food colourings
yellow and white jellybeans
banana sweets
1 marshmallow
1 black jellybean
2 orange jelly snakes

EQUIPMENT
32 cm (13 inch) square cake board

1   Do not level the cakes—leave them rounded. Cut one ring cake in half, with one end pointed for the beak, as shown. Cut a small piece from the middle of the other ring cake. Join the piece with the pointed end to the largest piece in the shape of a number three.

2   Tint ¹/4 cup of the buttercream bright orange-red. Tint the remaining buttercream bright yellow. Spread the orange icing over the end of the top cake for the beak. Add a couple more drops of red to the leftover orange beak icing and ice a strip along the bottom of the beak for the opening of the mouth. Ice the rest of the cake with yellow icing. Alternatively, you may prefer to ice all of the cake with the yellow icing first and then go over the beak area with the orange icing.

3   Cut the jellybeans and banana sweets in half lengthways. Leave a small space behind the beak for the eyes, then start laying jellybeans over the icing, cut-side-down and slightly overlapping. Stop when you reach the middle point of the three. Stick four rows of bananas in the middle of the cake. Add another five rows or so of jellybeans beneath the bananas, then add another three rows of bananas.

4   Cut a marshmallow in half and make eyes out of it. Cut the ends off a black jellybean and stick rounded-side-up on the marshmallows using a little buttercream to stick them in place. Add plumage by sticking a few bananas at a jaunty angle behind the eyes. Make three slits on the head end of the snakes to create feet and place them on the bottom of the cake as shown. Overlap some bananas on top of the legs to hide the top ends.

RACE YOU FOUR IT

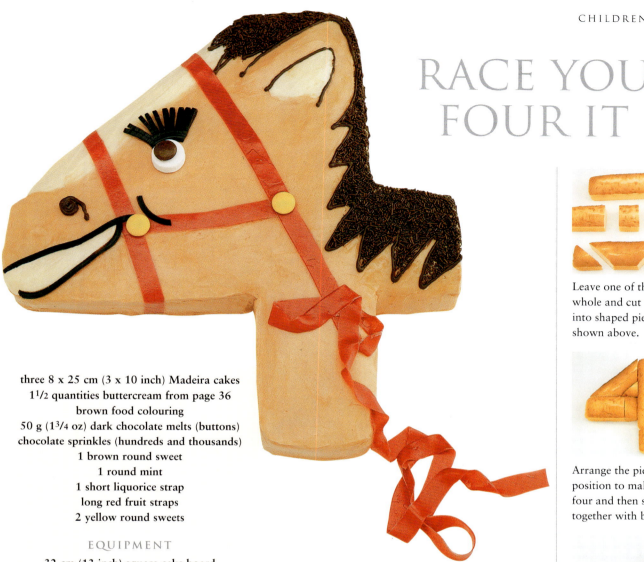

three 8 x 25 cm (3 x 10 inch) Madeira cakes
1¹/2 quantities buttercream from page 36
brown food colouring
50 g (1³/4 oz) dark chocolate melts (buttons)
chocolate sprinkles (hundreds and thousands)
1 brown round sweet
1 round mint
1 short liquorice strap
long red fruit straps
2 yellow round sweets

EQUIPMENT

32 cm (13 inch) square cake board
skewer

1   Position the cakes on the cake board. Leave one cake whole. Cut the second cake in half, then cut one of the halves in half again. For the last cake, cut a small slice from one end, then cut a triangle off each end of the larger piece. Arrange the cake pieces into the shape of a number four on a cake board as shown, levelling the cake if necessary and trimming any pieces that are a little too large. Join the edges with a little buttercream.

2   Reserve ¹/4 cup of the white buttercream and tint the remaining buttercream caramel brown. Spread the white buttercream down the nose of the horse. Spread brown buttercream over the rest of the horse and blend it neatly into the white icing.

3   Using a skewer, mark onto the icing the mouth, mane, the inside and outside of the ear, and the large comma shape for the nostril. Spread some of the white buttercream into the area you have

marked out for the mouth, then into the centre of the ear. Build up the height of the outer area of the ear with more brown icing.

4   Place the chocolate in a heatproof bowl. Bring a saucepan of water to the boil, then remove from the heat. Sit the bowl over the pan, making sure the base of the bowl does not sit in the water. Stir occasionally until the chocolate has melted. Spoon into a piping bag, then pipe over your skewer marks to form an outline around the mane, ear and nostril. Fill the mane with chocolate sprinkles. Continue the mane down the side of the cake by pressing sprinkles onto the side with a palette knife.

5   To make the eye, stick the brown sweet to the mint with a little buttercream and stick onto the face. Cut an eyelash out of a short piece of liquorice strap and place above the eye, fanning out the lashes and pressing gently into the cake. Cut thin strips from the liquorice straps and line the mouth of the horse. Arrange fruit straps in place for reigns and stick yellow sweets on the straps for the studs.

Leave one of the cakes whole and cut the others into shaped pieces as shown above.

Arrange the pieces into position to make a number four and then secure together with buttercream.

Spread white buttercream into the centre of the ear and then spread brown icing around it.

Continue the mane down the side of the cake by pressing sprinkles onto the side with a palette knife.

FIVE DOWN ON THE FARM

1

Cut the bar cake in half. Cut a piece from the ring cake that is almost a quarter of the ring.

1

Square off the rounded edges from the side and top of the removed piece of ring cake.

1

Arrange the pieces in the shape of a number five and join together with a little buttercream.

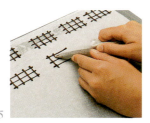

5

Pipe about 30 chocolate fences onto non-stick baking paper and then peel off when dry.

8 x 25 cm (3 x 10 inch) Madeira cake
20 cm (8 inch) Madeira ring cake
1¹/2 quantities buttercream from page 36
caramel and green food colourings
blue cake decorating gel
100 g (3¹/2 oz) dark or milk
chocolate melts (buttons)

EQUIPMENT

25 x 50 cm (10 x 20 inch) cake board
ruler
plastic farm animals

1   Cut the bar cake in half. Cut a piece from the ring cake that is almost a quarter of the ring. Next, square off this piece by neatly cutting off the rounded edges. Arrange the pieces on the cake board in the shape of a five, using the smaller offcuts to lengthen the bar of the number. Join each edge with a little buttercream.

2   Place ³/4 cup of the buttercream in a small bowl and tint light brown for the ground cover. Tint the remaining buttercream light green for the grass.

3   Mark out three sections for the paddocks and spread green buttercream over the top and bottom sections and brown over the middle section. Make a pond by piping blue food gel onto one of the green paddocks.

4   Place the chocolate in a heatproof bowl. Bring a saucepan of water to the boil, then remove from the heat. Sit the bowl over the pan, making sure the base of the bowl does not sit in the water. Stir occasionally until the chocolate has melted. Spoon the chocolate into a piping bag and create a mud bath for the pigs by piping some of the chocolate into the middle paddock.

5   Pipe the remaining chocolate onto a sheet of non-stick baking paper that has been placed on an oiled baking tray. Pipe about 30 fences 2.5 cm (1 inch) high and 5 cm (2 inches) wide (this will allow for any breakages). When set, carefully stick around the edge of the cake. Decorate the cake with farm animals.

UNDER THE SEA AT SIX

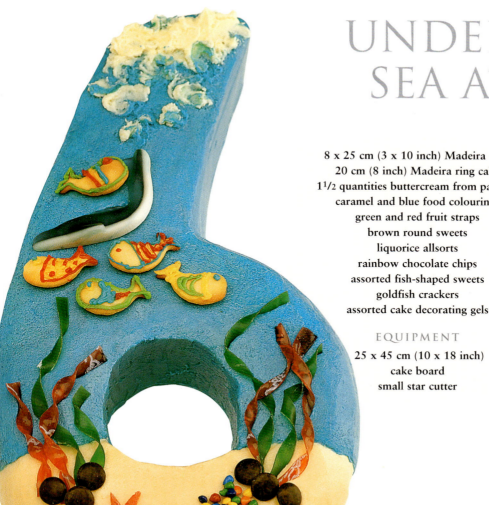

8 x 25 cm (3 x 10 inch) Madeira cake
20 cm (8 inch) Madeira ring cake
1¹/₂ quantities buttercream from page 36
caramel and blue food colourings
green and red fruit straps
brown round sweets
liquorice allsorts
rainbow chocolate chips
assorted fish-shaped sweets
goldfish crackers
assorted cake decorating gels

EQUIPMENT
25 x 45 cm (10 x 18 inch)
cake board
small star cutter

Cut a sharp curve in the bottom of the bar cake and a soft curve in the top. Discard the pieces.

Join the remaining bar cake to the ring cake with a little buttercream to make a number six.

Cut green and red fruit straps into lengths and then twist to look like strands of seaweed.

Cut away the coloured sections from the liquorice allsorts and, using a star cutter, make into starfish.

1   Leave the ring cake whole and cut the top and bottom from the bar cake as shown. Arrange the cakes on the board in the figure six, discarding the offcuts and joining with a little buttercream. Trim to neaten the edges and the top of the cake.

2   Reserve ¹/₄ cup white buttercream in a small bowl. Place a further ¹/₂ cup of buttercream in another small bowl and tint caramel to resemble sand. Tint the remaining buttercream blue.

3   Spread sand-coloured buttercream over the bottom of the six and cover the rest of the cake with the blue buttercream. Spread some of the white buttercream at the top to resemble a wave—use a palette knife to rough up the white buttercream so that it looks more realistic.

4   Cut green and red fruit straps into various lengths, then twist the strips a few times so that they look like seaweed strands. Stick the seaweed onto the cake, inserting into the sand-coloured buttercream. Place brown sweets at the base of each plant.

5   Cut the coloured section away from the liquorice allsorts and, using a small star cutter or small sharp knife, cut star shapes from them. Place the starfish on the sand. Sprinkle some rainbow chocolate chips onto the sand to add more colour. Arrange fish-shaped toys, sweets and crackers and use the coloured cake decorating gel or coloured buttercream to make patterns on the fish.

SEVENTH HEAVEN

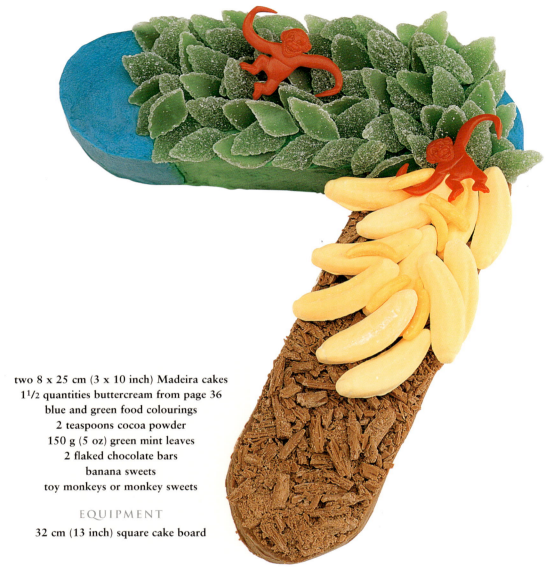

1

Trim the cakes so that the top bar cake has three corners cut off, but not the one that will be at the join.

1

Arrange the pieces on the board in a figure seven, joining each edge with a little buttercream.

3

Spread blue buttercream at the top corners for sky and green in the middle where the leaves will go.

4

Cut the mint leaves in half horizontally with sharp scissors and overlap on the green buttercream.

two 8 x 25 cm (3 x 10 inch) Madeira cakes
1½ quantities buttercream from page 36
blue and green food colourings
2 teaspoons cocoa powder
150 g (5 oz) green mint leaves
2 flaked chocolate bars
banana sweets
toy monkeys or monkey sweets

EQUIPMENT
32 cm (13 inch) square cake board

1 Trim the cakes as shown so that the top bar cake has three corners cut off (but not the corner that will join the bottom cake), and the second cake has a diagonal strip cut off one side and the corners cut off the other side. Arrange the pieces on the cake board in a figure seven, joining each edge with a little of the buttercream.

2 Place ¼ cup of the buttercream in a small bowl and tint blue for the sky. Divide the remaining buttercream in half. Tint one half green, and add the cocoa to the other half and mix together to create a deep brown.

3 Spread a 5 cm (2 inch) strip of blue buttercream at each end of the top of the seven and fill in the space with green buttercream. Then, cover the trunk with the brown buttercream.

4 Cut the mint leaves in half horizontally with sharp scissors and overlap on the green buttercream with a few edging over the blue buttercream—it looks best to have the leaves mainly sugar-side-up, but with occasional ones shiny-side-up. Break the flaked chocolate bar into flakes and sprinkle over the trunk of the tree, pressing down lightly into the buttercream so that they stay in place. Arrange assorted bananas in a bunch just below the leaves. Arrange the monkeys in the tree.

RACING AT EIGHT

two 20 cm (8 inch) Madeira ring cakes
2 quantities buttercream from page 36
green food colouring
2 liquorice metre straps
red liquorice laces
tiny bear biscuits
jelly babies
chocolate or toy cars
flags or liquorice allsorts and toothpicks

EQUIPMENT

30 x 50 cm (12 x 20 inch) cake board
ruler

1   Cut a small slice off each cake as shown so that they will sit flat against each other. Arrange the cakes on the cake board in the figure eight, joining each edge with a little buttercream. Trim to neaten the edges and the top of the cake. Tint the buttercream green, then spread evenly over the cake.

2   Use black liquorice to mark out the lanes of the track and add a strip across the finish line. Cut the red liquorice into short strips about 2.5 cm (1 inch) long (you will need about 35). Place the red strips in a line running down the centre of each lane. Place bear biscuits and jelly babies at the edges of the track for the cheering crowd. Place cars on the track and insert flags (paper or made from toothpicks and liquorice allsort slices) at the finish line and other points around the track.

Cut a small slice from the side of each cake so that they can sit flat against each other.

Arrange the cakes together on the board and join the edge where they meet with a little buttercream.

Use the straps of black liquorice to mark out the lines of the track and the finishing line.

Cut the red liquorice into short strips and place in a line down the centre of each lane.

161

LIFT OFF AT NINE

Leave the ring cake whole and cut a curve from the top of the bar cake, so that it will fit against the ring.

Arrange the cakes on the board in the shape of a number nine and glue the join with buttercream.

Slice off one side of the cone and then spread with buttercream. Roll in the dragees and sprinkles.

20 cm (8 inch) Madeira ring cake
8 x 25 cm (3 x 10 inch) Madeira cake
2 quantities buttercream from page 36
black and blue paste food colourings
500 g (1 lb) sugarpaste
1 ice-cream cone
silver dragees
twinkle sprinkles
1 ice-cream wafer
red and yellow fruit straps
1 coloured gum ball
sugar star decorations

EQUIPMENT
25 x 45 cm (10 x 18 inch) cake board

1   Leave the ring cake whole and cut a curve from the top of the bar cake, as shown. Arrange the cakes on a cake board in the figure nine, joining each edge with a little buttercream. Trim to neaten the edges and the top of the cake.

2   Divide the buttercream into six even amounts. Leave one portion white, tint one portion black and tint the others four shades of blue, from light to dark.

3   Spread the buttercream over the cakes, starting with the lighter colours at the bottom and moving up to the darker ones at the top. Blend each colour into the other at the edges.

4   Roll out half the sugarpaste with a rolling pin until it is a couple of millimetres thick. Cut out star shapes with a small star cutter or small sharp knife. Cut a circle for a planet.

5   To make the rocket, slice one side of the cone off so that it can sit flat. Spread the rocket with a little white buttercream and roll it on a plate filled with dragees and sprinkles. Carefully fill in any gaps that are left—tweezers makes this job much easier. To make the wings, cut a wafer in half along the diagonal and decorate as above. Sit the rocket's body halfway along the straight part of the nine and slide a wafer wing under each side.

6   Cut the fruit straps into thin strips for the flames and one thin curved strip for the ring around the planet. Add the 'flames' and the gum ball to the bottom of the rocket. Sprinkle the rocket with sugar star decorations. As the final touch, add the stars, planet and planet's ring.

AT LAST I AM TEN

22 cm (9 inch) round Madeira cake
two 8 x 25 cm (3 x 10 inch) Madeira cakes
2 quantities buttercream from page 36
assorted food colourings
30 g (1 oz) chocolate melts (buttons)
silver dragees

EQUIPMENT

30 cm (12 inch) square cake board
skewers or toothpicks

1　Level the tops off the cakes if necessary. Place the round cake on the cake board, cut in half crossways and move the pieces apart. Move one of the bar cakes into the middle. Cut off the over-hanging part of the bar cake. Sit the other bar cake to the left of the round cake and add the offcut to the bottom. Trace the templates from page 300.

2　Attach the adjoining cake pieces together with buttercream. Place the template of the paintbrush on the bar cake and secure with toothpicks. Mark the line between the bristles and the handle by piercing through the paper onto the cake with a skewer or toothpick. Cut to shape.

3　Place the template of the palette on the other cake and secure with toothpicks. To make the finger hole in the palette, you can either cut through the template with a sharp knife or mark the area with a skewer and cut it out after you have removed the template.

4　Leave half the buttercream white for the palette. Place one quarter of the remaining buttercream in a bowl and tint it caramel. Put 1/3 cup of the remaining buttercream in another bowl and tint it bright red. Leave the remaining buttercream white until needed. Spread brown buttercream over the bristles, making furrows for texture, and red over the handle. Spread the palette with the white buttercream.

5　Place the chocolate melts in a heatproof bowl. Bring a saucepan of water to the boil, then remove from the heat. Sit the bowl over the pan, making sure the base of the bowl does not sit in the water. Stir occasionally until the chocolate has melted. Spoon the chocolate into a piping bag and snip off the end. Pipe individual hairs over the brown icing, leaving a narrow strip at the bottom, wide enough to fit three rows of cachous. To finish the brush, carefully place three rows of cachous between the hairs and the handle.

6　Divide the remaining buttercream into small portions and tint each portion a different colour. Add dabs of the colours onto the palette to look like paints.

Cut the round cake in half and pull apart. Place the bar cake in the centre and cut off the overhang.

Spread brown buttercream on the bristles, red on the brush handle and white over the palette.

see template page 300

JUNGLE CAKE

Animals of any description appeal to most children. This simple creation, in buttercream and sugarpaste, is perfect for younger boys and girls. You can use any of the basic cakes except fruit (the flavour is not good with chocolate buttercream) or even use bought cakes.

2

Use a scalpel or knife to separate the horns in two.

3

Use a fine brush to paint red markings and black eyes and mouths.

5

Cut long shallow lines in the tree trunks for bark.

6

Position the green treetops overlapping slightly, alternating light and dark.

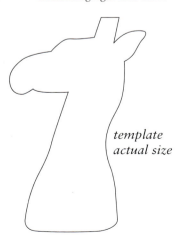

template actual size

---

two 15 cm (6 inch) round cakes

1 kg (2 lb) sugarpaste
yellow, red, black, brown, pale green and dark green food colourings
500 g (1 lb) chocolate buttercream

EQUIPMENT

fine paintbrush
cocktail sticks
23 cm (9 inch) round silver cake board
narrow green ribbon

GIRAFFES

1   To make the giraffes, colour 60 g (2 oz) of the sugarpaste yellow. Trace the giraffe template, left, onto non-stick baking paper and cut it out. Thinly roll out the yellow sugarpaste on a surface dusted with cornflour. Lay the template on the sugarpaste and cut around it. Make another giraffe, then turn the template over and cut out another two facing the other way. (One set acts as a spare.)

2   Using a scalpel or knife, cut between the horns to separate them. Roll small balls of yellow sugarpaste and secure to the ends of the horns with a damp paintbrush. Dampen the ends of the cocktail sticks and lay them under the base of each giraffe. Press down lightly to secure. Transfer to a sheet of non-stick baking paper and leave for 24 hours to dry. Wrap the remaining sugarpaste in plastic wrap.

3   Using a fine paintbrush and slightly diluted colourings, paint red markings and black facial features on the giraffes.

4   Slice the domed top off the cakes to give a level surface. Cut the cakes horizontally in half and sandwich the four layers together with a little of the buttercream. Place the cake on the board. Spread the top and sides with the remaining buttercream, smoothing it as flat as possible with a palette knife.

TREES

5   Colour 500 g (1 lb) of the remaining sugarpaste brown. Roll out a little to make a long sausage, roughly the same height as the cake. Flatten

slightly, then cut slits down one end and open out slightly for branches. Make bark markings with the tip of a knife and secure to the side of the cake. Make more trees in the same way, varying the sizes.

6   Colour 155 g (5 oz) of the remaining sugarpaste pale green and another 155 g (5 oz) dark green. Roll out a small ball of one colour to a 12 cm (4½ inch) circle. Pull up the edges and pinch together. Turn the piece of sugarpaste over and press into position on the top of the cake. Make more treetops in the same way. Arrange them on the cake so the colours alternate and overlap slightly.

FINISHING TOUCHES

7   Roll small balls of white icing and position around the cake in pairs to look like peering eyes.

8   Colour more trimmings grey and shape elephants' trunks. Press into the buttercream and secure to the trees with a dampened paintbrush.

9   Make brightly coloured snakes from the remaining trimmings and secure to the tree trunks. Make snakes' eyes from tiny balls of white sugarpaste. Paint the centres of the eyes and the snake markings with a fine paintbrush and black food colouring. Trim the board with green ribbon, securing with double-sided tape.

NOTE   Small, round, bought cakes are perfect for this if you don't have time to make your own. Stack three together as they tend to be shallower than home-made ones.

If you only have one green food colouring, make half the treetops, then darken the remaining green sugarpaste by adding extra green and a little black food colouring.

You can cut out extra giraffe shapes and press together to make double-sided giraffes with the cocktail sticks in the middle. Paint the markings on both sides.

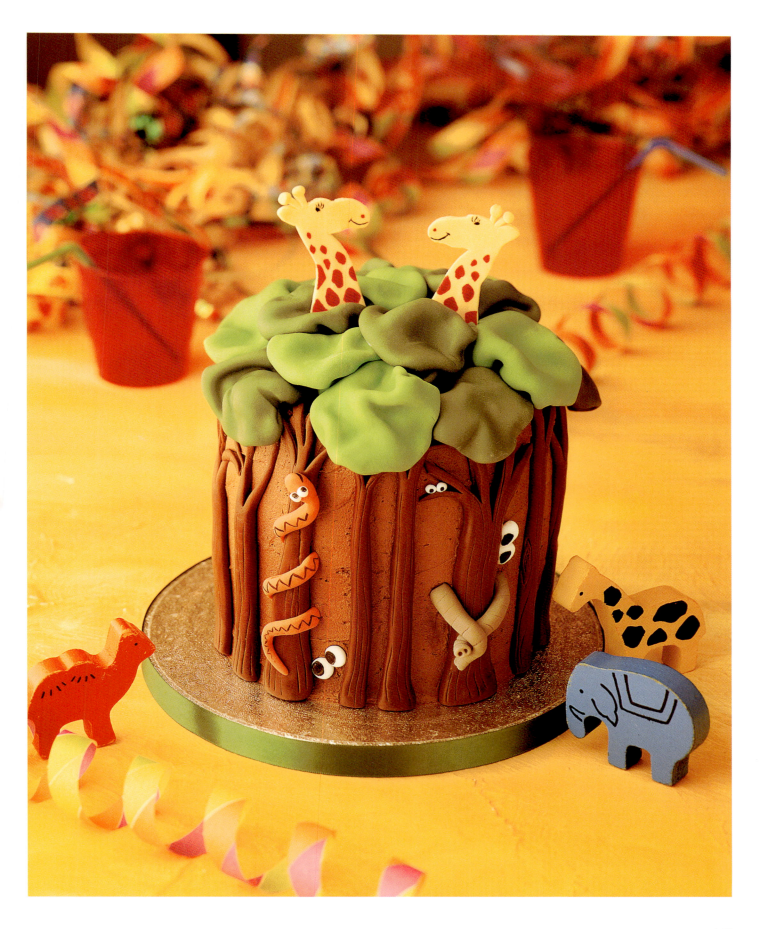

TEDDY BEAR CAKE

All children love teddy bears and this cake will be doubly popular with marzipan and chocolate lovers. Other animal cutters could be used in the same way. The cake itself is covered with a marbled mixture of marzipan and chocolate sugarpaste.

20 cm (8 inch) hexagonal cake (use mixture for 20 cm round cake)

625 g (1¼ lb) marzipan
500 g (1 lb) chocolate sugarpaste
250 g (8 oz) chocolate-coloured royal icing
500 g (1 lb) marzipan, extra
2 teaspoons gum tragacanth
brown powder food colouring
blue paste food colouring

EQUIPMENT

28 cm (11 inch) hexagonal cake board
numbers 1.5 and 2 piping tubes
large, medium and small bear cutters
9 cm (3½ inch) oval plaque cutter
plain round briar rose cutters
ribbon cutter

1   Slice the domed top off the cake to give a level surface. Blend 500 g (1 lb) of the marzipan with 250 g (8 oz) of the chocolate sugarpaste to create a marbled effect. Cover the cake with the marbled paste and leave to dry for 24 hours.

INLAY BEARS ON CAKE BOARD

2   Cover the cake board with chocolate sugarpaste and cut out and remove bear shapes around the edge with the small bear cutter. Roll out the remaining 125 g (4 oz) marzipan and cut out bear shapes with the same cutter. Insert the marzipan bears into the spaces on the board and smooth over gently with your fingers to seal.

3   Re-roll the marzipan trimmings and cut out an oval plaque with the plaque cutter. Leave to dry.

4   Secure the cake to the board with royal icing. Using chocolate-coloured royal icing and a number 2 tube, pipe a snail trail around the base of the cake.

5   Secure the plaque to the top of the cake with a little royal icing. Using chocolate-coloured royal icing and a number 1.5 piping tube, pipe a snail trail around the edge of the plaque.

CUT-OUT BEARS

6   Knead the extra 500 g marzipan well and add the gum tragacanth. Knead well to ensure the powder is completely worked into the marzipan. Cover with plastic wrap and leave for at least an hour before using. Roll out to approximately 2.5 mm (⅛ inch) thick and cut out 20 bears with the medium bear cutter. Dry in a warm place for at least 48 hours. You may not need all 20 bears, but it is useful to have some spares in case of breakages.

7   Roll out some more of the marzipan paste and cut out two bears with the large bear cutter, and three discs (one of each size) with the briar rose cutters. Also cut out a small triangular piece of paste as a support for the top decoration. Remove the arms and legs from one of the large bears with a craft knife or scalpel. Allow all the pieces to dry flat in a warm place for at least 48 hours.

8   Assemble the large bear by placing the different pieces one on top of the other, separated by small dots of royal icing. Allow the icing to dry before adding the next layer. Leave to dry for 24 hours.

9   Dust the bear with brown powder food colour. With chocolate-coloured royal icing and a number 1.5 piping tube, pipe in facial details and paw pads. Colour a little of the paste blue, roll it out very thinly and cut into strips with the ribbon cutter. Shape a bow and secure to the bear.

ASSEMBLY

10   Using a pencil and stiff card, draw around the medium bear cutter and cut out the shape. Use this template to indent the position of the feet for the bears on the board to help support them.

11   Using chocolate-coloured royal icing and a number 2 tube, pipe a little icing into the indents on the board and set the paste bears into them. Support with small pieces of foam until set. Fix the large bear to the top of the cake using the same method. Add the triangular piece of paste to support the bear from the back.

Cut out bears from the chocolate sugarpaste on the board and inlay with plain marzipan bears.

Assemble the large bear by placing the pieces on top of each other, separated by dots of royal icing. Dust with brown food colour.

Make indentations on the cake board and then fill with a little royal icing to support the paste bears.

6

Cut about 12 sunflowers from the flower paste. They should still be pliable when secured on the cake with royal icing.

9

Make noses from tiny cones of flower paste and attach to the faces with a little edible glue. Blend the join with a paintbrush.

11

This cake is great fun to make if you can match some of the characters to friends or family.

SUNFLOWER FACES

Bright sunflowers with smiling faces will bring a touch of summer to your celebration. Any large multi-petal cutter could be used instead of the sunflower cutters. The faces are great fun to make... especially if you can give them a resemblance to friends or family.

25 cm (10 inch) round cake

1 kg (2 lb) cream-tinted sugarpaste
1 kg (2 lb) marzipan
250 g (8 oz) cream-tinted royal icing
600 g (1¹/₄ lb) flower paste
selection of paste and powder food colourings, including flesh, cream, brown and shades of yellow
edible glue

EQUIPMENT

30 cm (12 inch) round cake board
crimpers
number 2 piping tube
large sunflower cutter
small oval cutter
ball tool
Dresden tool
pieces of foam
paintbrushes
narrow red ribbon

1   Cover the cake board with some of the cream sugarpaste and crimp the edge to neaten. Leave to dry.

2   Cut about 7.5 cm (3 inches) from one side of the cake so that it can stand on its side. Sit the cake flat again and cover the top and curved side with marzipan. Leave to dry for 24 hours.

3   Turn the cake over carefully onto non-stick baking paper and cover the other flat side with marzipan. Leave to dry.

4   Using the same method, cover both sides of the cake with cream sugarpaste. Secure the cake upright on the board with a little royal icing and neaten the sugarpaste joins with crimpers. Pipe a snail trail of cream royal icing around the base of the cake, using a number 2 tube.

SUNFLOWERS

5   Colour 185 g (6 oz) of the flower paste a pale flesh colour and store in a plastic bag. Colour the remainder in different shades of yellow.

6   Roll out the yellow pastes and cut out approximately 12 sunflowers. Soften the edges with a ball tool and mark veins with a Dresden tool. Allow the flowers to set slightly, but they should still be pliable when you attach them to the cake.

7   Attach the sunflowers to the cake with a little royal icing. You will need to lift and curve some of the petals so that they overlap and the flowers almost cover the surface. Allow some of them to stand up over the top edge and others to curve around onto the board. Some of the petals may need to be supported with pieces of foam while they are drying.

FACES

8   Roll out the flesh-coloured paste to approximately 2.5 mm (¹/₈ inch) thick and cut out the basic face shapes with a small oval cutter. Using your fingertips, smooth the edges and contour the shapes. Small pieces of paste can be tucked underneath to form cheeks, if necessary.

9   Make the noses from tiny cones of paste, attach them to the faces with a little edible glue and blend them onto the faces with a fine paintbrush. Nostrils can be marked in with the fine point of the Dresden tool. Eye sockets can be indented and the eyes painted in.

10   While the faces are still slightly soft, fix them to the sunflower centres with a little royal icing. Smooth into position and allow to dry. Paint in facial details with a paintbrush and pale brown food colour diluted with water or clear alcohol. By painting with a pale colour first you can erase any mistakes with a damp brush. When you are satisfied with the results, you can emphasise the features with a stronger colour.

11   Finish the faces off by adding hair, hats, collars, ties and bows. These can be piped with royal icing and brushed with a damp brush to give texture, or soft flower paste could be used. Try to give each face a different character, perhaps modelled on members of the family or friends. Leave the back of the cake plain or cover with more sunflowers. Trim the cake board with ribbon, securing in place with double-sided tape.

DREAM CASTLE

Fairy-tale castles are always popular with little girls. The turrets on these towers hide stacks of sweets that will delight party-goers. Make this cake a few days in advance so it can really dry well—it will keep for up to 10 days if needed. It needs to be Madeira cake for firmness.

Madeira mixture for 22 cm (9 inch) round cake

1.5 kg (3 lb) sugarpaste
250 g (8 oz) royal icing
apricot glaze
selection of round pastel-coloured sweets
gold dragees
yellow and pink food colourings
gold dusting powder

EQUIPMENT

20 cm (8 inch) round cake tin
3 empty 400 g (14 oz) clean food cans
25 cm (10 inch) round silver cake board
2.5 cm (1 inch) plain round cutter
number 2 piping tube
fine paintbrush
pink ribbon

BAKING THE CAKES

1 Preheat the oven to 160°C (315°F/Gas 2–3). Grease and line the cake tin and food cans with non-stick baking paper. Spoon the cake mixture into the cans, filling each one two-thirds full. Spoon the remaining mixture into the cake tin. Bake the cans for 30 minutes and the tin for 1¼ hours. Turn out onto a wire rack to cool.

CASTLE TOWERS

2 Roll out a little sugarpaste on a surface dusted with cornflour and cut out a 7.5 cm (3 inch) square. Transfer to a sheet of non-stick baking paper. Using a sharp knife, cut a small archway from one side and notches from the opposite side. Dry for 24 hours.

3 Cut the dome from the large cake to give a flat surface and secure to the board with royal icing. Cover the cake and board, using the all-in-one method, with 750 g (1½ lb) of the sugarpaste.

4 Level the tops of the small cakes by cutting off any domes. Cut a 2.5 cm (1 inch) slice off one cake and secure it with a little apricot glaze to another so that you have three towers of different sizes. Use a 2.5 cm (1 inch) plain round cutter to take a 5 cm (2 inch) deep notch out of one side of each of the two tallest towers. Brush with apricot glaze.

5 Cover the tower sides with sugarpaste and place on the cake. Cut out circles of sugarpaste to cover the tower tops. To make windows, cut crosses around the towers with a knife, then press the end of a piping tube into the ends of the arms of each cross.

6 Roll out two 5 cm (2 inch) squares of sugarpaste. Arrange a line of sweets down the centre of each. Wrap the icing around the sweets to cover them. Dampen one edge and secure the ends. Dampen the notched corners on the two towers, then press the mini-towers into position, with the joins facing inwards. Make windows in the mini-towers.

7 Secure the hardened sugarpaste archway against the front towers with royal icing. Make two more mini-towers and place one at each end of the archway. Leave to dry overnight.

TOWER TOPS

8 Cut an 18 cm (7 inch) round of non-stick baking paper into two semi-circles and shape into cones. Make a third cone from another round of paper. Pile sweets on top of each tower, then dampen the top edges of the towers. Gently rest the cones in position. Make smaller cones from 2.5 cm (1 inch) rounds of paper for the mini-towers.

9 Place the royal icing in a paper piping bag fitted with a number 2 tube and pipe a dot on top of each cone. Top with a gold dragee.

10 Roll out 2 cm (¾ inch) strips of sugarpaste. Cut out notches and secure a strip around each tower with the notched end uppermost. Place thinner notched strips around the mini-towers.

FINISHING TOUCHES

11 Dilute yellow food colouring with water and paint the lower third of each tower and each notched strip. Paint the lower area of the large cake. Dilute pink food colouring and use to paint the remaining areas of the towers.

12 Dust the cones and white areas of the lower cake with gold powder. Colour the remaining sugarpaste pale pink and shape into small boulders. Position around the base of the cake. Trim the board with ribbon, securing with double-sided tape.

Use a plain round cutter to remove a deep notch from one side of each of the two tallest towers, where the mini-towers will fit.

Mark crosses for windows. Press the end of a piping tube into the end of each arm of the cross to make a circular hole.

The mini-towers are rows of sweets wrapped in sugarpaste. Press them into the notched corners of the larger towers.

Pile sweets on top of the towers and then cover with cones of non-stick baking paper. Dust these with gold dusting powder.

PIANO

A nice touch for a music-lover is to copy out the notes of 'Happy Birthday to You' or a favourite song for the sheet music. For added detail, decorate the top of the piano with a sugarpaste candelabra or a vase of flowers. If you're feeling keen, make a piano stool too.

1 Cut out the keyboard base rectangle and ends, the piano legs and the music holder and leave to dry.

5 Roll out the remaining white sugarpaste and cut into a long strip. Mark keys and attach the black notes with a little water.

6 Support the keyboard with blocks of polystyrene until it is completely dry.

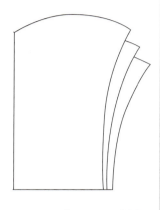

see template page 300

---

20 cm (8 inch) square Madeira cake

90 g (3 oz) pastillage
brown, chestnut, orange and black paste
food colourings
black food colouring pen
1.25 kg (2¹/2 lb) sugarpaste
orange dusting powder
125 g (4 oz) buttercream
90 g (3 oz) royal icing

EQUIPMENT

10 cm (4 inch) square rice (wafer) paper
ribbed rolling pin
30 cm (12 inch) square cake board
number 2 piping tube
small piece of polystyrene

CUTTING OUT THE PIECES

1 Colour the pastillage with brown and chestnut food colourings and roll out. Cut out the keyboard base rectangle the same width as the cake, the ends, the piano legs (a little over one-third the height of the cake when it is standing up on end) and the music holder and leave to dry. Make a tracing from the template on page 300 and cut out the music sheet from rice paper. Use a black food colour pen to draw on the musical notes and name of the tune.

COVERING THE BOARD

2 Colour 440 g (14 oz) of the sugarpaste orange and roll out. Texture the sugarpaste with a ribbed rolling pin, then cover the cake board. To make the board more attractive, tint randomly with orange dusting powder.

3 Cut the cake horizontally into three layers. Spread the layers with some of the buttercream and sandwich back together. Refrigerate to firm slightly. Stand the cake on its side and spread all over with a thin coating of buttercream. Reserve 75 g (2¹/2 oz) of the white sugarpaste and colour the remainder brown and chestnut to match the pastillage. Roll out the sugarpaste and cover the cake, easing away any pleats and folds with the palms of your hands.

4 Roll out the brown sugarpaste trimmings and cut into long narrow strips. Take time to make neat corners, cutting the strips at angles to create a mitred effect. Attach to the cake with water.

KEYBOARD

5 Roll out the remaining white sugarpaste and cut out a long narrow strip. Mark the keys using the back of a knife. Colour the sugarpaste trimmings black, roll out and cut the keys. Attach to the white keys by moistening with water.

ASSEMBLING THE CAKE

6 Colour the royal icing brown and fill a piping bag fitted with a number 2 tube. Position the cake on the board and secure in place with royal icing. Attach the keyboard base to the cake with the icing, and support the base with blocks of polystyrene. Attach the keyboard, keyboard ends, music holder and finally the legs. Continue supporting until all the joins are completely dry. Leave to dry, then place the sheet music on the holder.

NOTE If you need to make this cake in a hurry, use a piece of thin cake card under the keyboard and replace the pastillage legs with cake pillar dowels cut to size. This way the drying time is reduced and there is little need for supporting the keyboard.

PIECE OF CAKE

The colours on this giant slice of cake can easily be varied, as long as they remain very bright. A lot of the cake is trimmed off to make the 'wedge' shape; these trimmings can be frozen and used for making trifle or truffle paste later. Don't use a fruit cake for this recipe.

Attach teardrop shapes of pink sugarpaste to the top edge of the cake to represent drips of icing.

two 20 cm (8 inch) round cakes

1.5 kg (3 lb) sugarpaste
blue, red, pink, yellow and brown paste food colourings
1 length dried spaghetti
red piping jelly
4 tablespoons raspberry or strawberry jam
250 g (8 oz) buttercream

EQUIPMENT

33 cm (13 inch) round cake board
fine paintbrush
cocktail sticks
large paintbrush
large star piping tube

MAKING THE CANDLES

1   Colour 125 g (4 oz) of the sugarpaste pale blue. Reserve 15 g (1/2 oz) of the blue sugarpaste, then roll the remainder to a 2 cm (3/4 inch) thick sausage. Cut across into two 7 cm (2 1/4 inch) lengths and shape one end of each to look like the top of a melted candle. Snap off two pieces of dried spaghetti and singe the ends. Press one into each 'candle' top as a burnt wick. Make small teardrop shapes from the trimmed icing and secure down the side of each candle with a dampened paintbrush for drips.

2   Colour 60 g (2 oz) sugarpaste dark red and roll into two balls. Using the end of a paintbrush, make a dent in the top of each ball to make cherries. Paint with piping jelly to give a shine. Shape several tiny 'crumbs' of white sugarpaste. Leave the candles, crumbs and cherries on non-stick baking paper to dry for at least 24 hours.

SHAPING THE CAKE

3   Trace the template on page 307 onto non-stick baking paper. Slice the domes from the tops of the cakes to give a level surface and place one on top of the other. Lay the template over the top. Cut through both cakes to shape a wedge.

4   Thinly roll out 315 g (10 oz) white sugarpaste and use to cover the cake board. Roll out a long thin strip of sugarpaste, 4 cm (1 1/4 inches) in diameter. Dampen the edge of the board icing, then lay the strip around the edge to make the rim of the plate. Trim off the excess.

5   Sandwich the cake wedges together with the jam and 3 tablespoons buttercream. Reserve 4 tablespoons of buttercream and spread the rest over the cake.

'ICING' THE CAKE

6   Roll out half of the remaining sugarpaste and cover the flat sides of the cake. Colour the remainder dark pink. Use half to cover the outside of the wedge and the remainder to cover the top and hang over the edge. Using a cocktail stick, mark two bands of wavy lines along the sides to indicate areas of 'filling'.

7   Mix yellow and brown food colourings and dilute with water. Paint the 'sponge' areas on the cake sides and the shaped sugarpaste crumbs. Make more teardrop shapes from the dark pink trimmings and secure with a little water along the top edges as icing drips.

FINISHING TOUCHES

8   Thinly roll lengths of blue sugarpaste and secure in loops around the outside of the cake. Fill a piping bag fitted with a large star tube with the reserved buttercream and pipe swirls along the top edge. Paint lines of jam filling on the cake sides, and paint thin bands of pink and blue around the 'plate'. Position the candles, cherries and crumbs.

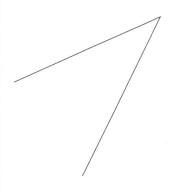

see template page 301

WOODCUTTER'S COTTAGE

This is a chocolate version of a gingerbread house. The cottage is hollow but, if you need to feed a lot of hungry children, you can build it around a buttercream-covered chocolate cake. You can use chocolate buttons instead of the flakes to make a tiled roof.

315 g (10 oz) plain flour
60 g (2 oz) cocoa powder
1/2 teaspoon baking powder
185 g (6 oz) butter, softened
185 g (6 oz) soft dark brown sugar
2 tablespoons black treacle
2 eggs
250 g (8 oz) dark chocolate
125 g (4 oz) white chocolate
270 g (9 oz) chocolate buttercream
30 g (1 oz) milk chocolate
60 g (2 oz) chocolate marzipan
4 large flaky chocolate bars
chocolate buttons (melts)
icing sugar

EQUIPMENT

25 cm (10 inch) round cake board
number 1 piping tube

THE HOUSE

1   Sift the flour, cocoa and baking powder together. Beat the butter and sugar together in a mixing bowl until just softened. Add the treacle and eggs with the flour mixture. Mix to a soft dough. Knead lightly, wrap in plastic and refrigerate for 30 minutes until firm. Trace the templates of the cottage walls and roof on page 296–7 onto non-stick baking paper and cut out.

2   Preheat the oven to 190°C (375°F/Gas 5). Roll out some of the dough on a lightly floured surface and lay it on a baking sheet. Cut around each template with a small sharp knife. Remember to cut out the windows. Lift away the excess dough. You will need two roof shapes, two end walls and one of each long wall. Bake the shapes for 10 minutes or until beginning to colour around the edges. Leave on the baking sheets for 5 minutes, then transfer to a wire rack to cool completely.

RUNOUT TREES

3   Trace the tree sections on page 296. You will need five tracings of the large tree and 10 each of medium and small trees. On a separate piece of paper trace 12 window shutters and one door, using the templates on page 297. Secure the tracings to a

flat surface with a smooth piece of non-stick baking paper on top. Melt the dark chocolate and spoon into a paper piping bag. Snip off the end and pipe into the outlines of the trees, shutters and doors.

4   Melt the white chocolate. Spoon a little onto the cottage walls. Spread with a palette knife, then make a swirled pattern over the chocolate with the tip of the knife. Leave to set.

5   Roughly spread a little of the buttercream all over the surface of the cake board.

ASSEMBLING THE HOUSE

6   Spread the inner ends of each wall with buttercream. Fix the four walls together, putting the cottage at the back of the board with the door facing the front. Rest one roof section in position so that the point at the top of the walls is level with the top of the roof. Repeat on the other side.

7   Melt the milk chocolate, put it in a piping bag fitted with a number 1 tube and pipe handles on the runout door and shutters. Shape a small chimney from chocolate marzipan. Carefully spread the roof with buttercream and position the chimney. Cut the chocolate bars into 2.5 cm (1 inch) pieces. Cut each lengthways into three or four flat sections. Starting from the bottom of the roof, secure the sections in position, with the chocolate overlapping.

8   Place 3 tablespoons of the remaining buttercream in a paper piping bag and snip off the end. Peel the runout shutters and doors away from the paper. Pipe a little buttercream on the back of each shutter runout and fix them in place. Fix the door, slightly ajar, with a little buttercream.

ASSEMBLING THE TREES

9   Peel the runout trees from the paper. Pipe several lines of buttercream up the straight edge of one tree section. Holding this vertically, secure four more tree sections to the first, then transfer the tree to the cake board. Make the remaining trees in the same way. Make a path from the chocolate buttons, then sift icing sugar over the cake and board.

NOTE   Chocolate runouts seldom break, but it is worth making a few extra just in case.

Make templates of non-stick baking paper and cut out the walls and roof.

Gently rest one roof section in position so that the point at the top of the walls is level with the top of the roof.

Spread the roof with buttercream and then secure overlapping pieces of chocolate flake.

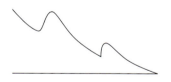

Pipe buttercream up the straight edge of a tree section. Secure four more sections to make a tree.

see templates page 296–7

177

FRILLY CLOWN

This colourful clown is modelled from sugarpaste. The garrett frill around the side of the cake is piped with tiny dots of royal icing and this cake is ideal for someone with a little experience of modelling and piping.

3

Scratch a fine line on the icing with a pin to mark the top of the template.

5

Position the sugarpaste on top of the cake as if the clown is resting against the dowel stick.

6

Mark 'creases' with a knife at the bottom of the clown's trousers.

11

Add the yellow strips of clown's 'hair' in overlapping layers.

see template page 286

20 cm (8 inch) round cake

125 g (4 oz) buttercream
1.5 kg (3 lb) sugarpaste
blue, red, green and yellow food colourings
250 g (8 oz) royal icing

EQUIPMENT

25 cm (10 inch) round cake board
pins
garrett frill cutter
7.5 cm (3 inch) wooden cake dowel
fine paintbrush
number 1 piping tube
plunger flower cutter
2 stamens

1　Slice the domed top off the cake to give a level surface. Slice the cake in half and sandwich with buttercream. Place the cake on the board. Cover the cake with 1 kg (2 lb) of the sugarpaste.

GARRETT FRILL

2　Cut a long, thin strip of non-stick baking paper measuring 71 x 5 cm (28 x 2 inches). Fold the strip in half, then in half twice more to give a rectangle of eight layers. Unfold. Trace the template on page 286 on to one of the end rectangles on the strip. Refold the paper and then cut out the shape.

3　Open out the template and wrap it around the cake, securing with pins. Using another pin, mark the curved outline on the cake. Remove the template.

4　Colour 250 g (8 oz) of the sugarpaste blue. Reserve a small piece and use a little of the rest to cover the cake board around the base of the cake. Roll out more blue icing and cut out frills with the garrett frill cutter. Position around the side of the cake with the unfrilled edge just covering the template line.

CLOWN

5　Press the dowel into the top of the cake, just off-centre, so that it sticks out at an angle. Shape 60 g (2 oz) sugarpaste into a sausage 7.5 cm (3 inches) long and flatten it slightly. Cut the sausage

lengthways in half from one end to the centre. Position the uncut end against the stick on top of the cake. Open out the cut pieces for the clown's legs. Lightly dampen the piece of icing with a paintbrush.

6　Thinly roll out a little more white sugarpaste on a surface dusted with cornflour to make a 7.5 cm (3 inch) square. Make a cut from one side into the centre. Wrap the square around the 'clown' on top of the cake, fitting it around the legs and tucking the excess around the back of the dowel. Mark creases on the trouser bottoms with a knife.

7　Colour a little sugarpaste pale pink. Shape some into a small ball and position for the clown's head. Shape two small hands. Shape two puffed sleeves from white icing and secure to the sides of the clown. Secure the hands to the ends of the sleeves.

8　Roll out the small piece of reserved blue sugarpaste and cut out a small frill. Attach it around the neck of the clown.

9　Attach two small dots of white icing for the eyes, then divide the remainder into three and colour red, green and yellow.

10　Put the royal icing in a paper piping bag fitted with a number 1 tube and pipe small dots over the blue frills. Pipe a snail trail around the base of the cake and around the top of the garrett frill.

11　To make the clown's hair, thinly roll out some yellow sugarpaste and cut it into strips about 5 cm (2 inches) long and 1 cm (1/2 inch) wide. Make cuts from one long side of each strip, almost through to the other side. Dampen the clown's head and secure the hair in position. Add a red nose and mouth.

12　Shape two large red boots and secure to the legs. Roll small balls of icing in different colours. Flatten and press onto the clown's clothes.

13　Shape small juggling balls, scarves and a hat from the icing trimmings. For the hat, wrap a strip of red icing around a flattened ball of green icing. Make two small blossom flowers with a plunger cutter. Push a stamen through each flower and press into the hat. Paint crosses onto the clown's eyes.

CROSS-STITCH BUILDING BLOCKS

These delightful blocks can be used as a first birthday or even a christening cake. Draw your own cross-stitch designs to suit the child, or, if you're not as confident at drawing, copy or trace from picture books or use letters of the alphabet. Not suitable flavours for fruit cake.

three 10 cm (4 inch) cubes of cake

1 kg (2 lb) sugarpaste
250 g (8 oz) pastillage
220 g (7 oz) royal icing
assorted paste food colours
250 g (8 oz) buttercream
edible glue

EQUIPMENT
fine ribbed rolling pin
graph paper
coloured pencils
three number 0 piping tubes
herb cutter (optional)
30 cm (12 inch) square red foil cake board

CROSS-STITCH PANELS

1 Blend 250 g (8 oz) of the sugarpaste with the pastillage, kneading well. Roll out the paste 2.5 mm (1/8 inch) thick and roll a ribbed rolling pin over it. Turn the paste through 90 degrees and re-roll with the ribbed pin to form tiny squares. Cut out twelve 10 cm (4 inch) squares and place on foam to dry.

2 Using graph paper, draw six different pictures to fit the cube sides. Colour with pencils, using only a few colours per design.

PIPING

3 Colour batches of royal icing in a selection of colours for each picture. Put into piping bags fitted with number 0 piping tubes. Start by finding the centre of the design and the centre square on the cut-out panel. Count the squares to find the top centre. Pipe tiny crosses in each square, starting from the top left of the design and working in a horizontal line. Count the rows, filling in with crosses and making sure that all the stitches are started in the same way. Change colours as required in each row. (Try not to change direction when piping.)

4 Allow to dry for 24 hours. Any facial features or additional straight lines are piped when the main cross stitches have dried.

ASSEMBLY

5 Coat the sides of the cake cubes with a thin layer of buttercream. Roll out the remaining sugarpaste and cover five sides of two cubes and six sides of one cube. Cover each side separately, trimming to fit. Allow to dry.

6 Colour 60 g (2 oz) of the blended paste blue, 60 g (2 oz) red and 60 g (2 oz) yellow. Roll out and cover the top square of each cube with a different colour. With a small amount of royal icing, fix a cross-stitch panel to two sides of each cube, making sure that the edges are level.

7 Roll out a strip of blue paste and cut with a herb cutter or knife into strips 5 mm (1/4 inch) wide. Stick strips of blue paste to the edges of the red-topped block with edible glue, covering the joins at the corners. Repeat for the remaining cubes, using the yellow and red pastes.

8 Place two blocks side by side on the board with the third block on top, positioning it at a slight angle and securing with royal icing.

NOTE The most efficient way to obtain the three cubes of cake is to bake two 20 cm (8 inch) square cakes and trim them into shape, sandwiching layers together with buttercream where necessary.

1

Run the ribbed rolling pin over the paste, then turn through 90° and roll again to make squares.

3

Draw your designs on graph paper and colour in. Pipe onto the icing by counting squares from the centre of the design.

7

Roll out a strip of paste and cut with a herb cutter or knife to make thin strips. These become borders to the designs.

3

Cover the pudding basin with foil and smooth the melted chocolate over the top to make a bowl shape.

4

Carefully peel the foil away from the set chocolate, leaving a case.

6

Spread the cake with buttercream and place the second cake on top.

8

Roll out the icing to cover the body, tucking the ends inside the chocolate bowl.

11

Pipe lines of buttercream hair, short at the fringe and longer at the neck.

BAGGY TROUSERS CLOWN

You will need a variety of different-sized pudding basins for making this cake to give the clown his lovely rounded shape—if you don't have the exact sized basins you can trim the cakes to shape or use any ovenproof bowls of a similar size.

1 quantity chocolate cake mixture for 25 cm
(10 inch) round cake
220 g (7 oz) dark chocolate, melted
375 g (12 oz) marzipan
peach, yellow, blue, red and green food colourings
270 g (9 oz) buttercream
700 g (1 lb 7 oz) chocolate sugarpaste
4 chocolate buttons (melts)
white chocolate chips
1 liquorice 'lace'
milk chocolate chips

EQUIPMENT

2 x 1.1 litre (2 pint) pudding basins
315 ml ($^{1}/_{2}$ pint) pudding basin
1.4 litre ($2^{1}/_{2}$ pint) pudding basin
23 cm (9 inch) square cake board
1 wooden cake dowel
paintbrush
cocktail stick
number 1 piping tube

MAKING THE CAKES

1   Preheat the oven to 160°C (315°F/ Gas 2–3). Grease the two 1.1 litre pudding basins and the 315 ml pudding basin. Line the bases with non-stick baking paper.

2   Spoon the cake mixture into the basins and bake the small basin for 35 minutes and the large basins for 1 hour 10 minutes. Turn out onto wire racks to cool. Trim off the top of the cake baked in the small basin to give a rounded shape for the clown's head.

CHOCOLATE 'TROUSERS'

3   Cover the outside of the 1.4 litre pudding basin with foil, tucking the ends neatly inside the bowl and pressing the creases as flat as possible. Spread the melted chocolate over the foil to within 5 mm ($^{1}/_{4}$ inch) of the basin rim. Leave to set.

4   Carefully lift away the foil tucked inside the bowl. Twist the bowl and remove it completely. With one hand gently resting in the base of the chocolate bowl, carefully peel away the foil lining to leave a chocolate case.

ASSEMBLING THE CLOWN

5   Colour half of the marzipan peach and two-thirds of the rest yellow. Colour some remaining pieces red and some blue, leaving a small piece plain. Shape two-thirds of the yellow marzipan into two flat boots. Place towards the front of the cake board.

6   Reserve 3 tablespoons of the buttercream for piping. Generously spread the rounded top of one large cake with buttercream. Gently drop it into the chocolate case. Position the case on the cake board, behind the feet, securing with buttercream. Spread the cake with buttercream and place the second large cake on top, towards the back so that the baggy trousers are emphasised.

7   Cut off one-third of the chocolate sugarpaste, reserving a small piece about the size of a plum. Divide the rest in half for arms. Roll into thick sausage shapes on a surface dusted with cornflour, tapering each 'sausage' at the end. Flatten slightly, then bend for arms. Cut off the thin ends for cuffs.

8   Keeping the plum-sized piece of sugarpaste aside, use the rest to cover the clown's body: on a surface dusted with cornflour, roll it out into a 25 cm (10 inch) round. Place over the top of the cake, tucking the ends inside the chocolate bowl. Ease the icing to fit around the back of the clown. Insert the dowel into the body, leaving enough poking out to support the head.

FINISHING TOUCHES

9   Secure the arms in position with a dampened paintbrush. Use a cocktail stick to mark elbow creases. Press chocolate buttons onto the front of the clown to make shirt buttons. Dot the shirt with white chocolate chips.

10   Roll a little of the peach marzipan into two balls for hands. Flatten slightly, then cut four slits for fingers, using a sharp knife. Attach the clown's left hand to the shirt cuff.

11   Roll out the remaining marzipan to a circle about 18 cm (7 inches) in diameter. Wrap around the reserved small pudding cake, easing the paste and smoothing the ends underneath. Secure to the cake to form the clown's head. Colour the reserved

buttercream green and place in a paper piping bag fitted with a number 1 tube. Starting from the top of the head, pipe vertical lines of hair, short at the front for a fringe and longer around the neck.

12 Shape the reserved chocolate sugarpaste into a small hat. Decorate the hat with a liquorice band and a small flower made from red and blue marzipan. Fix the hat on top of the clown's head.

13 To make braces, roll out two strips of blue marzipan, each about 28 cm (11 inches) long and 5 mm (¹/4 inch wide). Secure over the clown's shoulders so the ends just overhang the trousers. Press a milk chocolate chip into each end. Position the second hand clutching the brace. Roll out the

remaining yellow marzipan and cut out a wide collar. Position around the clown's neck and finish with a blue marzipan bow tie. Shape the mouth and nose from red marzipan.

14 For the eyes use plain marzipan rounds, pressing a milk chocolate chip onto each. Cut the remaining liquorice into short lengths and press into the boots for laces.

N O T E When the chocolate sugarpaste is placed over the cake, the excess will fall in folds. Make sure this is at the back of the cake. Trim off with a sharp knife, then gently smooth down, using hands dusted with icing sugar.

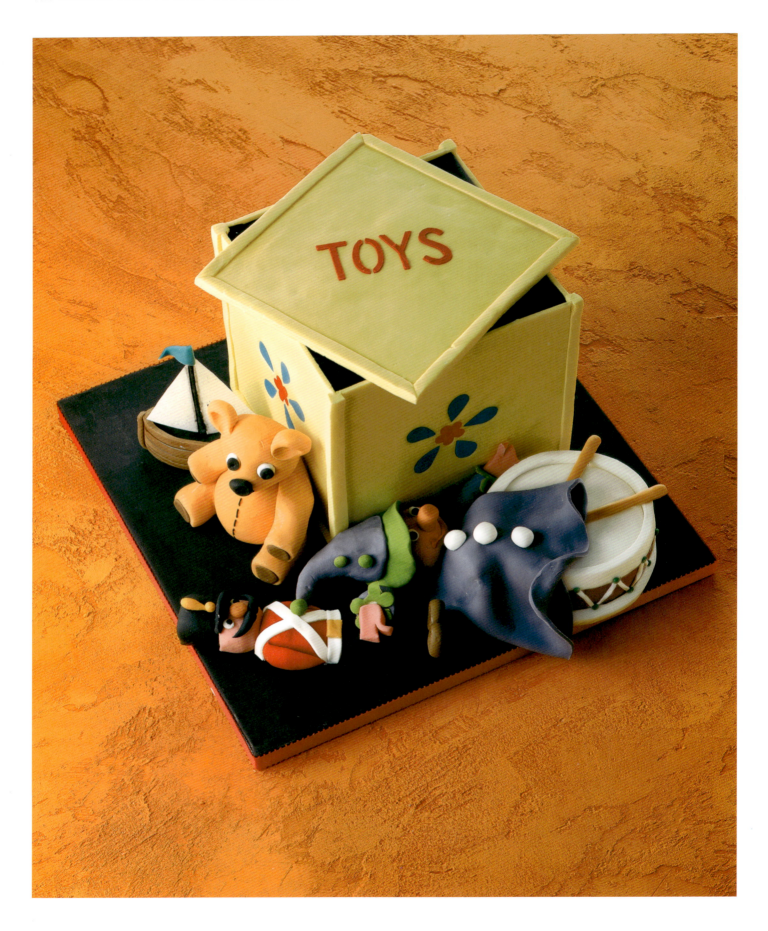

TOY BOX

This toybox conceals a solid cake centre (not suitable flavours for a fruit cake) and is simply made from squares of yellow sugarpaste decorated by inlay and stencilling. Use the guide in our modelling section (pages 92–103) to make toys to match the child's favourites.

three 15 cm (6 inch) square cakes

1.5 kg (3 lb) sugarpaste
blue, red, yellow and black paste food colourings
125 g (4 oz) royal icing
75 g (2¹/₂ oz) jam
300 g (10 oz) buttercream
1 kg (2 lb) sugarpaste in assorted colours, for toys

EQUIPMENT

flower cutter
petal or leaf cutter
36 cm (14 inch) square cake board
narrow red ribbon

INLAY FLOWERS

1   Colour 60 g (2 oz) of the sugarpaste blue and 60 g (2 oz) red and set aside. Colour 625 g (1 lb 4 oz) of the sugarpaste bright yellow. Make a template the size of one cake top, about 15 cm (6 inches) square. Roll out the yellow sugarpaste and cut out five squares. Lay the squares carefully on non-stick baking paper. While the sugarpaste is still soft, use the flower and petal cutters to remove a pattern from the centre of four of the squares. Roll out the red and blue sugarpaste. Using the same cutters, inlay shapes in the yellow sugarpaste, smoothing gently with your fingers to conceal the joins. Leave to dry on a flat surface.

STENCILLING THE TOP

2   Make a tracing of the word 'TOYS', right, for the lid and transfer onto thin cardboard. Using a sharp craft knife or scalpel, cut out the letters to make a stencil. Colour 30 g (1 oz) of the royal icing red and hold the stencil firmly over the undecorated square of yellow sugarpaste. Using a palette knife, spread the red icing thinly over the stencil to transfer the word to the yellow square.

ASSEMBLING THE BOX

3   Roll out the yellow sugarpaste trimmings and cut them into long narrow strips. Moisten the edges of the lid with water and attach the strips, using a small knife to cut neat mitred corners. Leave the lid to dry flat.

4   Cut the domed tops from the cakes to give a level surface. Layer the cakes with jam, one on top of the other to make a cube, ensuring that all the sides are equal. Trim if necessary. Cover the cake completely with a thin coat of buttercream.

5   Colour 750 g (1¹/₂ lb) of the sugarpaste black and roll out 125 g (4 oz). Cut out a square the size of the cake top and press gently on top of the cake—the buttercream will secure it in place. Roll out the remaining black sugarpaste to cover the board. Secure the cake to the board with buttercream.

ATTACHING THE SIDES

6   Carefully attach the toy box sides to the cake, securing them to the buttercream. Conceal the joins with strips of yellow sugarpaste. Attach the toy box lid with a dab of royal icing. Trim the board with ribbon, securing with double-sided tape.

FINISHING TOUCHES

7   Using the modelling instructions on pages 92–103, make sugarpaste toys from various colours of sugarpaste—rolled, textured, modelled and joined. Eyes and features can be piped on with royal icing. Rather than making the toys and letting them dry, make each one and position on the cake, securing with royal icing; in this way they look as if they have been casually dropped around the box and on top of each other.

Roll out the red and blue sugarpaste to the same thickness as the yellow sugarpaste and inlay the flower petals.

Use a stencil of thin card to write the word 'TOYS' on the top of the box with red royal icing.

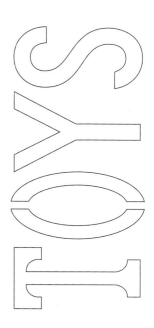

template actual size

185

3

Pipe the outlines of Mr and Mrs Noah with white royal icing then flood with coloured icing.

3

Pipe the outlines of the animals and then fill in with royal icing watered to runout consistency.

4

Flood the backs of the animals and leave to dry completely. Then remove from the paper and paint in the features and details.

4

Once the front of the ark is dry, turn over and flood the back, noting that it is different to the front.

NOAH'S ARK

This is a cake for the more committed decorator... the cake is coated with royal icing, then decorated with piping and animal runouts. Make a simpler version by coating the cake with sugarpaste and omitting the piping. For fuller details on runouts, turn to page 68.

30 cm (12 inch) round cake

1.25 kg (2¹/₂ lb) marzipan
1.25 kg (2¹/₂ lb) royal icing
assorted food colourings
125 g (4 oz) modelling paste
selection of petal dusts
90 g (3 oz) pastillage
30 g (1 oz) flower paste
egg white

EQUIPMENT

36 x 30 cm (14 x 12 inch) oval cake board
numbers 0, 2, 22 and 42 piping tubes
paintbrush and palette
veining tool
patterned rolling pin
foam pad and pieces
blossom cutter
small ball modelling tool

1 Cut the cake into a pointed oval measuring 30 x 23 cm (12 x 9 inches). Cover with marzipan and leave to dry thoroughly. Apply three coats of white royal icing to the cake. Coat the board separately with pale green royal icing. Leave to dry.

RUNOUTS

2 Photocopy the ark and Mr and Mrs Noah on page 297, enlarging to 105%. Trace the animals on page 297. Cover with non-stick baking paper. Secure on a smooth, flat board with masking tape.

3 Half-fill a piping bag with royal icing and pipe all the outlines with a number 0 piping tube and white royal icing. Outline two of each animal, but only one giraffe and one elephant as there is one of each already in the ark. Flood the sections with runout-consistency royal icing, using a selection of food colourings to tint the icing and trying to keep the colours as natural as possible.

4 When thoroughly dry, remove the runouts from the paper and turn them over. Flood the backs (note that the backs of the monkey, lion, penguin, Mr and Mrs Noah and the ark are different from the fronts). Paint in the details when dry.

5 Trace the design on page 297 for the doves and bow, covering it with non-stick baking paper and securing with masking tape over a curved surface (such as an oval tin). Complete the runouts in the usual way. When dry, paint in the detail.

6 Attach the cake to the board with royal icing, setting it back almost to the back edge of the board. Pipe a shell border around the top and bottom with a number 22 piping tube and pale green royal icing.

PATHS, RAMP AND BASE

7 Trace the templates on page 296 and cut out two paths from brown modelling paste. Mark paving with a veining tool. Dust with various shades of brown, cream and skintone petal dust.

8 Cut out the two parts of the ramp from thinly rolled out light brown pastillage. When dry, dust stripes across the pieces, using the colours used for the paths.

9 Cut out a base for the ark from the template on page 296 from white pastillage and, when dry, cover with green modelling paste, textured with a patterned rolling pin. This makes a stronger base.

TREES

10 Trace the template on page 296, cover with non-stick baking paper and secure on a board with masking tape. Pipe the outlines using a number 0 piping tube and white royal icing. You will need five trees. Flood the tree trunks with brown runout consistency royal icing, but pipe the leaves with a thicker consistency green-tinted royal icing. Leave to dry, then remove from the paper and flood the backs. Paint the trees with shades of green and brown when dry.

11 Pipe a row of eight shells in the centre of the ark base with a number 42 piping tube and pale green royal icing. Stand the ark upright on the base and support with pieces of foam. Leave to dry.

FINISHING TOUCHES

12 Secure the paths, ramp and ark on the cake and board with royal icing. Using petal dust, lightly dust blue sky and green grass on the sides of the cake, and dust grass on top of the cake. Attach the

animals and people by piping a small amount of royal icing on the underside of the feet and standing them in position. Support with foam until dry. Pipe royal icing on the base and back of the remaining trees and place around the cake.

13   Cut out many blossom shapes in pink, white and yellow flower paste, cup on pieces of foam with a ball tool and arrange in position around the top of the cake and the cake board. Secure with royal icing and pipe a white dot in the centre of each blossom with a number 0 piping tube.

14   Roll thin sausages of green flower paste to make grass. Fold each piece in half, put two together and attach to the cake and board with egg white or edible glue. Finally, pipe a green snail trail around the edge of the board with a number 2 piping tube and pale green royal icing.

see templates
pages 296–97

TEDDY WITH A BIG BLUE BOW

The cakes are baked in pudding basins to give the teddy his rounded shape. Madeira cake is best for this recipe because it holds up well to shaping and moulding. The stitching is piped black royal icing, although you could use fine strips of black sugarpaste.

2 quantities cake mixture for 20 cm
(8 inch) round Madeira cake

375 g (12 oz) buttercream
1.5 kg (3 lb) sugarpaste
brown and black paste food colourings
2 tablespoons royal icing
peach dusting powder

EQUIPMENT
two 15 cm (6 inch) diameter pudding bowls
two 13 cm (5 inch) diameter pudding bowls
1 wooden cake dowel
30 x 25 cm (12 x 10 inch) oval cake board
number 2 piping tube
1 large ribbon bow

BAKING THE CAKE
1 Preheat the oven to 160°C (315°F/Gas 2–3). Grease the base of the pudding bowls and line with circles of non-stick baking paper. Spoon the cake mixture into the bowls and level the surface. Bake the small bowls for 50 minutes or until firm, and the large bowls for 1 hour, or until firm. Turn out onto a wire rack and leave to cool.

2 Trim the domed top off the cakes and turn the cakes upside down to give a flat surface.

SHAPING THE CAKES
3 Slice the cakes in half and then sandwich together with buttercream. Then use the buttercream to join the two larger cakes and the two smaller cakes to make two ball shapes. The smaller cake may be left round, or you may prefer to sculpt it to more of an oval shape for the head. (Use a sharp knife dipped in warm water to make clean cuts. Chilling or part-freezing the cake prior to shaping makes the task easier.) Cover the cakes with buttercream.

COVERING THE CAKES
4 Colour 1.375 kg (2³/4 lb) sugarpaste light brown. Roll out separate circles and cover the cakes, easing the icing around the cakes carefully to prevent the icing pleating. Attach the head to the body by inserting the wooden dowel into the body and then pushing the head onto the dowel and securing with a little royal icing. Place the teddy on the board, securing with royal icing.

ARMS AND LEGS
5 Shape two arms and two legs from the remaining sugarpaste and stick to the body with royal icing (you can support them with foam until dry). Colour 30 g (1 oz) sugarpaste dark brown, roll out and cut out two small circles. Attach to the ends of the legs with royal icing.

6 Thickly roll out some more light brown paste and cut out a circle. Cut the circle in half and indent each with your thumb to form two ears. Stick them onto the head with royal icing.

FINISHING TOUCHES
7 Apply a light blush of dusting powder to the cheeks with a large brush. It is a good idea to make a temporary 'bib' of paper towels to catch any falling powder that may otherwise stain the body.

8 Make two small flat circles of black sugarpaste for the eyes and a small oval for the nose and attach to the face. Pipe the mouth and stitching on the teddy's tummy with a number 2 piping tube and black royal icing. Attach the bow to the teddy's neck with a dab of royal icing.

NOTE For many cake decorations, water is used to stick the various sugarpaste pieces onto the surface. However, due to the weight of the teddy's arms, you will need to use royal icing to attach them to the body.

Secure the head on the body with a cake dowel and a little royal icing.

Because of the weight of the teddy's arms and legs, you'll need to secure them to the body with dabs of royal icing.

Make a bib for the teddy from a piece of paper towel so that you don't drop colouring on the body while painting.

3 Cut a wavy edge to the circle of sugarpaste and lay over the cake to make a tablecloth, lifting and pinching the edge.

6 Sandwich a coloured sugarpaste filling between slices of white or brown sugarpaste bread and cut into tiny triangles.

7 For the sausage roll, lay a sausage of pink sugarpaste down the centre of a strip of brown sugarpaste and fold over. Seal and cut.

TEDDY BEARS' PICNIC

Once you've learnt to model sugarpaste food, you can let your imagination run wild creating the party spread of your dreams. We've chosen sandwiches, sausage rolls, jelly and cakes but your options are endless.

---

20 cm (8 inch) round cake

125 g (4 oz) jam, lemon curd or buttercream
375 g (12 oz) royal icing
1 kg (2 lb) sugarpaste
assorted paste food colourings
1 teaspoon red piping gel
caster and icing sugar
1 glacé cherry
5 chocolate-covered mini rolls
red and cream liquid food colourings

EQUIPMENT

30 cm (12 inch) round cake board
1.5 cm (5/8 inch), 2 cm (3/4 inch) and 3 cm
(11/4 inch) round cutters
number 2 paintbrush
numbers 0, 1, 2, 3 and 41 piping tubes
ball modelling tool
narrow pink ribbon

---

1 Trim the domed top from the cake. Slice the cake in half and then sandwich back together with your choice of jam, lemon curd or buttercream filling. Secure to the board, off-centre towards the back, with a little royal icing.

THE CAKE 'TABLE'

2 Colour 250 g (8 oz) sugarpaste pale blue. Roll out to 5 mm (1/4 inch) thick and cut a strip deep and long enough to cover the side of the cake.

3 Colour 250 g (8 oz) sugarpaste pink. Roll it out and cut a wavy-edged circle, at least 2.5 cm (1 inch) larger than the top of the cake. Lay the sugarpaste over the cake like a tablecloth. Pinch and lift the edge of the sugarpaste with your fingers.

TEDDY BEARS

4 Colour 250 g (8 oz) sugarpaste brown and use to make the bears. For each bear, shape a round body and pointed head. For the limbs, use four equal sized pieces of sugarpaste and roll out, tapering the ends. The legs should turn up slightly to represent feet and the arms taper then shape into basic hands. Brush with water and attach to the body.

PLATES

5 Colour 60 g (2 oz) sugarpaste pale green. Use the 3 cm (11/4 inch) cutter to make 17 large plates, the 1.5 cm (5/8 inch) cutter to make five small plates and the 2 cm (3/4 inch) cutter to make five saucers.

PARTY FOOD

6 Colour the remaining sugarpaste a variety of colours to make food. Make sandwiches by rolling out two colours of sugarpaste thinly. Sandwich the coloured paste between white or brown paste, brushing with a little water to stick them together. Cut into 1 cm (1/2 inch) strips, then into 1 cm (1/2 inch) squares. Cut in half diagonally. Stick to the plates with water.

7 For sausage rolls, roll out pale golden brown sugarpaste thinly. Cut into 10 x 1 cm (4 x 1/2 inch) strips. Make long sausages of pink sugarpaste and attach one to the centre of each strip with a little water. Fold one side of the strip over the sausage and stick to the other side. Seal with the end of a paintbrush. Cut into small rolls. Make slits in the rolls with a knife point.

8 Shape a small wedge of yellow sugarpaste to represent cheese, making holes with the end of a paintbrush. Pipe the mice with a number 2 tube and a little white royal icing. Pipe a small shell for the body, adding black eyes, brown ears and tail, and a pink nose when dry, using a number 0 tube.

9 Use a sterilized ballpoint pen lid to cut bases for the tiny cream cakes from rolled-out brown sugarpaste. Pipe on top of each one with a number 41 rosette tube and top with a spot of pink icing.

10 Make the jam tarts and swiss roll with tiny rounds of pale golden sugarpaste, indented with a ball modelling tool. For the swiss roll, roll out a thin strip of sugarpaste to about 4 x 1.5 cm (11/2 x 5/8 inch). Spread with red piping gel and roll up. Moisten the top and sprinkle with caster sugar. Cut a slice to lay beside the roll.

11 Model a fish out of orange sugarpaste, marking it with the piping end of a number 2 tube. Pipe éclairs with a number 3 tube. Pipe a short straight line of white royal icing, leave to dry, then

pipe a line of chocolate brown icing on the top of each one with a number 2 tube.

12   To make the jelly, cut a glacé cherry in half and pipe a dot of royal icing on top. Make a mini cake from a small round of sugarpaste and pipe around the edge with a number 41 rosette tube. Cut a candle short and place in the centre of the cake.

13   Model fruit with coloured sugarpaste. Roll the oranges and strawberries on a nutmeg grater to give them texture.

14   Sandwich two rounds of brown sugarpaste together with brown royal icing and dust with icing sugar to make the chocolate cake. Plait three thin

sausages of white sugarpaste to make the plaited loaf, then brush with brown food colouring. Model the teapot, milk jug, sugar bowl and cups out of green sugarpaste. Paint on a pattern when dry.

FINISHING TOUCHES

15   Colour some royal icing green and coat the board surrounding the cake. Stipple the icing to represent grass by dabbing it with a paintbrush held vertical to the surface. Attach the chocolate roll seats with a little royal icing. Fill a paper piping bag with any leftover green icing and pipe some grass around the bottom edge of the table and seats.

16   Trim the board with pink ribbon, securing with double-sided tape.

CHRISTMAS CAKES

No Christmas is complete without a cake and every experienced decorator looks forward to the festive season as a time to create memorable centrepieces for family and friends. For the newcomer to cake decorating, it is an excellent time to start, with cut-out holly and ivy being as simple as they come. But above all, Christmas is a time when the whole family can be involved with cake decorating, whether it's modelling figures, painting scenes or just fluffing up the icing to make snow for Santa's sleigh. It's a time of fun, thrills and inspiration in the world of cake decorating.

4

Cut out teardrop-shaped leaves for the mistletoe and dry on crumpled foil for a realistic effect.

MISTLETOE GARLAND

The stunning blue colouring is what makes this cake stand out, although in design it is very traditional and uses no difficult techniques. The mistletoe is made using cutters and the rope from twisted sugarpaste. If you prefer classic Christmas colours, leave the sugarpaste white.

20 cm (8 inch) round fruit cake

1 kg (2 lb) marzipan
3 tablespoons royal icing
1.5 kg (3 lb) sugarpaste
dark blue, pale green, dark green and cream
food colourings
gold dusting powder

EQUIPMENT

30 cm (12 inch) round cake board
small piece of foam sponge
4.5 cm (1³/4 inch) mistletoe cutter
fine paintbrush
gold ribbon

1   Cover the cake with marzipan and leave to dry. Secure to the cake board with a little royal icing. Reserve 500 g (1 lb) of the sugarpaste and cover the cake and board with the rest. Leave to dry for three days.

2   Cut a strip of non-stick baking paper the same length as the circumference of the cake and about 1 cm (¹/2 inch) wide. Fold it in half and then in half twice more to make a strip of eight thicknesses. Unfold the paper and secure around the top edge of the side of the cake with pins. Use a pin to mark around the top edge of the cake at each fold.

3   Dilute a little blue food colouring. Dip in the sponge and use to lightly stipple the cake and board.

MAKING MISTLETOE

4   Colour 90 g (3 oz) of the remaining sugarpaste pale green, another 90 g (3 oz) dark green and a further 30 g (1 oz) cream. Roll out the pale green icing and cut out small mistletoe leaves with the cutter. Mark veins down the centre and leave to harden on crumpled foil. Repeat with the dark green sugarpaste to make 24 of each colour. Shape the cream icing into small balls for berries.

ROPE EDGING

5   Thinly roll a little of the remaining sugarpaste to form two long thin sausages, then twist them together to make a rope. Using a fine paintbrush,

dampen the icing, just underneath the pin marks. Cut a 10 cm (4 inch) length of rope and secure around the side of the cake, with the ends meeting the pin marks. Repeat around the cake, securing a ball of icing at each point. Make long ropes and secure first around the base, then the board edge. Leave to dry.

6   Mix a little gold dusting powder with clear alcohol or water. Using a fine paintbrush, paint dots on the cake and board. Carefully paint all the ropes.

7   Secure the leaves and berries to the board with a little royal icing. Trim the board with gold ribbon, securing with double-sided tape.

NOTE   For an even quicker version of this cake, use bought fabric rope instead of sugarpaste rope. Secure in position with a little royal icing.

FROSTED FRUITS

For something a little different at Christmas time, sugar-frost a collection of berries, currants and tiny stone fruit and pile them high on this traditional fruit cake. The cake does need to be served within a few hours of decorating.

18 x 25 cm (7 x 10 inch) oval fruit cake (use mixture for 25 cm round cake)

selection of seasonal fruits such as white and dark cherries, red or white currants, blackcurrants, apricots or tiny plums or pears
2 egg whites (kept separate)
caster sugar
1–3 teaspoons lemon juice
125 g (4 oz) icing sugar

SUGAR-FROSTING THE FRUIT

1   Wash the fruit and make sure it is completely dry before starting (if possible, wash beforehand and leave for several hours). Line a tray with paper towel. Place one of the egg whites in a shallow bowl and whisk until just foamy. Put some caster sugar on a large plate. Work with one piece of fruit at a time, except for the berries which can be sugared in small bunches. Brush the egg white lightly over the fruit, making sure the entire piece of fruit is covered but not too heavily.

2   Sprinkle the sugar over the fruit and shake off any excess, then leave on the tray to dry. The drying time will depend on the humidity. Always frost more fruit than you need, so you have a good selection to choose from when arranging.

ICING THE CAKE

3   To make the icing, whisk the other egg white until just foamy. Beat in 1 teaspoon of the lemon juice. Add the icing sugar gradually, beating well after each addition. The icing should be thick and white—add a little more lemon juice if necessary, but don't make it too runny.

4   Place the cake on a serving plate or stand. Working quickly, pour the icing over the top. Using a palette knife, carefully smooth the icing to the edge of the cake, allowing it to run slowly down the side. Leave the cake for 10 minutes to let the icing set a little. Arrange the frosted fruits on top of the cake.

NOTE   The fruits will keep for a few hours after frosting, but the cake should be served as soon as it is iced and decorated.

Paint the fruit with a little egg white, then sprinkle with the caster sugar.

To make the icing, whisk the egg white, then add the lemon juice and icing sugar.

Smooth the icing over the cake, allowing it to run slowly down the side.

2

Cover the tops of the cakes and then roll in rectangles of marzipan to cover the sides.

3

Shape pea-sized pieces of coloured sugarpaste into teardrops. Moisten the backs to secure to the sides and tops of the cakes.

4

Use the number 2 tube to pipe an outline around each teardrop. Then paint the outline with gold.

JEWELLED BOXES

These little cakes make lovely Christmas presents. The recipe makes enough for six cakes. The shiny glazing is created by painting over the sugarpaste 'jewels' with piping jelly. A little piping is required, but it can be loose and artistic and does not require much experience.

1 quantity mixture for 18 cm (7 inch) round fruit cake

1 kg (2 lb) marzipan
250 g (8 oz) royal icing
1.5 kg (3 lb) sugarpaste
icing sugar and cornflour
red, blue and green food colourings
gold dusting powder
1–2 tablespoons clear piping jelly

EQUIPMENT

six empty, clean 440 g (14 oz) food cans with both ends removed
six 10 cm (4 inch) round gold cake cards
number 2 piping tube
fine paintbrush

BAKING MINIATURE CAKES

1   Place the food cans on a baking tray and line with non-stick baking paper as you would a round cake tin. Divide the cake mixture among the cans and bake for about 1 hour or until a skewer inserted into the centres comes out clean. Cool in the tins.

2   Cover the tops of the cakes with marzipan. Roll out the remaining marzipan and cut out six rectangles, each the circumference and depth of the cakes. Roll the cakes in the rectangles of marzipan to cover the sides. Secure the cakes to the cake cards with a little royal icing. Leave to dry.

DECORATING WITH 'JEWELS'

3   Divide 1 kg (2 lb) of the sugarpaste into six portions and use to cover the cakes. Leave to dry for three days. From the remaining sugarpaste, colour 250 g (8 oz) red, 125 g (4 oz) blue and 125 g (4 oz) green. Take pea-sized balls of the colours and shape into small teardrop shapes. Use to decorate the top and sides of the cakes, moistening the backs, pressing down gently and leaving small gaps between the decorations. Leave the centre top of each cake clear for the ribbons.

OUTLINING THE 'JEWELS'

4   Place the royal icing in a piping bag fitted with the number 2 tube. Use to pipe an outline around each coloured shape. Leave overnight to dry.

5   Mix a little gold dusting powder with water or clear alcohol until it has the consistency of thin paint. Using a fine paintbrush, carefully paint over the piped icing outlines. Lightly beat the piping jelly, then paint it over the coloured teardrops to glaze.

MAKING THE BOWS

6   To make a bow, thinly roll some red sugarpaste and cut out a long strip about 3 cm (1 1/4 inches) wide. Cut the strip into two rectangles. Dampen the ends, then fold the rectangles over to form loops. Position on the cake, leaving a small gap between the loops and tucking rolls of paper towel inside them to hold them in shape. Cut more long strips of the same thickness for bow ends. Finish the ends that will trail neatly with a knife. Pinch the other ends together and secure between the loops. Cut a square of sugarpaste, doming it slightly in the centre. Secure over the centre of the bow to hide all the ends. Remove the paper towel once the bow has dried. To add a touch of glamour, paint thin lines of gold along the edges of the ribbons to finish.

NOTE   Another easy way to decorate miniature cakes is to impress the sugarpaste with small festive cutters and then paint the shapes.

HOLLY GARLAND

The colours and modelling on this cake are traditional and it is a very rewarding cake for beginners. The candy canes and parcels are easy to make but effective and the garland of holly around the cake is simply attached to a sugarpaste base.

25 cm (10 inch) petal-shaped fruit cake (use mixture for 25 cm round cake)

1.25 kg (2^1/2 lb) marzipan
2 kg (4 lb) sugarpaste
red, dark-green and blue food colourings
2 tablespoons royal icing
silver dusting powder

EQUIPMENT

33 cm (13 inch) petal-shaped silver cake board
large and small holly cutters
fine paintbrush
fine cord

1   Cover the cake with marzipan, pressing it into the flutes of the petal shape, and leave to dry. Cover the cake with 1.3 kg (2^3/4 lb) of the sugarpaste and leave to dry for three days.

2   From the remaining sugarpaste, colour 185 g (6 oz) red, 250 g (8 oz) green and 60 g (2 oz) blue, leaving the remainder white. Secure the cake to the board with a little royal icing. Use the red sugarpaste to cover the cake board, trimming off the excess and reserving the trimmings.

HOLLY AND CANDY CANES

3   Thinly roll a little green sugarpaste and cut out eight large holly leaves. Mark the central veins with a knife, then lay them over crumpled foil to set in curved positions. To make the candy canes, very thinly roll a little white sugarpaste under the palms of your hands. Thinly roll a little red sugarpaste to the same thickness. Twist the rolls together, then roll them together. Cut into 3 cm (1^1/4 inch) lengths and bend over the tops. You will need 12 altogether. Make four or five thicker longer canes in the same way for the top of the cake.

MAKING THE PARCELS

4   From the blue icing, shape 12 small squares, about 5 mm (1/4 inch) in diameter and four larger squares, about 2 cm (3/4 inch) in diameter. Very thinly roll out the red icing trimmings and use to shape ribbons for the larger parcels. From the remaining white icing, roll 48 tiny

balls of icing and 10 larger balls, about 1 cm (1/2 inch) in diameter. Leave all the decorations to dry for 24 hours.

MAKING THE GARLAND

5   Roll out some green icing under the palms of your hands to a make a 1 cm (1/2 inch) thick sausage. Cut a section of the icing and secure around one petal of the cake, so that the end comes 1 cm (1/2 inch) from the top edge of the cake and the lowest part comes about 2 cm (3/4 inch) from the base. Secure with a dampened paintbrush. Repeat around all the cake.

6   Thinly roll out more green icing and cut out holly leaves with the small cutter. Mark the central veins with a knife. Dampen the underside of the leaves, then secure them to the green ropes around the sides of the cake to make a garland.

FINISHING TOUCHES

7   Lightly brush the small and large balls with silver dusting powder. Secure the small baubles, candy canes and parcels to the garland around the sides of the cake with dots of royal icing.

8   Use the larger decorations to make an attractive arrangement on the top of the cake, first securing the leaves and parcels with dots of royal icing, propping them up on small balls of foil until dried in position. Then arrange the candy canes and baubles. Arrange the cord around the base of the cake, securing with a little royal icing.

To make the candy canes, twist and then roll strips of white and red sugarpaste together.

Dampen the backs of the holly leaves and secure, at an angle, across the green ropes to make a garland.

CHRISTMAS NATIVITY

The design of this cake is effective in its simplicity. Both the stable and figures are exceptionally easy to shape and are ideal for a newcomer to sugarpaste modelling. For experienced sugarcrafters, more detail can be painted on with a fine brush.

1 Cut around the stable template and then carefully lift away the excess brown sugarpaste.

4 The simple figures are made from cone-shaped bodies with balls for heads and circular cloaks.

5 Make the donkey from nine pieces of grey sugarpaste, assembling them in a sitting position.

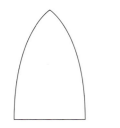

see template page 301

---

25 cm (10 inch) square fruit cake

1.25 kg (2¹/2 lb) marzipan
125 g (4 oz) royal icing
2.5 kg (5 lb) sugarpaste
brown, purple, red, black, dark- and light-blue, green and yellow food colourings

EQUIPMENT

30 cm (12 inch) square cake board
small star cutter
4 and 5 cm (1¹/2 and 2 inch) plain round cutters
cocktail stick
fine paintbrush
cream cord
sage green ribbon

MAKING THE STABLE

1 Cover the cake with marzipan and secure to the board with royal icing. Colour 250 g (8 oz) of the sugarpaste dark brown. Trace and cut out the stable templates on page 301 onto non-stick baking paper. Thinly roll the brown icing and lay on a sheet of non-stick baking paper. Lay the templates over the icing and cut around them, then carefully peel away the excess paste. (You will need two roof templates and two side templates.) Roll and cut out a small star from white icing. Leave the star and stable to dry for 48 hours.

2 Colour the remaining sugarpaste as follows: 90 g (3 oz) purple, 90 g (3 oz) red, 90 g (3 oz) pale pink, 90 g (3 oz) grey, 60 g (2 oz) dark blue, 60 g (2 oz) pale blue and 30 g (1 oz) green. Leave 30 g (1 oz) white, then colour the remainder yellow.

MARBLING THE SUGARPASTE

3 Reserve 90 g (3 oz) of the yellow sugarpaste. Roll the remainder to a thick sausage. Dot with 30 g (1 oz) of the brown icing. Fold the ends of the icing into the centre and roll again so that the yellow icing becomes marbled with the brown. Continue rolling and folding until the colours are fairly evenly distributed. Roll out the sugarpaste and use to cover the cake and board. Trim off the excess sugarpaste from the board edge. Leave to dry for three days.

MAKING THE FIGURES

4 To shape a 'king', make a small piece of purple-coloured sugarpaste into a cone. Shape two curved sections for the arms and secure to the cone with a little water. Shape head and hands from pink sugarpaste. For the cloak, cut a 5 cm (2 inch) circle of sugarpaste with the large cutter. Cut away an area for the neck, and position around the body. Shape a small circle of brown sugarpaste for the hair, then add the crown and gifts. Shape two more kings in the same way. Shape 'Mary' as above, draping a 4 cm (1¹/2 inch) circle of dark blue icing over her head.

5 Shape the remaining characters in the same way, using a cocktail stick for the centre of the shepherd's crook. For Jesus in the manger, shape a simple base of brown icing. Roll a tiny ball of flesh-coloured sugarpaste for the head and lay it on a thinly rolled square of white icing. Wrap the white icing around the head and lay it on the base. For the donkey, shape the grey sugarpaste as shown in the margin photograph, left, and assemble so that the donkey is in a sitting position.

6 Colour the royal icing dark brown and place in a piping bag. Snip off the tip. Pipe a little icing down one side of the stable back. Secure one side piece to the back and position on the cake. Position the other side piece and then the roof sections in the same way. Pipe another line of icing around the base of the stable.

7 Use a little more icing to pipe the donkey's mane. Secure the star to the stable roof. Using a little diluted brown colouring, paint simple features onto the faces then secure the figures on the cake with royal icing. Tie the cord around the cake and secure at the back with a little icing. Trim the board with ribbon, securing with double-sided tape.

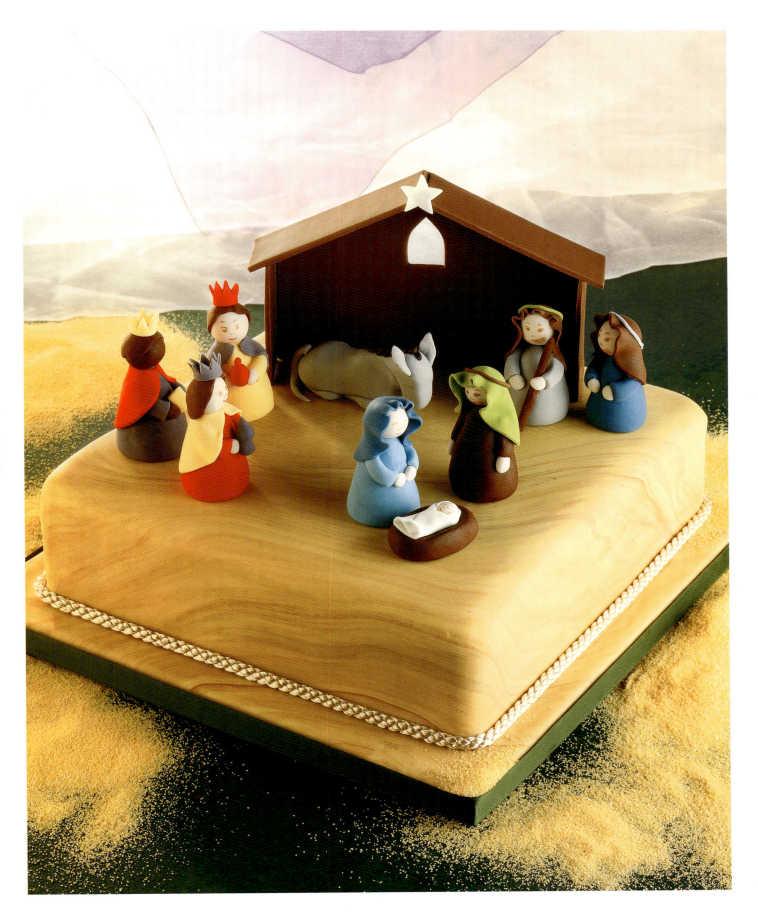

WINTER WONDERLAND

This cake is decorated with runout Christmas trees. They are made using the template traced from page 286 and are not difficult but, because of the number needed, can be time-consuming. Always make a few extra in case of breakages.

two 15 cm (6 inch) round fruit cakes

4 tablespoons apricot glaze
1 kg (2 lb) marzipan
500 g (1 lb) royal icing
1.5 kg (3 lb) sugarpaste
blue and pearlized or white dusting powder

EQUIPMENT
33 cm (13 inch) petal or round silver cake board
number 1 or 2 piping tube
cocktail sticks
large soft paintbrush

1   Brush the cakes with apricot glaze, then position one cake over the other, filling in the gaps left around the middle with marzipan. Secure the cake to the board with a little royal icing. Cover the cake with marzipan and leave to dry. Cover the cake with 1 kg (3 lb) of the sugarpaste and leave to dry for three days.

COVERING THE BOARD
2   Position small mounds of the remaining sugarpaste on the board around the cake, varying them in height and diameter. Roll out half the remaining sugarpaste to a long curved strip. Trim the inner edge of the strip. Dampen the base of the cake around the mounds, then lay the strip in position so that the trimmed edge rests against the side of the cake. Cover the other half of the board in the same way, smoothing out the joins and trimming off the excess around the edge.

MAKING RUNOUT TREES
3   To make the trees, trace five of each tree template on page 286 onto non-stick baking paper. Beat some of the royal icing, adding a little water or lemon juice so that it just holds its shape. Place in a piping bag fitted with a number 1 or 2 piping tube. Lay a large sheet of non-stick baking paper over the large template and pipe over the outline. Move the templates under the paper and trace 35 more large trees. Use the same technique for the other trees, making about 60 of the medium-sized and 40 of the small.

4   Thin more of the royal icing with water until the surface is smooth and level when left to settle for several seconds. Place in a piping bag and snip off the merest tip. Pipe the icing into the tree outlines, easing the icing into the corners with a cocktail stick. Leave to dry for 2 days.

COLOURING THE CAKE
5   Mix together a little blue and pearlized or white dusting powder. Using the large soft brush, gently dust the sides of the cake, making the colour slightly more dense near the base. (Practise on spare icing first to check that the blue is not too deep.) Pipe small dots of icing over the top and side of the cake to resemble snow, making the dots more dense near the base of the cake.

POSITIONING THE TREES
6   Carefully peel the paper lining away from the icing trees. To assemble the trees, pipe a line of icing along the straight edge of a large tree shape. Gently secure the shape to the cake, letting the shaped edge stand slightly away from the cake. Position another tree section against the cake so that the straight edges almost meet. Build up the tree with three more sections. Repeat around the cake, using large and medium sections.

7   For the trees that stand away from the cake, pipe a dot of icing where the tree is to stand. Secure two tree sections together and position on the icing. Gradually build up the tree with more sections. (You will need six to seven for each tree.) Continue adding trees to the cake, arranging some in clusters. Use a medium-size tree to decorate the top of the cake. Once set in position, dust the trees with a little sifted icing sugar.

NOTE   If any of the trees will not readily stand unsupported, prop them up with a piece of foam or crumpled paper towel or plastic wrap until set.

Cover the cake board with sugarpaste, concealing the mounds beneath.

Pipe the royal icing into the tree outlines, easing it into the corners with a cocktail stick.

Dust the side of the cake with blue and white or pearlized dusting powder.

To assemble the trees, pipe icing along the straight edge and press onto the cake.

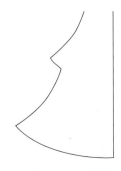

see template page 286

CAROL SINGERS

This lovely cake will be a great success if there are children in the house. The cake itself is very easy, with the scarf tied around the outside made from sugarpaste. The figures can be as simple or complex as you choose depending on your expertise and confidence.

22 cm (9 inch) round fruit cake

1 kg (2 lb) marzipan
1 tablespoon royal icing
2 kg (4 lb) sugarpaste
red, dark green, light green, yellow, blue and black assorted food colourings

EQUIPMENT

30 cm (12 inch) round silver cake board
medium Christmas tree cutter
cocktail sticks
fine paintbrush

1   Cover the cake with marzipan and secure to the cake board with a little royal icing. Leave to dry, then dust a circle in the centre of the cake, about 23 cm (9 inches) round, with cornflour. Brush the rest of the cake with clear alcohol. Colour 1.25 kg (2½ lb) of the sugarpaste red and cover the cake.

REMOVING THE CENTRE PANEL

2   Place a small bowl or saucer with a diameter of 12 cm (5 inches) on the centre of the cake, or make a paper template of that size and secure to the top of the cake with pins. Cut around it and then lift out the red sugarpaste from the centre. Re-roll the red trimmings and use to cover the cake board, reserving the trimmings.

3   Roll out 185 g (6 oz) white sugarpaste to the same thickness as the red sugarpaste and cut out a 12 cm (5 inch) circle using the bowl or paper template. Brush the centre of the cake with clear alcohol and ease the white sugarpaste into the hole, smoothing out gently with the palms of your hands. Reserve the white trimmings.

4   Taking the remaining icing, colour 185 g (6 oz) dark green, 125 g (4 oz) light green, 60 g (2 oz) yellow, 60 g (2 oz) blue, 30 g (1 oz) pale pink and the remainder black.

MAKING THE SCARF

5   Thinly roll half the dark-green icing and cut out a 38 x 5 cm (15 x 2 inch) rectangle. Thinly roll half the pale-green icing and cut out several

Christmas trees with the cutter. Lay the trees over the dark-green strip then gently roll with the rolling pin so that the trees are secured to the icing (moisten with a little water if they aren't sticking well). Trim the edges of the strip. Lightly moisten one side of the cake and wrap the rectangle around it, pinching the ends together around the front to create a tie in the scarf. Cut out and secure another rectangle around the other side of the cake. Shape two smaller scarf rectangles and secure to the front of the cake for the scarf ends.

6   Roll more pale-green icing under the palms of the hands to 7.5 cm (3 inch) lengths. Bend the lengths and make knife marks to resemble threads of wool. Secure to one scarf end and finish with flattened balls of icing along the edge. Repeat on the other scarf end.

MAKING THE FIGURES

7   To make a figure, shape a small pair of boots from black icing. Mould a rounded cone shape for the body and mark a line down the front. Position the body over the boots and secure together by pressing a cocktail stick right through to the base of the boots so that the figure stands upright. Add moulded arms, gloves and scarf. Roll a ball of icing and position for the head, adding a tiny ball of icing for the nose. Shape a hat and gently press in place.

8   Shape the other figures in the same way, varying their clothes and colours. Secure to the cake with royal icing. Dilute a little red and brown food colouring and use to paint the faces. Press the figures onto the cake then sprinkle lightly with icing sugar as if it has been snowing.

3

Remove the circle of red sugarpaste from the centre of the cake and replace it with a circle of white sugarpaste.

6

Bend lengths of green sugarpaste and score with a knife to resemble wool for the fringe of the scarf.

7

Build the boots and body of the figure on a cocktail stick, adding the other features afterwards.

TIERED CHRISTMAS CAKE

This lavishly decorated centrepiece is not actually two tiers. It is made by cutting the centre from a large cake and raising it up—a simple technique with stunning results. The bright red icing makes the cake eye-catching, but for a traditional look you could use white.

1 Cut around a small tin or saucer, holding the knife upright, to remove the centre of the cake.

2 Lay the marzipan over the ring cake and ease it into the cavity before you trim off the excess.

4 Use the end of a paintbrush to make indentations in the stars before you paint them.

8 To make tassels, cut squares of thin sugarpaste, make cuts on one side, then roll up from the top.

22 cm (9 inch) round fruit cake

2 tablespoons royal icing
1.5 kg (3 lb) marzipan
1.5 kg (3 lb) sugarpaste
red and purple food colourings
gold dusting powder
2 tablespoons clear piping jelly

EQUIPMENT
13 cm (5 inch) round cake card
30 cm (12 inch) round cake board
5 cm (2 inch) star cutter
fine paintbrush
2 metres green paper ribbon
2 metres red wired ribbon
florist's wire
glass tumbler, about 12 cm (5 inches) tall
several bunches of bay leaves
6 small gold fir cones
large handful of hazelnuts

MAKING TWO TIERS

1 Place a small tin or saucer measuring 13 cm (5 inches) in diameter on top of the fruit cake. Using a knife held upright, cut out the centre of the cake. Carefully ease out and secure on the small cake card with a little royal icing.

2 Secure the outer ring of cake on the large board with a little royal icing. Use 375 g (12 oz) of the marzipan to cover the smaller cake, easing to fit around the side and trimming off the excess. Roll out the remaining marzipan to a 30 cm (12 in) round. Lay it over the ring cake and ease around the side to fit. Trim off the excess around the base. Press the marzipan over the central cavity inwards to gauge the inner edge of the cake, then remove the excess with a knife. Re-roll all the trimmings and use to cover the inner side of the cake.

3 Reserve 125 g (4 oz) of the sugarpaste and colour the remainder deep red. Roll out 375 g (12 oz) of the red sugarpaste and use to cover the small cake. Roll out the remaining icing and use to cover the large cake, using the same technique as for the marzipan. Use the trimmings to cover the board.

GOLD STARS

4 To make the gold stars, thinly roll 60 g (2 oz) of the white sugarpaste and cut out 10 stars with the cutter. Transfer to a sheet of non-stick baking paper. Roll small balls of icing, flatten them slightly, moisten the backs then press gently onto the centres of the stars. Using the tail-end of a paintbrush or a skewer, impress holes around the edges of the stars.

5 Paint the centres of the stars with purple food colouring. Mix a little gold dusting powder with clear alcohol or water until it has the consistency of thin paint. Use to paint the stars. Once the purple paint has dried, brush the stars with piping jelly to make them shine.

RIBBON DECORATIONS

6 To make the ribbon decorations, cut both ribbon types into 25 cm (10 inch) lengths. Bend in half, then pinch together. Tie with a little florist's wire, twisting well to secure. Bend back the ribbon ends attractively.

7 Invert the tumbler into the centre of the large cake then position the small cake over the tumbler. Pipe a little royal icing onto one of the ribbon ends, then secure to the small cake, if necessary supporting with a pin until the icing hardens a little. Secure more ribbons and bay leaves between the two tiers and over the top of the cake.

TASSELS

8 Secure the fir cones and nuts in the same way, filling in the gaps between the ribbons. Secure the gold stars in prominent positions, allowing room for the tassels to hang down. For each tassel, very thinly roll a little white sugarpaste to a 4 cm (1¹⁄₂ inch) square. Using a fine-bladed knife, make cuts along the square, leaving the icing intact at one side. Lightly dampen the uncut area of icing then roll up the tassel and cut off the excess uncut area.

9 Roll small balls of icing and secure with the tassels to the points of the stars. Leave to harden. Use a little more of the dusting powder and alcohol mixture to paint the tassels with a fine brush.

CHRISTMAS ROSES

Although this cake is royal iced, the finish does not have to be perfect, making this an ideal cake for those new to royal icing. The ring of white Christmas roses and rich ribbon collar give this cake an elegant simplicity.

20 cm (8 inch) round fruit cake

1 kg (2 lb) marzipan
750 g (1¹/2 lb) royal icing
60 g (2 oz) flower paste
yellow dusting powder
white stamens

EQUIPMENT

28 cm (11 inch) round cake board
medium rose petal cutter
cocktail sticks
piece of foam sponge
soft paintbrush
75 cm (28 inches) firm gold ribbon, about 5 cm (2 inches) wide
2 metres fine green or red wired ribbon
1 metre narrow gold ribbon

COVERING THE CAKE

1   Cover the cake with marzipan and leave to dry. Secure on the cake board with a little royal icing. Reserve 4 tablespoons of the royal icing. Spread the remainder over the top and side of the cake until it is covered in one even layer. Work a palette knife around the side of the cake, then over the top to neaten. Leave to dry.

CHRISTMAS ROSES

2   To make the Christmas roses, roll some strips of foil, then shape into rounds about 5 cm (2 inches) in diameter. Place on a sheet of non-stick baking paper. You will need 11 altogether, allowing one spare for breakages. Take a little flower paste and roll as thinly as possible on a surface lightly dusted with cornflour. Cut out five petals with the cutter. Roll a cocktail stick over the edges of the petal to give a delicate, lightly curled edge. Press each petal onto a piece of sponge to lightly cup it.

3   Lightly dampen one side of each of the five petals. Arrange the petals, slightly overlapping, inside a foil ring so that the rose is supported by the foil. Make the remaining roses in the same way and leave to dry for 24 hours.

4   Using the soft brush, lightly colour the centre of each rose with dusting powder. Place the reserved royal icing in a piping bag and snip off the tip. Pipe a dot of icing into the centre of a rose. Cut about a dozen stamens down to 1 cm (¹/2 inch) depth and press several at a time into the royal icing. Finish the remainder in the same way.

POSITIONING THE ROSES

5   Secure the roses in a ring around the edge of the cake with a dot of royal icing. Tie the firm gold ribbon around the cake and secure with a dot of icing. Loosely pleat the wired ribbon concertina-fashion between the fingers and thumbs. Secure over the gold ribbon. Trim the board with narrow gold ribbon, securing with double-sided tape.

NOTES   Plastic apple trays and shallow tartlet tins make good moulds for the roses to dry in. Positioning the stamens can be tricky with your fingers—try using tweezers.

Cover the cake with royal icing, working a palette knife around it to neaten the finish.

Cut out the petals, then roll the edges with a cocktail stick to thin and curl them.

Lightly dampen one side of each petal and arrange them, slightly overlapping, inside a foil ring.

Pipe a dot of icing into the centre of each rose, then add a dozen stamens, a few at a time, using tweezers if you find it too fiddly for fingers.

WHITE CHRISTMAS

The plain white colouring on this festive cake makes it both stylish and classic. The technique is very simple, with the leaves being cut out and the beading easy to attach to the cake. A little piping is required, for outlining the leaves with royal icing.

2 Attach the pearl beading to the base of the cake, securing it with dabs of royal icing at intervals.

3 Attach the leaves to the cake by moistening with water. Group the holly leaves together and graduate the ivy by size.

4 Pipe an outline of white royal icing around the leaves, adding loops and trails around the ivy to link the leaves together.

25 x 18 cm (10 x 7 inch) oval fruit cake (use mixture for 23 cm round cake)

1 kg (2 lb) marzipan
1.5 kg (3 lb) sugarpaste
250 g (8 oz) royal icing
pearlized white dusting powder

EQUIPMENT

30 x 22 cm (12 x 9 inch) oval cake board
number 1 piping tube
45 cm (18 inches) pearlized beading for top of cake
1 metre pearlized beading for base of cake
small, medium and large ivy leaf cutters
medium and large holly cutters
leaf veiner
fine paintbrush
narrow white ribbon
white candles

1 Cover the cake with marzipan and leave to dry. Cover the cake and board with 1 kg (2 lb) of the sugarpaste. Secure to the cake board with a little royal icing and leave to dry for three days.

BEADING

2 Cut out an oval template measuring 15 x 10 cm (6 x 4 inches) from non-stick baking paper. Lay it on the centre of the cake and mark the outline with a pin. Beat the royal icing, adding a little water or lemon juice until it is softly peaking. Place in a piping bag fitted with the number 1 tube. Trim the beading for the top of the cake so that it fits neatly over the marked line. Press it gently down, securing at intervals with a dot of royal icing. Arrange the beading around the cake base, securing at intervals with dabs of royal icing.

CUTOUT LEAVES

3 Roll out a little of the remaining sugarpaste and cut out ivy and holly leaves in various sizes. Mark each with a veiner or knife, then secure to the cake with a little water, bunching two or three holly leaves together and graduating the strings of ivy leaves from small to large.

PIPING

4 Pipe a fine outline around all the leaves with royal icing, then add decorative trails of icing around the ivy leaves, particularly where there are large gaps between them.

BERRIES

5 Roll small balls of sugarpaste to represent holly berries and secure with a little icing to the holly leaves. Mix a little of the dusting powder with enough clear alcohol to give the consistency of thin paint. Use to paint over the holly berries. Gently press the white candles into the top of the cake. Trim the edge of the board with the ribbon, securing with double-sided tape.

NOTE If you do not have an oval cake tin, and cannot hire one from a cake-decorating shop, this cake can be made equally successfully using a 23 cm (9 inch) round tin. Use a 12 cm (5 inch) circle to mark the position for the beading on top of the cake.

HOLLY IN THE CHRISTMAS SNOW

Hanging icicles add a delicate finishing touch to this traditional Christmas cake—they are piped to a strip of sugarpaste secured around the edge of the cake. The holly leaves are simply made, using cutters, and the red berries add a splash of colour.

22 cm (9 inch) round fruit cake

1.5 kg (3 lb) sugarpaste
green and red food colourings
1 kg (2 lb) marzipan
250 g (8 oz) royal icing

EQUIPMENT
fine paintbrush
1 cm (^{1}/2 inch) holly cutter
number 2 piping tube
large paintbrush
30 cm (12 inch) round cake board

HOLLY LEAVES

1   To make sugarpaste holly leaves, colour 60 g (2 oz) of the sugarpaste green. Roll a little out into a long, thin strip on a surface dusted with cornflour. Roll out another strip of white sugarpaste. Brush one edge of each strip with a dampened paintbrush and press together. Roll lightly to secure. Using the holly cutter, press out 16 half green and half white leaves. Bend the leaves slightly, then transfer to a sheet of crumpled foil to dry.

2   Roll out more green and white icing in the same way and cut out four large petal shapes, each about 6 cm (2^1/2 inches) long and 3 cm (1^1/2 inches) wide (only three are used—one is a spare). Using the wide end of the number 2 tube dipped in cornflour, cut out semi-circles from around the petals to give them holly-leaf shapes. Lightly mark veins on each leaf with a knife. Leave overnight to dry.

COVERING THE CAKE AND BOARD

3   Cover the cake with marzipan and secure to the cake board with a little royal icing. Colour 15 g (^{1}/2 oz) of the sugarpaste red. Reserve 315 g (10 oz) of the white sugarpaste and use the remainder to cover the cake.

4   Use small pieces of the reserved white sugarpaste to make 'mounds' on the board around the base of the cake at irregular intervals. Roll out half the remaining white sugarpaste to make a long curved strip. Trim the inner edge of the strip. Dampen the base of the cake around the mounds, then lay the strip in position so that the trimmed edge rests against the side of the cake. Cover the other half of the board in the same way, smoothing out the joins and trimming off the excess around the edge.

PIPING THE DECORATIONS

5   Cut out a 22 cm (9 inch) circle of non-stick baking paper. Fold the circle into eight sections, then open it out and lay it over the cake. Make pin marks around the top edge of the cake, at the point where each crease in the paper meets the edge. Thinly roll out the remaining white icing and cut out eight thin strips, each 11.5 cm (4^1/2 inches) long and 5 mm (^{1}/4 inch) wide. Dampen the icing on the side of the cake under the pin marks, and then secure the strips so the ends meet at the pin marks to form scallops around the side.

6   Place a little royal icing in a paper piping bag fitted with the number 2 tube. Pipe a small dot of icing on the edge of one strip. Pull the tube away from the cake until the icing breaks, allowing it to hang like an 'icicle'. Pipe more 'icicles' of varying lengths all around the cake.

7   Pipe a snail trail around the base of the cake. Pipe tiny dots around the base and on the side and top of the cake to resemble snow. Secure the holly in position with small dots of icing. Roll berries from the red sugarpaste and position on the cake.

NOTES   To achieve a realistic colour for the holly leaves, use a leaf or gooseberry green rather than a bright green.
When securing the large holly leaves on the cake, you may need to prop them up with crumpled paper towel or foam so that they set in a raised position.

Use the wide end of the piping tube as a cutter to give the holly leaves their fluted edges.

The 'icicles' are made from strands of piped royal icing that will hang down from the strips without breaking.

SNOWMAN

The snowman on this cake is made using the bas-relief technique and is not difficult although the finish will be more professional with practice. Alphabet cutters are an easy alternative to piping letters—you could replace 'Noel' with a child's name for a winter birthday cake.

6 Roll out a small piece of white modelling paste and cut out the scarf, then emboss with a dishcloth.

7 Roll tiny balls of black paste and insert into the holes made for teeth, eyes and buttons.

19 Colour a little modelling paste green and then stamp out the word 'Noel' with alphabet cutters.

see template page 289

---

20 cm (8 inch) round fruit cake

1.25 kg (2¹/₂ lb) marzipan
1.5 kg (3 lb) sugarpaste
60 g (2 oz) royal icing
green, black, tangerine, dark brown, cream, yellow, paprika and red paste colourings
90 g (3 oz) modelling paste
edible glue
brown and blue dusting powders
60 g (2 oz) sugarpaste

EQUIPMENT

28 cm (11 inch) round cake board
scriber
paintbrush
small ball tools
Dresden tool
new dishcloth
number 1 piping tube
Garrett frill cutter
tiny holly cutter
alphabet cutters
narrow dark green ribbon

---

1 Cover the cake with marzipan and leave to dry. Cover the cake and board with sugarpaste and secure the cake to the board with a little royal icing. Leave to dry for three days.

2 Trace the template on page 289 onto non-stick baking paper and then scribe onto the top of the cake with a scriber or pin. Paint the fir trees with diluted green paste colouring, leave to dry, then paint on darker green shadows to create the foliage. Paint the other trees with a lighter green, leave to dry, then paint on the branches in a darker tone. Leave to dry.

3 Cover the design with tracing paper and use as a guide when making the snowman and animals.

SNOWMAN'S HEAD

4 Roll a grape-size piece of modelling paste between the palms of your hands and flatten. Place on the tracing paper and pinch and push into shape. Attach to the cake with edible glue.

SNOWMAN'S BODY

5 Roll a piece of modelling paste, roughly the size of a small plum, into a ball, then form a cone and flatten. Shape and position below the head. Indent with the ball tool where the arms, rabbit, racoon and snowballs are to be placed. Indent the eyes, nose and buttonholes with the end of the paintbrush. Mark the creases around the eyes and cheeks with the Dresden tool. Create holes in which to place the teeth with the cocktail stick.

SCARF

6 Roll out a small piece of white modelling paste and cut out the scarf shapes marked A, B and C on the template. Emboss by texturing with a dishcloth and secure piece A in place with edible glue.

EYES, TEETH, BUTTON AND NOSE

7 Colour a grape-size piece of paste black. Roll small balls of paste and insert into the eye sockets and buttonholes. Make tiny balls of black paste and insert into the holes made for the teeth. Colour a small piece of paste tangerine, roll into a ball, then into a long cone. Mark a few grooves with the scalpel, upturn the tip and place in the nose socket.

ARMS

8 Roll a grape-size piece of modelling paste into a smooth sausage. Bend, mark the creases for the wrist and bend in the arm and pinch the elbow. For the small arm, form an elongated cone. Attach scarf section B around the neck and finally section C.

HAT

9 Colour a large grape-size piece of modelling paste black. Roll out a little, not too thin, and cut out the back hat brim. Attach to the cake with glue. Cut out the remaining hat brim shapes and cover with plastic so that the paste does not dry out. Roll the remaining paste into a fat sausage, flatten and place on the traced design. Cut to shape. Smooth and round any cut edges with fingers. Place against the top of the head. Roll out a small piece of white paste and, using the template, cut out the hat band and attach with edible glue. Place the remaining hat brim shapes in position to form one continuous shape. Pipe slightly thinned royal icing onto the top of the hat to represent snow.

RABBIT

10   Colour a large grape-size piece of modelling paste with a little dark brown paste colouring. Roll two-thirds into a ball for the main body, then form a cone. Indent the line for the hip and a channel where the arm will be placed with the Dresden tool. Roll out a tiny piece of the paste and cut out a triangular shape for the back ear. Fix in place with water.

11   Roll a grape-size piece of the paste into a ball for the head, then form a cone. Indent an eye with the cocktail stick or tiny ball tool. Make a small hole in which to place the other ear.

12   To make the ear, make a tiny cone with the dark brown paste. Add a little cream colouring to a pea-size piece of brown paste and make a smaller cone. Flatten both cones and place one on top of the other. Flatten again. Pinch the pastes at the base of the ear together and trim away the excess at the back. Fix in position on the head with water.

13   Make a small ball of black paste and insert into the eye socket. Roll a grape-size piece of dark brown paste into a long thin sausage for the arm and bend to form a gentle curve.

RACOON AND MOUSE

14   Repeat steps 10, 11, 12 and 13 but changing the colours. Use mixed cream and brown paste colourings for the racoon and grey for the mouse. Make the racoon's tail the same way as his arms.

BIRDS

15   Colour a pea-size piece of paste brown with dusting powder and a similar size piece of paste pale blue. Roll out thinly. Cut out the back wing and attach to the cake, then cut out the head, body and tail as one shape and attach. Cut out the upper wing. Attach to the bird by the inner edge only so that the feathers can be lifted up slightly to give movement. Roll a tiny ball, flatten and place on the head to give a three-dimensional effect. Indent an eye with the number 1 piping tube. Repeat for the second bird.

FINISHING TOUCHES

16   Place paste snowballs at the base of the snowman and for the rabbit's tail. Paint stripes on the scarf and features on the animals. Dust shadows on the animals. Dust the sky pale blue. Paint some fine brown lines on the foreground and, when dry, dust with blue to create depth. Pipe tiny beaks on the birds with a little yellow royal icing and a tail and feet on the mouse with pale paprika. Pipe noses on the animals with black royal icing. Pipe snow on the fir trees.

17   Pipe a snail trail around the base of the cake with white royal icing. Roll 60 g (2 oz) of the sugarpaste thinly on a surface dusted with cornflour. Cut out rounds with the garrett frill cutter. Frill with a cocktail stick and attach to the base of the cake with water. Pipe tiny dots of icing on the top edge.

18   Colour a grape-size piece of modelling paste green. Roll out thinly and cut out tiny holly shapes with the cutter. Place at the top of each frill and pipe some red berries between the leaves. Place a holly leaf in the mouth of the bluebird.

19   Colour a little modelling paste green. Roll out and stamp out 'Noel' with alphabet cutters. Attach to the cake with water. Trim the cake board with ribbon, securing with double-sided tape.

2 Cover the cake with marzipan, creating folds and ridges by indenting with finger and thumb.

3 Roll the new dishcloth over the red sugarpaste to give it texture.

7 Make two cuts in the top of each ball of sugarpaste to make bells. Paint with gold paint.

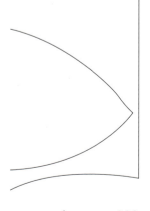

see template page 288

SANTA'S STOCKING

This is a wonderful cake if there are children coming for Christmas tea. The stocking itself is easy to make and can be used just on its own. If you have a lot of time and experience, make toys and dolls from modelling paste to match your child's favourites.

20 x 30 x 5 cm (8 x 12 x 2 inch) cake

1.25 kg (2^{1}/2 lb) marzipan
250 g (8 oz) sugarpaste
1.5 kg (3 lb) red-tinted sugarpaste
30 g (1 oz) royal icing
gold dusting powder
modelling paste and paste colourings

EQUIPMENT

33 x 38 cm (13 x 15 inch) cake board
new dishcloth
ribbed sports sock or cuff of cotton jumper
pastry wheel or scalpel
small ball tool
number 1 paintbrush
holly leaf cutter
narrow red ribbon

CUTTING THE CAKE TO SHAPE

1 Copy the template on page 288 and enlarge by 195%. Position on the cake and cut to shape. Round the top and bottom edges with a knife so that when the cake is covered the shape will appear to be rounded. Cut into the inner edge of the top of the stocking to create a curve.

COVERING THE CAKE

2 Cover the cake with marzipan, by placing the template on the marzipan. Leave 5 cm (2 inches) around the template to allow for covering the sides of the cake and cut the marzipan to shape. Cover the cake in the usual way, making sure the bottom edge turns under the cake. Create folds in the marzipan by indenting with fingers and thumbs. Exaggerate the indentations as they will become less evident when the cake is covered with sugarpaste. Cover the cake board with white sugarpaste and leave to dry.

CREATING THE STOCKING TEXTURE

3 Make a template of the stocking by laying a sheet of paper towel over the cake. Draw around the cake, omitting the heel and toe areas. Transfer this rough template onto tracing paper. (The template is a guide only, as the size will not be accurate.) Roll out the red sugarpaste. Place the new dishcloth on

top and indent it into the paste by rolling over firmly once with a rolling pin to create a knitted texture. Place the template on the sugarpaste and cut out. Drape carefully over the marzipan and ease into place, taking care not to spoil the textured effect. Use paper towel to make a pattern for the heel and toe in the same way. Cut out in the textured paste and place in position on the cake, leaving a 5 mm (1/4 inch) gap between the heel and foot join.

4 To make the ribbed toe section, cut the sock or jumper cuff vertically and open up to form a strip. Place on the red sugarpaste and texture as before. Cut and place the sugarpaste on the cake, leaving a 5mm (1/4 in) gap between the joins.

5 To fill the gaps between the shapes, roll a long thin section of red paste, flatten slightly and attach to the gaps. Make two lines of 'stitching' with the pastry wheel or tip of a scalpel. Leave the cake to dry, then secure to the board with royal icing.

6 Lay paper towel over the top of the stocking and make a template for the zig-zag shape, allowing an extra 2.5 cm (1 inch) to roll over the top edge. Roll out all the red sugarpaste and texture with the dishcloth. Cut out, pinching the edges of the pointed shape with the cloth to eliminate the cut look. Attach to the stocking, taking care not to damage the textured effect. Roll over the top edge and turn in the corners. Twist and curve the points to create an interesting and natural look. Leave to dry.

BELLS

7 Roll six small grape-size pieces of white sugarpaste into balls for the bells. Make two cuts in the top of each with a kitchen knife. At each end of the cuts, indent a small hole with the ball tool. Indent a small hole at the top of the bell and insert the zig-zag points. Mix gold dusting powder with clear alcohol until it has the consistency of thin paint. Paint the bells gold. Leave to dry. Attach to the stocking with royal icing. Support the underneath of the bells on the board or cake with royal icing.

8 Use coloured modelling paste to make toys and holly. Place 'inside' the top of the stocking, arranging so that some hang over the edge. Trim the board with ribbon, securing with double-sided tape.

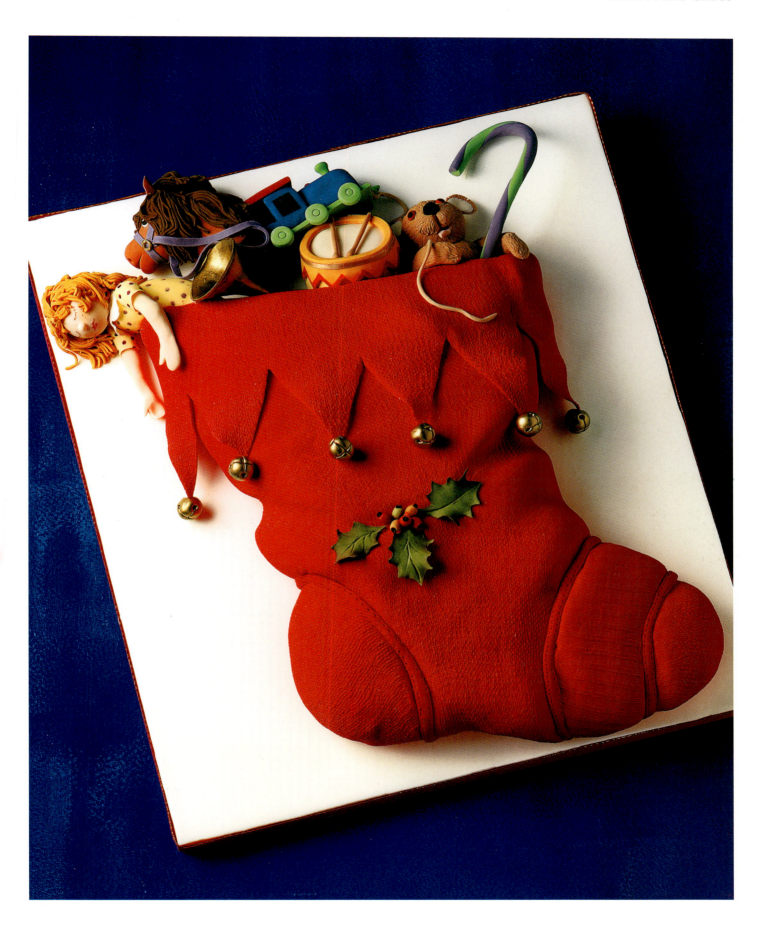

PASTORAL PEACE

A painted pastillage plaque is inserted into the centre of the cake and framed by Christmas foliage. The techniques for this cake are a little more advanced, requiring painting, rather more complicated layered stencils, brush embroidery and runouts.

20 cm (8 inch) round fruit cake

125 g (4 oz) pastillage
1.25 kg (2¹/₂ lb) marzipan
1.25 kg (2¹/₂ lb) sugarpaste
90 g (3 oz) royal icing
cream, browns, greens and black paste colourings
60 g (2 oz) modelling paste
1 teaspoon piping gel
30 g (1 oz) flower paste
edible glue
grey, green and lilac dusting powders
red powder colour

EQUIPMENT

10 cm (4 inch) round cutter
23 cm (11 inch) round cake board
numbers 1 and 2 piping tubes
scriber
paintbrushes
holly and Christmas rose veiners
ball tool
yellow stamens
narrow red ribbon
narrow green ribbon

PASTILLAGE PLAQUE

1   Roll out the pastillage and cut out a 10 cm (4 inch) round plaque with the cutter. Leave to dry.

2   Cover the cake with marzipan and leave to dry. Cover the cake with sugarpaste, leaving a circle in the centre clear when you brush the marzipan with clear alcohol. Using the same cutter, remove a 10 cm (4 inch) circle from the centre of the sugarpaste while it is still soft. Secure the cake to the board with a little royal icing and cover the board with sugarpaste. Leave to dry for three days. Pipe a snail trail around the base of the cake with a number 1 piping tube.

3   Trace the template on page 293 onto non-stick baking paper. Scribe the church onto the plaque and paint with paste colour, keeping the brush as dry as possible and the colours muted. Secure the plaque into position in the hollow circle on the cake with royal icing. Pipe small dots of royal icing over the scene with the number 1 tube to represent snow.

OVERLAPPING TEMPLATE

4   Using the template, scribe the main design onto the top of the cake around the plaque. Roll out the modelling paste thinly. Trace the overlapping base template, place on the paste and carefully cut around the shape. Leave to dry thoroughly. Secure on the cake, matching the design, with royal icing.

PAINTING THE ROSES AND HOLLY

5   Starting at the back, paint on the light leaves. For the holly leaves in the foreground, colour a large grape-size piece of modelling paste with a little green, a little dark brown and a touch of black paste colourings. Using the template, cut out the leaves, vein, then place on a foam pad. Curve between the points of the holly with the ball tool and twist to give movement. Place the leaves in position, support with small pieces of foam if necessary and leave to dry.

6   Stir the piping gel into 60 g (2 oz) of the royal icing to slow the setting time. Outline the Christmas rose bud with the number 2 piping tube, then brush the icing downwards to the base of the bud. Colour a little of the icing with a touch of green and black to give a grey/green colour and pipe the calyx at the base of the bud in the same way.

MODELLING THE FLOWERS

7   Roll out the flower paste so it is thicker at the base of the petal. Using the template, cut out the Christmas rose, then vein. Thin the cut edge with the ball tool. Curl some of the edges with the cocktail stick to give a natural effect. Leave to dry. Working from the back forwards, attach the holly leaves and Christmas roses to the cake with edible glue.

8   Colour a little royal icing with the merest touch of cream and green to make a yellow/lime colour. Pipe a small bulb in the middle of each flower. Curve some fine yellow stamens by dragging a thumbnail along the cotton. Place in the bulb of icing with tweezers. Dust the background around the flowers and leaves with grey/green and grey/lilac.

9   To make the holly berries, colour a little modelling paste red. Roll into small balls and attach with royal icing. Paint on black dots. Trim the base of the cake with red ribbon and the board with green ribbon, securing with double-sided tape.

Use the template to scribe the church onto the plaque. Paint with muted colours and a dry brush.

Pipe small dots of white royal icing over the plaque to represent falling snow.

Trace the overlapping base template onto modelling paste and secure to the cake. Paint the light leaves and then attach the holly leaves in the foreground.

see template page 293

6 The angel is made from modelling paste and secured to the wings with royal icing.

8 To make the baubles, roll tiny balls of paste then tease out at the base. Hold steady on cocktail sticks while you paint them.

10 Cut out a drape, using the template. Soften the edges with the ball tool and then fold under the top and bottom edges.

12 Cut away part of the back of each present so that it will sit at an interesting angle under the tree.

CHRISTMAS TREE

This tree is cut from a slab cake and decorated with a mix of cut-out, moulded and shaped decorations. The decorations require a steady hand with a paintbrush rather than expertise, but the angel is modelled and requires a little more experience.

20 cm (8 in) square fruit cake

1 kg (2 lb) marzipan
1.75 kg (3½ lb) sugarpaste
green, browns, melon, black and
cream paste colourings
60 g (2 oz) royal icing
185 g (6 oz) modelling paste
burgundy and red powder colours
edible glue
cream and gold dusting powders
gold and silver food colourings

EQUIPMENT

36 x 40 cm (14 x 16 inch) rectangular cake board
scalpel and cocktail sticks
very fine paintbrush
number 1 piping tube
Dresden tool
wooden cake dowels
small ball tool
small bell mould
medium plunger cutter
narrow red ribbon

1   Copy the template on page 292 onto non-stick baking paper and cut the cake into a tree shape. Cover with marzipan and leave to dry. Colour 1 kg (2 lb) of the sugarpaste green and use to cover the cake. Cover the board with white sugarpaste and leave to dry. Secure the cake to the board with royal icing, leaving enough space to attach the tub to the base of the tree. Leave to dry.

2   Colour 90 g (3 oz) of the sugarpaste dark brown, roll out thinly and cut out the tub, using the template. Attach to the base of the tree. Mark in the wood texture with a knife. Cut out and fix darker brown strips to represent iron bands.

ANGEL'S HEAD

3   Colour 15 g (½ oz) modelling paste a skintone colour. Mould into a doll's head following the instructions on page 95. Make nostrils with the point of a cocktail stick. Cut between the lips with the point of a sharp scalpel to open up the mouth. Place the head on a cocktail stick to hold it steady and

paint on the features. Colour a small amount of royal icing a light golden brown and pipe onto the head to represent hair.

ANGEL'S DRESS

4   Colour a large grape-size piece of modelling paste with the burgundy powder. Make a large ball, then roll into an elongated round cone. The top of the cone will form the shoulders so do not roll into a point. Open up the base of the cone with the end of the paintbrush to thin out and frill. Form crease lines in the skirt with the point of the Dresden tool. Roll the cone between the two index fingers, one-third down from the shoulders, to form the waist. Mark in the creases for the upper bodice with the Dresden tool. Place on a piece of dowel to dry. Roll out a long fine strand of white modelling paste, making the ends pointed. Wrap around the upper body, criss-crossing in front and taking around the waist. Butt together in front and let fall down and open. Leave to dry, then paint gold.

ANGEL'S ARMS

5   Roll a pea-size piece of flesh-coloured modelling paste into a sausage. Flatten one end between thumb and finger. Cut out a wedge to create a thumb and curl the hand to look natural. To form a wrist, roll the paste between the fingers. Continue to roll and pinch out an elbow. Bend the arm and cut away a wedge on the inside of the upper arm so that it will sit well when attached to the body. Leave to dry. Roll out a little burgundy paste and cut a rough sleeve shape. Wrap around the upper arm and cut away the excess. Leave to dry. Attach the arms and head to the body with edible glue.

ANGEL'S WINGS

6   Thinly roll out a grape-size piece of white modelling paste. Using the template on page 292, carefully cut around the wings. Soften the cut edge with the ball tool. Mark the division between the feathers with the edge of a palette knife. Curve and support the wings in position with foam and leave to dry. Paint fine grey lines onto the feathers as shown, using black paste colouring. Dust the edges of the wings with cream and gold dusting powders and leave to dry. Attach the wings to the cake board with a little royal icing. Secure the angel onto the wings with a little royal icing.

BELLS

7   Shape a grape-size piece of modelling paste into a cone. Open up the end with a piece of dowel. Dust the outside with cornflour and drop into the mould. Continue to push the paste against the mould with the fingers until the paste is thin. Cut away the excess around the bottom of the bell. Using the scalpel, cut in half while still in the mould. Leave to dry, remove from the mould and paint gold. Make 10 bells and attach to the cake with royal icing.

BAUBLES

8   To make simple balls or elongated baubles, roll pea-size pieces of modelling paste into balls, then simply tease the paste out at the base by tweaking and pinching. Elongate by rolling between your index fingers. Cut away a slice at the back of each bauble so that it will sit on the cake. Place on cocktail sticks to hold while you paint patterns over the baubles with a fine brush.

9   To make the silver clasp, use a medium plunger cutter to create the shape. Rotate on the inside with the ball tool to exaggerate the cup shape. Paint silver and leave to dry. Attach to the top of the bauble with a dot of royal icing. Roll a thin strand of modelling paste and attach to the top of the bauble to form a ring. Leave to dry, then paint silver.

DRAPES AND BOWS

10   Colour 90 g (3 oz) modelling paste with red powder. Using the templates, cut out each drape. Soften the cut edges with the ball tool. Fold under the top and bottom edges. Form into folds with a cocktail stick and Dresden tool. Secure to the cake with edible glue. Trim and flatten the edge where the bow is to be attached so that it will sit neatly.

11   Using the templates, cut out all the bow shapes in red paste, soften the cut edges and attach with edible glue. Attach the baubles to the cake with royal icing. Using red modelling paste, form a fine strand. Thread through the silver ring on the bauble to form a circle. Attach another fine strand in a figure of eight. Shape to form a bow and fix to the cake with edible glue.

PRESENTS

12   Make an assortment of simple parcels and presents in modelling paste (see page 100–1). Cut away part of the back so that each shape will sit at an angle under the tree. Make some of the parcels in white or pastel colours and paint with interesting wrapping paper designs or decorate with a ribbon or bow. Trim the cake board with the ribbon, securing with double-sided tape.

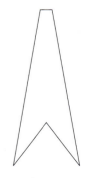

see templates page 292

3 Pipe the thinned royal icing into the different areas of the design, working from the back.

4 Flood the collar sections with thinned royal icing, piping straight lines onto the open section. Pipe dots between the straight lines.

5 Remove the kings from the paper and secure to the top of the cake with dots of royal icing.

see templates page 287

THREE KINGS

This beautiful, sophisticated cake is for those who are experienced at working with royal icing. The cake and board are both royal iced to give a sharp clear finish and the kings and collars are made using the runout technique.

20 x 15 cm (8 x 6 inch) oval fruit cake (use mixture for the 23 cm round cake)

1.25 kg (2^1/$_2$ lb) marzipan
1.5 kg (3 lb) royal icing
green, blue and gold food colourings

EQUIPMENT

25 x 20 cm (10 x 8 inch) oval cake board
glass or perspex square
number 1 piping tube
fine paintbrush
narrow pale blue ribbon

1   Cover the cake with marzipan and leave to dry. Cover the cake and board with royal icing and leave to dry. Secure the cake to the board with a little royal icing. Trace the template on page 287 onto non-stick baking paper.

RUNOUT KINGS

2   Attach the template to the glass or perspex with double-sided tape. Cover with non-stick baking paper or runout film, ensuring that there are no creases, and secure with tape.

3   Outline the figures with a number 1 tube and royal icing. Set aside a little icing for piping the collars, then thin the remainder with water until you can draw a knife through it and it will become smooth again after a count of ten. Colour a little of the icing with a touch of green food colouring and a little with a touch of blue. Leave the rest of the icing white. Put the icing into paper piping bags, snip off the ends and pipe into the different areas of the design, working from the back forwards. Ease the icing into the corners with a paint brush. Dry each area under a lamp to ensure it dries with a slight sheen. Leave to dry completely, then paint the patterns on the clothing with a fine, fairly dry brush. Paint in the gold areas. Leave to dry.

RUNOUT COLLARS

4   Trace the two collar templates from page 287 onto non-stick baking paper. Secure to glass or perspex with tape. Cover with non-stick baking paper or runout film, ensuring there are no creases, and secure with tape. Beat the reserved royal icing to stiff peak and use to outline each section and pipe the straight lines on the open sections. Flood each section with thinned white royal icing and dry under the lamp. Pipe dots between the straight lines. Leave to dry, then paint the dots gold. Pipe dots around each section to give a neat finish and leave these white. Leave to dry completely.

FINISHING TOUCHES

5   Remove the base collar sections from the non-stick baking paper with a palette knife and attach to the board with dots of royal icing. Remove the kings from the paper, position on top of the cake and secure in place with royal icing. Finally, carefully remove and attach the upper collar sections to the edge of the cake, using a little more royal icing for support. Trim the cake board with blue ribbon, securing in place with double-sided tape.

NOTE   Gold food colouring can sometimes be difficult to buy. If so, blend gold dusting powder with a little clear alcohol until it has the consistency of paint.

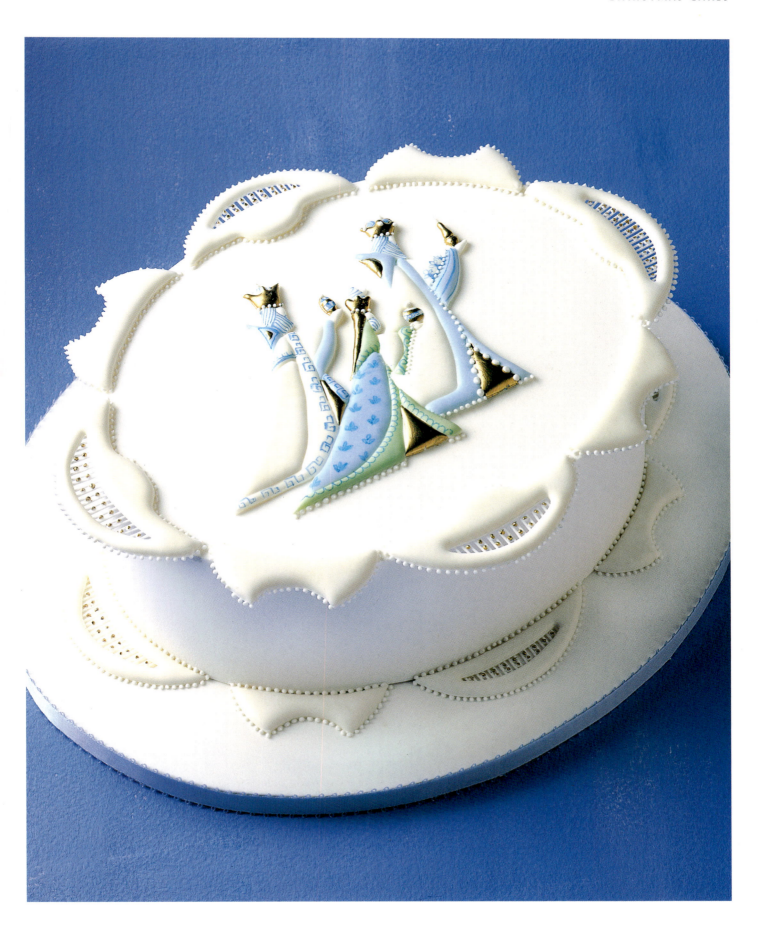

WEDDING CAKES

The cutting of the cake is a symbol of good luck for the bride and groom—the groom traditionally using his sword to help the bride cut through the royal icing. Classic wedding cakes are usually rich fruit cakes, covered with marzipan and white royal icing. Today's cakes come in many more guises—they can be decorated with bright sugarpaste, shaped into individual cake 'parcels', or even created from many-tiered chocolate mud cakes. Do remember though, that fruit cakes were traditionally used because they store well: an important consideration if the decorating is going to take some time or you want to keep the top tier of the cake.

1 Press your finger into the rounded end of each petal, making a hollow.

2 Prepare five petals for each flower, overlapping them slightly. Then gently roll them together, pinching the ends.

2 Put the flower into a padded egg carton to protect it while it dries and ease open the petals.

FRANGIPANI WEDDING CAKE

This cake is excellent for a beginner to decorating. The frangipani are simple flowers, requiring neatness and care rather then previous experience. Once dried, they can be stored in an airtight container for a month with chalk or a little rice to absorb any moisture.

30 cm (12 inch) and 15 cm (6 inch) round cakes

500 g (1 lb) flower paste
yellow chalk and green, brown and yellow food colourings
1.5 kg (3 lb) marzipan
1.5 kg (3 lb) cream-tinted sugarpaste
1 tablespoon royal icing

EQUIPMENT

medium frangipani petal cutter
medium long leaf cutter
40 cm (16 inch) and 15 cm (6 inch) round cake boards
4 wooden cake dowels
wide ribbon

FRANGIPANI

1 Roll a small amount of flower paste to 2 mm (1/8 inch) thick on a bench lightly dusted with cornflour. Working quickly, cut out petals with the frangipani cutter. Only cut 10 petals at a time (enough for two frangipani) and cover with plastic wrap. Dust your fingers lightly with cornflour and smooth the cut edges of the petals. Gently press your finger into the rounded end of the petal and make a slight hollow by easing your finger towards you.

2 Place a dab of water at the point of each petal and press the next petal, slightly overlapping, onto this. When you have prepared all five petals, gently roll together, pinching the ends to join. Put in a padded egg carton and ease the petals open to form a full flower. Make at least 20 flowers, all at varying degrees of opening. Make buds by rolling cigar shapes and pressing lines down the outside, then give a gentle twist. When the flowers are dry, dust the centres with a little yellow chalk.

LEAVES

3 Knead green food colouring into a little flower paste. Roll out thinly on a bench lightly dusted with cornflour and, with the long leaf cutter or a sharp knife, cut out leaves about 5 cm (2 inches) long. Gently press in half, then open out and mark veins on either side with the back of the knife. Twist at angles and leave to dry. Paint with green and brown colouring and a little water. Leave to dry for at least 24 hours.

ASSEMBLY

4 Cover the cakes with marzipan and leave to dry. Cover the cakes with cream sugarpaste and leave to dry for one day.

5 Secure the cakes on the boards with a little royal icing. Insert the wooden dowels into the centre of the larger cake, equally spaced so they will be covered by the top cake. Cut off the dowels level with the icing. Place the small cake on top, hiding the dowels.

6 Trim the base of each cake with ribbon, securing with a little double-sided tape. Arrange the frangipani flowers, buds and leaves on the cakes, securing with royal icing.

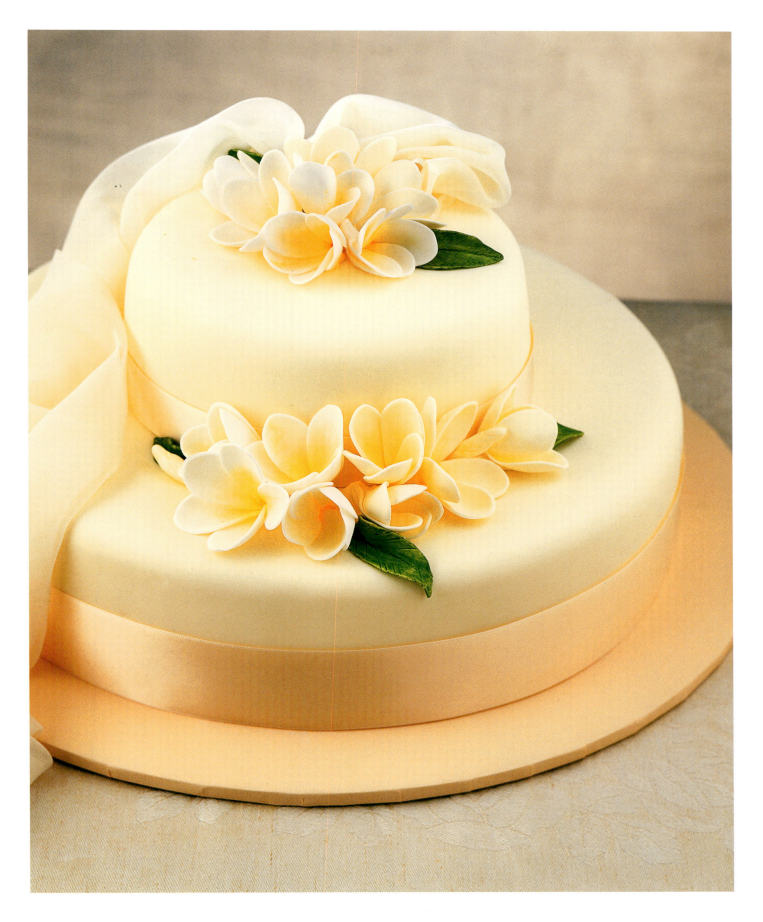

WRAPPED PRESENTS WEDDING CAKES

Add ribbon or white flowers to these wonderful individual wedding cakes. The cakes decorated with ribbon can be stored in an airtight container for two weeks. Decorate with fresh flowers close to the serving time.

1 Trim the edges of the cake and cut neatly into four smaller square cakes.

1 Mould the icing over the cakes, smoothing with your hands. Trim the excess icing.

2 Cut two lengths of ribbon long enough to reach from one side of the cake the the other and secure with royal icing.

23 cm (9 inch) square cake

500 g (1 lb) marzipan
500 g (1 lb) sugarpaste
ribbon and fresh flowers
1 tablespoon royal icing

1 Trim the edges of the cake neatly and turn upside down. Cut into quarters to make four small square cakes. Divide the marzipan and sugarpaste into four and use to cover the cakes. Leave the icing to dry for 24 hours before decorating. Decorate two of the cakes with ribbon bows and two with flowers.

DECORATING WITH RIBBON

2 Cut two lengths of ribbon long enough to reach from one side of the cake to the other, crossing over the top, and secure in place with royal icing. Cut another length and tie into a bow, sticking with icing. Secure the ribbon with pins while the icing dries, then stick the bow on the top of the cake.

DECORATING WITH FLOWERS

3 For the flower-decorated cakes, wrap a length of ribbon around the base of the cake and attach with royal icing, securing with pins until dry. Trim the flower stems, wrap the ends in plastic and arrange on top of the cake, securing with royal icing.

WHITE IVY

These simple roses and ivy leaves are made with cutters. The perspex cake boards mean decorative ivy can be seen under the cakes.

25 cm (10 inch), 20 cm (8 inch) and
15 cm (6 inch) teardrop-shaped cakes

2.5 kg (5 lb) marzipan
2 kg (4 lb) sugarpaste
30 g (1 oz) flower paste
185 g (6 oz) modelling paste
125 g (4 oz) royal icing

EQUIPMENT

varying sizes of ivy leaf cutters and leaf veiner
ball tool
6 cm (2¹/₂ inch) ring cutter
cloud-shaped perspex, 65 cm (26 inches) long x
55 cm (22 inches) at the widest point
narrow white satin ribbon
numbers 1 and 2 piping tubes
6 wired lily leaves
teardrop-shaped perspex, 50 cm (20 inches) long
perspex tubing or cake stand
silk variegated ivy and thin white paper ribbon

1   Cover the cakes with marzipan and leave to dry. Cover the cakes with sugarpaste and leave to dry for three days.

IVY LEAVES

2   Thinly roll out a medium-sized ball of flower paste and cut a selection of each size of ivy leaf. Soften the edges with a ball tool and dry slightly curved. You will need about 18 of each size leaf.

ROSES

3   Roll out a large ball of modelling paste and cut out five 6 cm (2¹/₂ inch) circles. Cover with plastic wrap. Take one circle and fold in half. Bring both corners down and into the centre to form a petal shape. Arrange the petals in a circle, overlapping slightly if necessary, and secure with water. Make five more petals and attach inside the first set.

4   Cut three more circles and fold two of them as above. Fold and roll the remaining circle into a tight bud shape, then wrap the two petals around it. Roll to thin the base and remove any surplus paste. Secure this in the centre of the other petals with water. Make five roses in this way.

5   Secure the largest cake to one end of the large piece of perspex with royal icing. Trim the base of the cake with white satin ribbon, securing with double-sided tape. Use the number 2 tube to pipe a snail trail of royal icing around the base of the cake.

POSITIONING THE IVY

6   Using the number 1 tube and royal icing, pipe a trailing ivy stem from the centre of the recess, around the curve of the cake and down onto the perspex. Attach the ivy leaves at intervals along the piped stem, starting with three large leaves in the recess, medium around the curve and then small ones on the perspex. Repeat on the other side.

POSITIONING THE ROSES

7   While still reasonably soft, position a rose in the curve of the teardrop so that it fits quite snugly. Secure with royal icing. Fold two lily leaves in half and tuck one in behind each side of the rose.

8   Attach the middle-sized cake to the other end of the perspex and decorate in the same way. Attach the smallest cake to the teardrop-shaped perspex and decorate in the same way. Attach a rose to the top of the smallest and largest cake with royal icing.

ASSEMBLY

9   Use perspex tubing or a clear stand to raise the lower tier. Raise the top tier above it with tubing or a clear glass. Arrange the silk ivy sprays under the perspex and twine the white paper ribbon around it. Or, drape the ivy and ribbon around the cakes.

Make the roses by folding circles in half, then bringing down the corners to make a petal.

Pipe a trailing ivy stem over the cake and onto the perspex, then attach the ivy leaves at intervals.

STENCILLED BOXES WEDDING CAKE

The all-over stencilling makes this an eye-catching design, perfect for those who feel that flower-making is not for them. Use paper or a covered board to practise stencilling and gauge the depth of colour before working on the cake.

30 cm (12 inch) and 20 cm (8 inch) square cakes

3.5 kg (7 lb) marzipan
3 kg (6 lb) cream-tinted sugarpaste
60 g (2 oz) soft-peak royal icing
cream dusting powder
375 g (12 oz) cream-tinted modelling paste
edible glue

EQUIPMENT

38 cm (15 inch) and 18 cm (7 inch) square thin
gold cake boards
large flower stencil
number 2 piping tube
narrow stiff gold net ribbon
florist's wire
spray of fresh or silk yellow roses

1   Cover the cakes with marzipan and leave to dry. Cover the cakes with the cream sugarpaste and leave to dry for three days. Attach the cakes to the boards with a little royal icing.

2   Hold the stencil firmly against the large cake and, using cream dusting powder lightened with cornflour if necessary, brush the colour onto the cake through the stencil. Lift the stencil away carefully without smudging the colour. Leave to dry, then place the small cake on top of the back corner of the larger cake and secure with royal icing (use wooden cake dowels to support it if you feel the bottom cake might begin to sag).

3   Using the number 2 piping tube and white or cream soft-peak royal icing, pipe a snail trail around the base of both cakes.

RIBBONS

4   Roll out the modelling paste quite thinly and cut a strip 3.5 cm (1½ inches) wide and long enough to fit up and over the side of the large cake. Secure with royal icing. Cut another strip and attach over the other side of the cake.

5   Roll out more modelling paste to cut ribbons for the smaller cake, but stencil and colour before cutting and attaching to the cake.

RIBBON LOOPS

6   You will need at least 25 loops of assorted sizes to achieve the size of bows shown. Some of the loops are stencilled and some are plain—the number and variety will depend on whether you want a largely plain bow or a highly patterned one. Cut strips 2.5 cm (1 inch) wide and 7.5 to 10 cm (3 to 4 inches) long, using an icing ruler to give straight edges. Brush one end of the strip with edible glue and wrap around small pieces of foam to form loops. For patterned loops, stencil the strips before folding.

ASSEMBLING THE BOWS

7   Arrange a minimum of five large loops in a circle (the foam can be left in) overlapping the flattened edges to join. Using royal icing or edible glue, attach further loops to the inside, decreasing in size, until a large bow is formed. Mix and match the stencilled and plain loops. When the loops are firm, remove the foam.

8   Cut pieces of gold net ribbon and form loops slightly smaller than those made of the paste. Use florist's wire to twist the ends together. Position these loops in the finished bow.

9   Arrange the spray of roses along one side of the cake board.

Hold the stencil firmly against the large cake and brush on the colour. Lift the stencil away carefully.

Stencil the ribbon for the small cake before cutting out the strips and attaching to the cake.

Make a variety of plain and stencilled loops, in different sizes.

GARLANDS AND TULLE WEDDING CAKE

This cake is really a matter of careful measuring and making dried flower garlands. If you are not confident at taping flowers together, turn to page 90. Bake the hexagonal cakes using the mixture quantities for the same diameter round cakes.

4 Fold the tulle into a long cylinder and then measure into lengths, tying off at intervals with ribbon.

5 Position the ribbon and tulle on the dab of royal icing at the corner of the cake and secure with a pin until dry.

6 Use a compass or draw around cake boards on a piece of paper in decreasing circles to make templates for the garlands.

9 Measure the depths of the largest three cakes and add a little to the measures. Transfer these to the hidden pillars.

30 cm (12 inch), 25 cm (10 inch), 20 cm (8 inch) and 15 cm (6 inch) hexagonal cakes

5 kg (10 lb) marzipan
5 kg (10 lb) ivory-tinted sugarpaste
150 g (5 oz) royal icing
ivory paste food colouring

EQUIPMENT

40 cm (16 inch), 30 cm (12 inch), 25 cm (10 inch), 20 cm (8 inch) hexagonal cake boards
number 1 piping tube
5.5 metres of 15 cm (6 inch) wide eggshell tulle
2.5 metres of 3 mm (^{1}/8 inch) wide ivory ribbon
24 glass-head pins
A3 paper, pencil and compass
silk flowers: 40 sprigs ivory gypsophila,
30 dark green ivy leaves, 19 large and 28 small dusky pink rosebuds, 16 large and 3 small claret rosebuds, 18 large and 13 small ivory rosebuds, 26 small pink rosebuds and 39 ivory pink freesias
wire cutters
dark green and white florist's tape
20-, 26- and 28-gauge dark green wires
28-gauge white wire
posy holder
9 hidden pillars
4.5 metres of 15 mm (^{5}/8 inch) wide ivory ribbon

1 Cover the cakes with marzipan and leave to dry. Cover the cakes with sugarpaste and leave to dry for one day. Secure the cakes to their boards. Gather up the icing trimmings and roll out into thin strips to cover the exposed parts of the boards, trimming off any excess. Leave to dry.

HAIL SPOTS

2 Colour the royal icing with the ivory food colouring to match the sugarpaste. Using a piping bag with a number 1 tube, pipe small dots all over the surface of each cake. When piping, use a gentle stabbing motion so the tube actually touches the cake. Keep an even pressure on the bag as you work, instead of squeezing and releasing. Leave to dry.

TULLE

3 To calculate for the pinched tulle around the base of each cake, measure across one side of each cake and multiply by six to get the circumference, then add 4 cm (1^1/2 inches) for an overlap. Cut four strips from the length of tulle measuring 125 cm (49 inches), 105 cm (41 inches), 90 cm (35^1/2 inches) and 72 cm (28 inches), leaving the rest for the top arrangement. Cut the 3 mm (^{1}/8 inch) ivory ribbon into 24 lengths of 10 cm (4 inches).

4 Take the longest length of tulle for the large cake and lay it out flat. Fold the long edges into the centre to make a long cylinder. Turn it over so the ends are underneath and measure 21 cm (8^1/2 inches) in from the left. Use your fingers to gather the tulle across its width at this point and tie a piece of ribbon around it into a double knot. Measure and tie off the tulle at five intervals, spaced 19 cm (7^1/2 inches) apart (if your measurements differ from this use your own measurements instead). Pipe a dab of icing on one of the corners at the back of the cake.

5 Position the first ribbon and tulle on the royal icing at the corner and secure with a glass-head pin. (Remove the pins when dry.) Work around the cake, securing at each corner in the same way until you get to the last corner. Place a piece of ribbon on the board (this is easier than threading the ribbon underneath and around with one hand), then overlap the ends of the tulle so that they meet at a corner and pinch the tulle together. Lift up the ends of the ribbon from behind and tie the ends around the tulle in a double knot. Trim the ends of the tulle close to the ribbon, and then trim all the ribbon ends to the same length. Repeat for the other cakes, tying ribbon at the following intervals: 16 cm (6^1/2 inch) intervals for the 25 cm (10 inch) cake, 13 cm (5 inch) intervals for the 20 cm (8 inch) cake and 9.5 cm (3^3/4 inch) intervals for the 15 cm (6 inch) cake (use your own measurements if different). Add 2 cm (^{3}/4 inch) onto the first interval to allow for the overlap.

FLOWER GARLANDS

6 Using a compass or round cake boards, draw four circles on a piece of paper in the following sizes: 30 cm (12 inches), 25 cm (10 inches), 20 cm (8 inches) and 11 cm (4^1/2 inches). These will make the templates for the flower garlands.

7   Commercial silk flowers either have very long stiff-wired stems or plastic floppy stems, neither of which bend very easily. To make them easier to work with, pull out the existing wire and replace it with a more pliable one. Take a piece of green wire and bend it in two, leaving a circle of wire at the bent end. Thread the two cut ends of wire into the centre of the flower and pull through: the circle of wire should stop it from going all the way through.

Wrap green tape along the length of the stem as close to the base of the flower as possible. Re-wire the large rosebuds with 26-gauge wire, the medium rosebuds with 28-gauge wire and snipped off single ivy leaves with 28-gauge wire. The smallest rosebuds do not need re-wiring—just tape them over. You will need 40 small sprigs of gypsophila on 28-gauge wire with white floristry tape, and 30 separate ivy leaves.

Refer to the chart (below) for the correct number of flowers per garland.

8   Wire the garland for the largest cake with 20-gauge wire. Tape a few larger flowers to the wire, and then a couple of the filler flowers, ivy and gypsophila. Every so often lay the wired flowers over the 30 cm (12 inch) template and bend to follow the curve. Group the larger flowers at evenly spaced intervals. When you have completed a circle, trim the wire, leaving about 5–8 cm (2–3 inches), and tape this securely to the starting point. Repeat for the other cakes. For the 15 cm (6 inch) cake, leave about 5 cm (2 inches) of wire at the beginning and the end, then tape them together to stick out at an angle of 90° to the garland, and insert the wire into a posy holder.

POSITIONING THE PILLARS

9   Measure the depth of the three largest cakes. Add 5 cm (2 inches) to the depth of the two largest cakes, and 4 cm (1¹/₂ inches) to the 20 cm (8 inch) cake, then transfer these measurements to the hidden pillars. Allow three pillars per cake. Mark a line around each pillar and follow this line when cutting, using a sawing motion, to create a level pillar.

10   Lay the garlands on each cake and place the pillars inside the garlands, inserting them into the cake. Insert the smallest garland into the top cake with a posy holder. Tie the remaining tulle into a bow. Thread 28-gauge white wire through the back and fix to the garland. Trim and neaten the tulle. Trim the cake boards with the wider ivory ribbon, securing with double-sided tape.

Garland sizes	30 cm (12 inch)	25 cm (10 inch)	20 cm (8 inch)	11 cm (4¹/₂ inch)
Gypsophila	12	12	8	8
Ivy	8	8	8	6
Dusky pink rosebuds				
Large	6	6	4	3
Small	12	6	4	6
Claret rosebuds				
Large	6	6	4	/
Small	/	/	/	3
Ivory rosebuds				
Large	12	6	/	/
Medium	/	6	4	3
Pale pink rosebuds				
small	8	6	6	6
Ivory pink freesia	15	6	12	6

CHOCOLATE ROSES WEDDING CAKE

For colour contrast, the flowers and leaves could be made in white chocolate or, for a winter wedding, the whole cake can be made in white chocolate and dusted with icing sugar. If you have never made chocolate paste roses before, turn to page 80 for full instructions.

15 cm (6 inch), 20 cm (8 inch) and
25 cm (10 inch) round chocolate or mud cakes

2.25 kg (4¹/₂ lb) marzipan
2.25 kg (4¹/₂ lb) chocolate sugarpaste
2 tablespoons royal icing
180 g (6 oz) chocolate modelling paste
250 g (8 oz) dark chocolate, melted
36 chocolate leaves in various sizes (page 116)

EQUIPMENT

20 cm (8 inch), 25 cm (10 inch) and 30 cm
(12 inch) round silver cake boards
6 wooden cake dowels
6 clear cake pillars
number 0 or 1 piping tube

1   Cover the cakes with marzipan and leave to dry. Cover the cakes with chocolate sugarpaste and secure on the boards with a little royal icing. Gather up the icing trimmings and roll out into thin strips to cover the exposed parts of the boards, trimming off any excess. Leave the icing to dry for three days.

CHOCOLATE ROSES

2   Gently knead the chocolate modelling paste until firm but pliable. Pull off a grape-sized piece of paste and shape into a cone. Press onto a work surface and form a 'waist' in the cone near the base. Take another piece of paste about half the size of the cone and press it as flat as possible, to make a petal. Secure this around the cone, from the waist upwards. Shape another, slightly larger, petal and wrap this around the first, overlapping it slightly.

3   Continue building up the rose, making each petal slightly larger than the previous one, until you have a rose with about seven or eight petals. Bend and tuck the outer petals into a realistic shape. Once complete, cut off at the 'waist' just below the petals. Vary the sizes of the roses a little. Make buds using just three or four petals and securing them tightly around the cone. You will need about 18 roses.

POSITIONING THE PILLARS

4   Mark the position for the dowels and pillars on the middle and bottom tiers of the cake, by cutting a 10 cm (4 inch) circle of paper and folding it into thirds. Open out the circle again and lay over the centre of the middle tier. Prick around the edge of the paper where each crease ends, to mark three points for the dowels. Repeat this for the bottom tier, using a 13 cm (5 inch) circle of paper.

5   Press the dowels down to the base of the cake through the marks. Place the pillars over the dowels and mark the top of the pillar on the dowel. Remove the pillar and cut off the dowel at that point. Replace the pillars over the dowels.

PIPING THE EDGING

6   Cut out a strip of greaseproof paper to fit the circumference of each cake. Fold each strip in half 3 times so that when the paper is unfolded, it will be neatly marked into 8 sections. Open out the end section and lay it over the template on page 289. Trace along the dotted line. Refold the template and cut along the dotted line so that the strip is scalloped when opened out. Use a pin to fasten the paper template around the base of each tier, with the straight edge against the base. Then prick out the scalloped line with another pin.

7   Melt the dark chocolate. Put a little of it in a piping bag fitted with a number 0 or 1 tube. Pipe a snail trail around each cake base and scalloped line. Leave to set.

ASSEMBLY

8   Arrange the chocolate roses and leaves around the pillars and on the top of the cake, securing them with a little piped melted chocolate. Assemble the smaller cakes on their pillars.

NOTES   Before decorating, you can drizzle the cakes with brandy or an orange-flavoured liqueur.
The chocolate roses can be made several weeks in advance and stored in an airtight container. Chocolate leaves can be stored for up to three days.
If you prefer solid cake pillars to clear ones, trim the dowels level with the top of the icing and sit the pillars over the top.

Press the dowels into the cake and cover with pillars. Mark the top of the pillar on the dowel.

Prick out a scalloped line on the cake with a pin and template. Pipe a snail trail around the base and over the scalloped line.

Use melted chocolate in a piping bag to secure the roses around the pillars. Arrange the leaves around the roses.

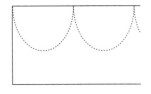

see template page 289

237

3 Lay the paste over the negative side of the mould, then press the positive side on top. Remove and trim.

4 Attach the lace pieces over the corners of the cake and in the centre of each side. Attach a second piece at each corner.

VICTORIAN LACE WEDDING CAKE

This cake is decorated with full lace sections and roses made from a mixture of sugarpaste and white chocolate sugarpaste—easier to work with than chocolate sugarpaste but retaining the chocolate flavour.

15 cm (6 inch), 20 cm (8 inch) and
25 cm (10 inch) square cakes

3 kg (6 lb) marzipan
1.75 kg (3¹/₂ lb) sugarpaste
1.75 kg (3¹/₂ lb) white chocolate sugarpaste
1 tablespoon royal icing
edible glue
red petal creams
green paste food colours

EQUIPMENT

23 cm (9 inch), 28 cm (11 inch) and 36 cm
(14 inch) square cake boards, covered with
dark pink foil
clay gun with discs, optional
silicone lace mould
8 wooden cake dowels
8 cake pillars
plastic sheets
small and medium rose leaf cutters
narrow dark pink ribbon

1 Cover the cakes with marzipan and leave to dry. Knead together the sugarpaste and white chocolate sugarpaste. Roll out on a work surface dusted with icing sugar and cover the cakes. Remove the excess chocolate sugarpaste mix, keeping the trimmings wrapped in plastic. Leave to dry for three days. Secure the cakes to the boards with royal icing.

BASE BORDERS AND LACE

2 Using a clay gun or by hand, make thin twisted ropes of chocolate sugarpaste mix and attach with edible glue to the base of each cake.

3 For the lace, roll out some chocolate sugarpaste mix 2.5 mm (¹/₈ inch) thick and lay it over the negative side of the mould, pressing the paste into the mould. Place the positive side of the mould on top and press. Remove the paste section from the mould and trim to size. The number of lace pieces needed will vary according to the size of the cake and mould. Hold the mould against each cake to work out how many pieces you will need and whether they will need to be trimmed to fit. Most cakes will need 12 pieces of lace.

4 With edible glue, paint the underside of each piece of lace and attach around the sides and on the corner of each cake. Position a lace piece at the corner of each cake, then another piece in the middle of each side. Then attach another piece at the corner of each cake, creating a layered effect.

POSITIONING THE PILLARS

5 Insert four wooden dowels into the centre of each of the two larger cakes, equally spaced so they will be covered by the cake above. Cut off the dowels level with the icing and place a pillar over the top of each dowel. Cut out four extra sections of lace for the top of each cake (for the flowers to be placed on) and arrange on top of the cakes, positioning neatly between the pillars.

ROSES AND BUDS

6 Shape a cone of chocolate sugarpaste mix and shape eight balls the size of marbles. Cut another piece that is twice as large as the others to form the bud petal. The size of the cone and balls of paste will determine the size of the finished rose.

7 Place the balls of paste between plastic sheets and thin half of each with your thumb or finger. It is important to leave the base of each petal thick. Remove the top sheet of plastic and peel off the 'bud' petal. For the cream-coloured roses, tint the edge of the petal slightly by gently rubbing with a small amount of red petal cream.

8 Place the cone a quarter of the way in from the left-hand edge of the petal and 2.5 mm (¹/₈ inch) down from the top edge. Wrap the left-hand half of the petal around the cone to the front, making sure that the bud forms a sharp point at the top. Wrap the larger right-hand half around to the front, curling the edge of the petal back when you have completely enclosed the cone.

9 For a bud, roll the base between your fingers and cut off the excess paste. For a full rose, release another petal from the plastic, tint the edge as before and place on the bud, covering the curled back edge of the first petal and cupping around the bud. Add two more petals to encircle the bud. Each petal should overlap the previous one slightly. The bud and petals should be at the same height.

10 Attach another five petals, curling their edges back slightly and tinting to give an open look. Dry for a few minutes, then roll the base of the rose between your fingers and cut off the excess paste.

LEAVES

11 Colour 60 g (2 oz) chocolate sugarpaste mix pale green. Roll out and cut a selection of rose leaves. Thin the edges, vein and pinch into shape with your fingers. Leave to dry. With a small amount of red petal cream on your fingers, wipe the set leaves to shade the edges.

ASSEMBLY

12 Arrange the roses, buds and leaves in the centre of each cake, on top of the lace pieces, securing with a little melted white chocolate. Trim the cake boards with the ribbon, securing with double-sided tape.

NOTE If you don't have a lace mould, impress the soft paste with a piece of lace and cut out.

AUTUMN GOLD CHOCOLATE WEDDING CAKE

More brides are choosing their cakes for flavour as well as looks and chocolate cakes are becoming ever more fashionable. This two-tiered cake doesn't use dowels for support. We've chosen golden yellow chrysanthemums but you can make them any colour you like.

18 cm (7 inch) and 25 cm (10 inch) round cakes

1.5 kg (3 lb) marzipan
750 g (1¹/₂ lb) sugarpaste
850 g (1 lb 12 oz) dark chocolate sugarpaste
2 tablespoons royal icing
edible glue
250 g (8 oz) white chocolate sugarpaste
paste food colourings

EQUIPMENT

36 cm (14 inch) round cake board, covered with
bronze foil
clay gun with discs, optional
plastic sheets
small bow cutter
set of 3 daisy cutters
ball tool
foam pads
chrysanthemum leaf cutter set
Dresden tool

1   Cover the cakes with marzipan and leave to dry. Knead the sugarpaste with 750 g (1¹/₂ lb) of the dark chocolate sugarpaste. Roll out on a work surface dusted with icing sugar and cover the cakes, keeping the trimmings. Leave to dry for three days. Secure the large cake to the board with royal icing.

2   Divide each cake into eight equal sections by cutting a piece of paper the size of the top of each cake. Fold the paper into quarters then open out over the cake. Mark with a pin at the end of each fold. Cut a disc of non-stick baking paper smaller than the small cake and place it on top of the large cake, off-centre. Place the small cake on the disc.

3   Roll out the trimmings of the chocolate sugarpaste mix and cut two strips 5 mm (¹/₄ inch) wide. Secure around the cake bases with edible glue.

ROPE CORDS

4   Using a clay gun or by hand, make rope cords with 100 g (3¹/₂ oz) of the dark chocolate paste trimmings. Twist the rope. Make eight lengths of 15 cm (6 inch) twisted rope, and eight lengths of 10 cm (4 inch) rope for the small cake. Cover.

5   Brush edible glue on each of the eight marks around the tops of the cakes. Drape a piece of rope between two of the marks, attaching it at each end. Trim the ends. Repeat with the remaining ropes.

BOWS

6   Roll out the remaining dark chocolate sugarpaste and cut out 16 bows with the cutter. Secure a bow to every point where the ropes meet.

CHRYSANTHEMUMS

7   Colour most of the white chocolate sugarpaste in a couple of shades, using paste colours. To make the first chrysanthemum, roll some paste to 2.5 mm (¹/₈ inch) thick. Using graduated daisy cutters, cut out three large, three medium and two small daisies. Cut each petal in half, so each daisy has 16 petals.

8   Lightly dust your hand with cornflour and place a large daisy in your palm. With a ball tool, gently draw each petal from the centre out to the tip to lengthen and widen. Keep the petal moving so the paste doesn't stick. Place on a firm foam pad and, with the small end of the ball tool, draw each petal from the tip in towards the centre to cup the ends. Place on a work surface dusted with cornflour.

9   Repeat with the remaining two large daisies. Glue the centre of the first daisy and place the second on top, turning to stagger the petals. Gently fix with the large end of the ball tool. Add the third large daisy, then repeat with the medium and small daisies. As the petals become smaller, cup the ends more, to create a tighter array that hides the centre of the flower. Make as many chrysanthemums as you need.

LEAVES

10   Tint the rest of the white chocolate sugarpaste green and cut a selection of different-sized leaves. Place on a firm foam pad. Using a Dresden tool, mark veins on the leaves and, with the large end of the ball tool, thin the edges slightly. Place on a soft foam pad to shape and leave to dry.

ASSEMBLY

11   Position the leaves and flowers first on a board, angling the large flower heads with a wedge of chocolate paste. Attach the leaves to the cake first, and then the flowers with edible glue or royal icing.

Use the cutter to make bows of dark chocolate sugarpaste and place where the ropes meet.

Use a set of three graduated daisy cutters to make chrysanthemums, curling the petals with a ball tool.

LILIES AND LARKSPUR WEDDING CAKE

Yellow and white make a pleasant change from the more traditional white wedding cake. The lily theme is reflected in the royal icing runouts. The edging is made by folding the soft icing with a skewer and the lilies are made using the runout technique.

2 Use squared paper and a pin to mark the cakes and boards. Pipe the clusters of dots with royal icing.

4 Press the skewer onto the centre of the raised paste to make two folds. Repeat down the length of the paste, leaving uneven gaps.

8 Pipe the outline of the run-out with soft peak icing and then thin down the icing to flood the flowers. Work on alternate petals.

see templates page 298

---

25 cm (10 inch) round cake and
20 x 15cm (8 x 6 inch) oval cake (use mixture
for 20 cm round cake)

250 g (8 oz) sugarpaste
2.5 kg (5 lb) marzipan
2 kg (4 lb) yellow-tinted sugarpaste
125 g (4 oz) soft-peak royal icing
yellow colouring
125 g (4 oz) yellow-tinted modelling paste

EQUIPMENT

33 cm (13 inch) round cake board
28 x 23 cm (11 x 9 inch) oval cake board
1 cm (1/2 inch) squared paper
glass-head pin
numbers 0 and 1 piping tubes
wooden skewer
spray of fresh lilies and larkspur
wired ribbon loops and organza bows
narrow yellow ribbon
perspex cake stand

1   Cover the cake boards with the white sugarpaste and leave to dry. Cover the cakes with marzipan and leave to dry. Cover the cakes with yellow sugarpaste. Leave to dry for three days. Attach the cakes to the boards with royal icing.

2   Using squared paper and a glass-head pin, prick through the paper onto the surface of the cakes and the boards, marking 2.5 cm (1 inch) squares.

3   Using soft-peak royal icing and a number 0 tube, pipe clusters of three tiny dots, making sure one dot covers the pin prick. Pipe white dots on the yellow cakes and then tint the icing yellow to pipe the dots on the cake boards.

EDGING THE CAKES

4   Roll out 30 g (1 oz) yellow modelling paste and cut a strip 2.5–5 cm (1–2 inches) wide. Slide a wooden skewer under one end of the strip of paste and lift a small section. Holding the paste, press the skewer down onto the centre of the raised section to form two folds. Repeat down the length of the paste, leaving small, uneven gaps between the folds.

5   Fold the paste in half widthways and press the long edges lightly together. Press the folded side of the paste against an icing ruler to lift. Attach to the cake board with the flat edge tucked against the base of the cake. Continue around the edge of both cakes. To join sections, leave one end open and fold the edges under. Pinch the end of the section to be attached, form into a point and slot into the open end of the first section.

LILY RUNOUTS

6   Trace the two lily templates on page 298 onto two separate pieces of paper. Place on a piece of perspex or glass and cover with non-stick baking paper. Smooth out until perfectly flat and secure with masking tape. Using soft-peak royal icing and the number 1 tube, pipe the outline of the designs.

7   Thin some royal icing with water. Half-fill a medium piping bag with the run-out icing (no tube is required). Snip off the end of the bag (to the size of a number 2 tube) and squeeze the icing into another bag to get rid of the air bubbles.

8   Cut the same amount off this bag and pipe inside the outline to flood the lilies. Work on alternate petals so that they can dry slightly and crust over without running into each other. Dry under a lamp to obtain a sheen. Leave to dry completely, then carefully remove from the paper and attach to the cakes with a little royal icing.

ASSEMBLING THE CAKE

9   Wire the lilies, leaves, larkspur and wired ribbon loops together to make two similar sprays. Secure them to a piece of modelling paste directly on the large cake board, with one spray standing up behind the other. Attach wired organza bows to hide the paste and cover the base of the sprays. Trim both boards with the yellow ribbon, securing with double-sided tape. Arrange the top cake, slightly offset, on a perspex stand.

SPRINGTIME DAFFODILS WEDDING CAKE

Tiny daffodils and elegant pleats make a striking combination with a spring theme. The sugar daffodils and filler flowers can be found on page 78, but to make this cake suitable for those without much experience, simply arrange a spray of fresh flowers on the top cake.

25 cm (10 inch), 20 cm (8 in) and 15 cm (6 inch) hexagonal cakes (use mixture for same size round cakes)

4 kg (8 lb) marzipan
3 kg (6 lb) cream-tinted sugarpaste
125 g (4 oz) soft-peak royal icing
500 g (1 lb) cream-tinted modelling paste
30 g (1 oz) yellow-tinted flower paste
green and yellow food colourings

EQUIPMENT

33 cm (13 inch), 28 cm (11 inch) and 23 cm (9 inch) hexagonal cake boards
foam pad and thin wooden skewers
small snowdrop cutter
edible glue
number 0 and two number 1 piping tubes
8 wooden cake dowels
8 clear perspex pillars
20 wired daffodils (page 78)
15 white filler flowers
12 small white buds
wired green and cream ribbon loops
wired tulle and gypsophila
narrow white ribbon

1   Cover the cakes with marzipan and leave to dry. Cover the cakes and boards with the cream sugarpaste. Leave to dry for three days. Attach the cakes to the boards with a little royal icing.

PLEATING

2   Cut thin card templates twice as long as one side of each cake and slightly less than half the depth in width. Scribe a line around the sides of the cakes using the template and a pin.

3   Roll out a large ball of cream modelling paste and cut a strip using the template. Put the paste on the foam pad. Hold a wooden skewer in each hand and, working from the top, press the skewers down firmly into the paste. Slide the bottom skewer up to meet the top one. This will make a pleat. Move the skewers down and repeat until the full section of paste is pleated. Press firmly along one side to hold all the pleats in place. Trim to give a straight edge.

4   Attach the strip of pleating to the cake with a little water along the scribed line, starting in the middle of one side to ensure there will be no joins on the corners. Continue all the way around the cakes and leave to dry overnight.

DAFFODILS

5   Roll out a small ball of yellow flower paste quite thinly. Using the snowdrop cutter, cut six flowers. Ball around the edges and pinch at the tip to form a point, then glue one flower on top of another so that six petals are visible.

6   To make a trumpet, form a tiny cone of paste, then open up and thin the narrow end with the celpin. Attach to the top of the six petals to finish the daffodil. Repeat to make 18 flowers. Leave to dry. Attach one daffodil with royal icing to the centre of each side of the cakes, just above the pleating.

SIDE PIPING

7   Half-fill a piping bag fitted with a number 0 tube with white royal icing. Colour half the remaining icing green and half yellow and fill two paper piping bags fitted with number 1 tubes. Pipe two buds on either side of each daffodil with the yellow icing, and white dots and green and lemon buds around the sides.

POSITIONING THE PILLARS

8   Insert four wooden dowels into the centre of each of the two larger cakes, equally spaced so they are centred below the cake above. Cut off the dowels level with the icing and place a pillar over the top of each dowel.

ASSEMBLING THE CAKE

9   Make up a posy with the wired daffodils, filler flowers, buds, ribbon loops, tulle and gypsophila. Place in the centre of the small cake and attach a tiny strip of pleating around its base.

10   Trim the cake boards with the white ribbon, securing with double-sided tape. Layer the cakes on their pillars.

NOTE   If you can see the top of the dowels through the clear pillars, paint them to match the sugarpaste.

Attach the strip of pleats to the cake with water, ensuring there are no joins on the corners.

Cut flowers with the snowdrop cutter, then ball around the edges of the petals. Glue another flower on top.

Pipe two yellow buds on either side of each daffodil and white dots, green and yellow buds around the sides of the cake.

LOVE'S DREAM WEDDING CAKE

Pink is a popular choice for many brides, often matching the colour of the bridesmaids' dresses or the bridal bouquet. The soft pleating and subtle brush embroidery make this a very pretty cake for those with some previous experience of sugarcraft.

2

Measure around each cake to determine how much of the stencil design will fit into each quarter.

6

Pleat the pink modelling paste with wooden skewers. Flatten down one long side and trim to a neat edge.

7

Moisten the icing where the cake meets the board and attach the pleated strip with a little water.

25 x 20 cm (10 x 8 inch), 20 x 15 cm (8 x 6 inch)
and 15 x 10 cm (6 x 4 inch) oval cakes (use mixture
for 25 cm, 20 cm and 15 cm round cakes)

2.75 kg (5$^{1}/_{2}$ lb) marzipan
2 kg (4 lb) pale pink-tinted sugarpaste
125 g (4 oz) soft-peak royal icing
1$^{1}/_{2}$ teaspoons piping gel
250 g (8 oz) pale pink-tinted modelling paste

EQUIPMENT
33 x 28 cm (13 x 11 inch), 28 x 23 cm
(11 x 9 inch) and 23 x 18 cm (9 x 7 inch) oval
cake boards
flower side stencil (see Note)
number 1 or 0 piping tube
foam pad
thin wooden skewers
assorted fresh or sugar flowers, buds and leaves
sprays of fresh or sugar ivy
claret florist's wire
narrow white ribbon
perspex cake stand

1   Cover the cakes with marzipan and leave to dry. Cover the cakes and boards with sugarpaste. Leave to dry for three days. Attach the cakes to the boards with a little royal icing.

2   Measure the circumference of each cake to determine how much of the stencil design will fit into each quarter. Hold the stencil carefully against the side of the cake with the bottom edge resting on the board. Transfer the design to the side of the cake by scribing around the inside edge of the pattern. Adjust the position of the stencil to centre the design within each quarter section of the cake.

BRUSH EMBROIDERY
3   Add the piping gel to the royal icing and fill a small parchment piping bag fitted with a number 1 or 0 piping tube (either tube is quite acceptable for brush embroidery—the choice will depend on your skill and confidence in piping with a number 0 tube).

4   Have ready a damp cloth, a small container of water and a fine paintbrush. Working on one leaf or

flower shape at a time, pipe around the scribed outline. Pipe a second line on top of the first. Dampen the paintbrush, flatten the tip between finger and thumb and draw the second piped line into the centre. Lift off any surplus icing with the paintbrush. Repeat around all the cakes.

5   Tilt the cakes and pipe the scribed underline with the number 1 tube. Add three small dots to the line work above each reverse design.

PLEATING
6   Roll out a piece of pink modelling paste. Place an icing ruler or strip of card lightly on the paste and cut a strip of paste. Lift the strip onto a foam pad. Hold a wooden skewer in each hand and, working from the top, press the skewers down firmly into the paste. Slide the bottom skewer up to meet the top one. This will make a pleat. Move the skewers down and repeat until the full strip of paste is pleated. Flatten a little along one side to hold all the pleats in place. Trim to give a straight edge.

7   Moisten the icing where the cake joins the board with water and attach the pleated section, with the flattened edge touching the cake.

8   Repeat the pleating until the base of each cake has been trimmed.

ASSEMBLING THE CAKE
9   Wire together the flowers and leaves to make three sprays (page 90). Loop the florist's wire at the back of each spray and leave trailing, slightly twisted, at the front with the ivy. Secure a small ball of soft modelling paste or sugarpaste to each cake. Arrange a spray, offset in the ball of paste, on the top of each cake. Trim the cake boards with the ribbon, securing with double-sided tape. Arrange the cakes off-set on a perspex stand.

NOTE   There are many different designs available for side stencilling. Simply choose one that suits your choice of flowers for this cake.

BRODERIE ANGLAISE WEDDING CAKE

Soft pinks are in order for this dainty cake. Add the colouring to the icing a drop at a time to ensure subtle pastel colours. The broderie anglaise design adds colour and texture and requires an experienced hand with the piping bag.

20 cm (8 inch) and 15 cm (6 inch) round cakes

1.75 kg (3½ lb) marzipan
1.25 kg (2½ lb) sugarpaste
500 g (1 lb) pink-tinted sugarpaste
60 g (2 oz) soft-peak royal icing
250 g (8 oz) pink-tinted modelling paste
edible glue
claret food colouring

EQUIPMENT

28 cm (11 inch) and 23 cm (9 inch) round
cake boards
plaque cutter
plunger blossom cutters
small leaf cutter
numbers 0, 1, 2 and 3 piping tubes
celpin
4 wooden cake dowels
4 clear perspex pillars
10 large pale pink silk roses
about 12 sugar or silk leaves
8 pink net ribbon loops
gypsophila
posy holder
narrow white ribbon

1   Cover the cakes with marzipan and leave to dry. Cover the cakes with white sugarpaste and leave to dry for three days. Cover the cake boards with pink sugarpaste and leave to dry. Attach the cakes to the boards with a little royal icing.

BRODERIE ANGLAISE

2   Roll out a golf ball size piece of pink modelling paste and, using the plaque cutter, cut one shaped piece. Cut in half lengthways with a sharp knife.

3   Cut out a centre flower from the plaque, using the largest of the plunger blossom cutters, then cut out two small leaves on either side. Cut out tiny holes around the top edge using the number 3 piping tube or a drinking straw. Prick the paste in between these holes with the celpin. Make 16 plaques and cover with plastic wrap to prevent drying out.

4   Measure the circumference of the large cake and divide into quarters. Mark the quarters on the side of the cake near the base. Now mark quarters on the top of the cake, falling between the quarters marked on the side. Repeat with the smaller cake.

5   Brush the backs of the plaques sparingly with edible glue and attach four to the top of the large cake, placing each plaque over a marked point. Attach four more plaques around the base of the cake over the marked points, with the flat edge touching the board. Repeat with the smaller cake, decorating with the remaining eight plaques.

6   Using a number 0 or 1 tube and white royal icing, pipe a flower, dot and scroll design around the edges of the plaques. Pipe the same design between the plaques on the base of the smaller cake.

7   Colour some royal icing pink with a touch of claret food colouring. Using the number 2 tube, pipe a snail trail around the base of the cakes between the plaques. Repeat the flower and dot design in pink icing between the plaques on top of the cakes.

POSITIONING THE PILLARS

8   Insert four wooden dowels into the centre of the larger cake, equally spaced so they are centred below the cake above. Cut off the dowels level with the icing and place a pillar over each dowel.

ASSEMBLING THE CAKE

9   Make up a posy with the roses, leaves, ribbon loops and gypsophila and attach to the top of the small cake with a posy holder. Trim the cake boards with the white ribbon, securing with double-sided tape. Arrange the cakes on their pillars.

NOTE   If you can see the top of the wooden dowels through the clear pillars, paint them to match the sugarpaste.

Cut out the eight shapes with the plaque cutter then cut each in half length-ways to make 16 plaques.

Decorate the broderie anglaise by cutting a central flower, then leaves on either side. Use a piping tube or straw to cut holes.

Attach four plaques of broderie anglaise around the top of each cake and pipe a design below each.

4   Turn over the paste with the stencil still attached and sponge the leaves green and the roses pink.

9   Pipe the scalloped bridge-work until it has seven lines and then pipe a flower and leaf design above the scallops.

10   Pipe extension lines down from the scribed top line to connect with the outer edge of the bridge work. Keep the lines straight.

ROSEBUD WEDDING CAKE

Delicate coloured piping and extension work complement the rosebud sprays and striking stencilled side decoration. Piping extension work with royal icing is a technique for experienced decorators, with more instructions on page 75.

25 x 20 cm (10 x 8 inch), 20 x 15 cm (8 x 6 inch) and 15 x 10 cm (6 x 4 inch) oval cakes (use mixture for 25 cm, 20 cm and 15 cm round cakes

2.75 kg (5$^{1}/_{2}$ lb) marzipan
2 kg (4 lb) cream-tinted sugarpaste
125 g (4 oz) soft-peak royal icing
tiny amount each of white petal cream and white vegetable fat
green and claret paste colourings
60 g (2 oz) cream-tinted modelling paste

EQUIPMENT
33 x 28 cm (13 x 11 inch), 28 x 23 cm (11 x 9 inch) and 23 x 18 cm (9 x 7 inch) oval cake boards
rose embosser
miniature wreath stencil (rose design)
pale pink sugar roses and buds
white sugar blossoms and buds
assorted sugar leaves and filler flowers
wired ribbon loops
narrow pink and white ribbon

1   Cover the cakes with marzipan and leave to dry. Cover the cakes and boards with cream sugarpaste. Emboss the sugarpaste around the edge of the boards with the rose embosser. Leave to dry for three days. Secure the cakes to the boards with a little royal icing.

2   Measure around each cake and lightly mark the centre front, back and sides at the base. Trace the templates on page 300 and scribe onto the sides of the cakes, using the centre side mark to position.

ROSE STENCIL
3   Mix together the white petal cream and white vegetable fat on a scraper. Add a small amount of green paste to half to tint it pale green. Tint the other half pale pink with the claret colouring.

4   Press a small piece of modelling paste onto the stencil firmly enough for the raised design to show through the cut-out sections. Turn over the modelling paste with the stencil still attached and, using a small piece of sponge dipped in the green,

dab lightly to colour the leaf sections. Colour the rose cut-outs pale pink with a clean sponge.

5   Carefully remove the stencil and cut out the wreath shape with a craft knife or scalpel. Place on foam and leave to dry.

6   Colour and cut a further five wreaths so you have six in total (two for each cake). When dry, attach one to the front and back of each cake with a little royal icing.

7   Use a number 2 tube and soft-peak royal icing to pipe a snail trail around the base of each cake.

BRIDGE WORK
8   Using a number 1 tube and soft-peak royal icing, begin piping the bridge work over the scribed lines on the sides of the cakes (see page 75). Raise the cake so that you can work at eye level if possible. Work on the sides of each cake until each scallop has its first base line. Leave to dry. Pipe a second line on top of the first, using a fine damp paintbrush to guide any loose ends into place. Clean the tube before commencing each new line to prevent bulbs forming. The bridge work should consist of seven lines. Leave to dry completely.

9   Using a number 1 tube and pink- and green-tinted royal icing, pipe small pink and green flower and leaf designs above the scallops. This will show through the completed extension work.

EXTENSION WORK
10   Start piping lines from the scribed top line of the design down to the outer edge of the bridge work. Pipe the lines as close together as you can—the gap between the lines should be the same width as the piping. Keep the lines completely straight.

11   When the extension work is complete on all the cakes, finish the bottom edge by piping an additional scalloped line over the top of the extension work. Pipe over the top edge of the middle scallops and pipe a second scallop slightly below, resting on the extension work. Repeat the coloured flower and leaf design on the outer edges of the extension work and above the highest points of the scallops.

ASSEMBLING THE CAKE

12   Wire together the flowers and leaves to make two sprays for the larger cakes (see page 90). For the top tier make two small mixed sprays, secure to a piece of modelling paste and curve in at the top to make a horseshoe shape. Attach to the centre of the top tier and attach more flowers, leaves and ribbon loops at the base. Attach the sprays to the centre of the other two tiers, poking them into small balls of soft sugarpaste. Trim the large and small cake boards with pink ribbon, securing with double-sided tape, and the middle board with white ribbon. Arrange the cakes offset on perspex stands.

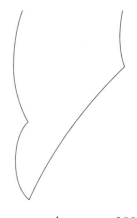

see templates page 300

LILY-OF-THE-VALLEY WEDDING CAKE

This small but elegant wedding cake is ideal for those who are confident with their piping techniques. The cake is iced with royal icing to give a smooth sharp finish and then the icing pattern built up using a template and piped lines of decreasing width.

20 x 15 cm (8 x 6 inch) oval cake (use mixture for a 20 cm round cake)

900 g (1 lb 13 oz) marzipan
1 kg (2 lb) royal icing
green food colouring

EQUIPMENT

25 x 20 cm (10 x 8 inch) oval cake board
numbers 0, 1, 2, 3, 42 and 44 piping tubes
narrow cream ribbon

1   Cover the cake with marzipan and leave to dry. Apply three layers of royal icing, drying between coats. Coat the board with royal icing and leave to dry. Secure the cake to the board with royal icing.

PIPING THE EDGING AND FLOWERS

2   Trace the top design template on page 298 onto non-stick baking paper, cut out and secure in position on top of the cake. Fit a piping bag with a number 3 tube and pipe a line of royal icing around the edge of the template. Then pipe a line inside the first line, using a number 2 tube. Finally, pipe a line inside the second line, using a number 1 tube.

3   Following the curves of the linework, pipe one large 'S' and two 'C' scrolls with a number 44 tube. For the 'S' scroll, start with strong pressure and rotate the tube towards the centre of the cake in an up and over movement. Decrease the pressure to form the end of the scroll, finishing by pulling the icing into a tail. For the 'C' scroll, pipe a 'C' shape, beginning with a bulb and rotating the tube out, decreasing the pressure so that the icing forms a fine tail. Following the remaining curve, pipe a row of shells with a number 44 tube along the opposite edge of the cake.

4   Pipe the mirrored pattern on the base edge of the cake and board with a number 44 tube.

5   Overpipe the 'S' and 'C' scrolls with a number 42 tube, holding the tube in a vertical position and pressing very slightly onto the scroll shapes to fill in any gaps and produce a flat surface for overpiping.

6   Overpipe the shells and scrolls with a number 3 tube, then a number 2 tube, then a number 1 tube as before. You can also pipe lines along the side of the cake. To make piping on the side of the cake easier, place a solid, flat object under the edge of the front of the board to tilt the side upwards and provide a flatter surface for piping.

7   Complete the design with green stems and leaves, piped following the shape of the template. (Trace and scribe the designs on page 298 for guidance, if required.) Pipe small lily-of-the-valley directly onto the cake and graduated bulbs to finish the design on the top and sides of the cake.

8   Trim the cake board with cream ribbon, securing with double-sided tape.

NOTE   When attaching ribbon to the edge of a cake board, the best method is to apply double-sided sticky tape to the board before attaching the ribbon. (Alternatively, use an ordinary glue stick.) Do not use royal icing on the cake board as the ribbon will fall away when the icing dries.

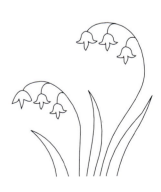

see templates page 298

4

Roll out the green flower paste and cut ribbon strips with the quilling cutter. Cut the ends at an angle.

5

Attach the tails to the side of the cake, hanging down. Attach the ribbon loops along the top edge, on either side of the tails.

8

Form the roses around a cone of red flower paste threaded onto a piece of wire. The wire is removed when the rose is dry.

11

To support the cake top ornament, make a base with a circle of icing and four leaves on top of it.

CORNELLI AND ROSES WEDDING CAKE

Tiny red roses and leaves highlight the clean lines and cornelli work on this royal-iced cake. The heart-shaped cake top ornament is made from pastillage. This is a sophisticated cake for those with plenty of experience of working with royal icing.

25 cm (10 inch) and 20 cm (8 inch) round cakes

2.5 kg (5 lb) marzipan
1 kg (2 lb) soft peak royal icing
30 g (1 oz) each light green, dark green and white flower paste
edible glue
125 g (4 oz) red flower paste

EQUIPMENT

33 cm (13 inch) and 28 cm (11 inch) round cake boards
assorted sizes scalloped templates
numbers 0 and 1 piping tubes
quilling cutter
26-gauge wires
2.5 cm (1 inch) blossom cutter
tiny rose leaf cutter
Dresden tool
heart-shaped template
medium plain leaf cutter
1.5 cm ($^5/8$ inch) round cutter
narrow white ribbon

1   Cover the cakes with marzipan and leave to dry. Cover with royal icing and leave to dry. Secure the cakes to the boards and cover the boards with royal icing. Leave to dry.

CORNELLI WORK

2   Measure the circumference of each cake and divide into five sections, marking the top edge of the cake. Using the templates, scribe five scallops around the side of each cake.

3   Using the number 0 tube and slightly softened royal icing, pipe cornelli work beneath the scallops and all over the boards. Tilt the cakes and pipe a line over the scribed scallops on the sides of the cakes.

RIBBONS

4   Roll out a small ball of light green flower paste quite thinly and cut ribbon strips with the quilling cutter. These should be slightly shorter than the depth of the cakes with the ends cut at an angle. Use edible glue to attach two strips to each place where the scallops meet.

5   To make the loops, cut another strip of paste 7.5 cm (3 inches) long. Fold one end over to form a small loop and secure with edible glue. Lift the centre of the strip and secure to form a second loop which is slightly shorter and sits on top of the first loop. Attach along the top edge of the cake to one side of the tails. Cut and fold another strip the same length and attach to the other side of the tails in a bow. Repeat around both cakes.

6   Using the number 1 tube and royal icing, pipe a snail trail around the top edge of the cakes between the bows.

ROSES AND LEAVES

7   Cut some pieces of wire 7.5 cm (3 inches) long. Form a tiny cone of red flower paste on the end of a wire. Repeat to make 10 more. Dry for a few hours.

8   Roll out a small ball of red flower paste very thinly and cut two blossoms. Take one of the blossoms, ball around the edges to soften and thread a cone through the middle. Lightly brush some glue on the blossom and wrap the individual petals to form a tiny rose: wrap one petal completely around the cone, two alternate petals into the centre around the first, then the remaining two to overlap the previous two. Ball the second blossom and attach to the underside of the flower, curving the petals back slightly. Repeat to make 11 roses. When the outer petals are dry, gently slide each rose off the wire and set aside to dry completely.

9   Roll out a small ball of dark green flower paste and cut 22 tiny rose leaves. Mark a centre vein with the Dresden tool. Use royal icing to attach a rose to the centre of each bow and a leaf to either side.

CAKE TOP ORNAMENT

10   Roll out a medium-sized ball of white flower paste to 2.5 mm ($^1/8$ inch) thick. Cut a narrow strip and lay it around the outline of the heart template. Overlap the ends slightly and join with edible glue. Make a small hole at the point of the heart and insert a small piece of uncooked dried spaghetti. Set aside to dry for at least 24 hours. Drying the heart shape on a piece of foam or sponge will ensure that both sides dry evenly.

11   Roll out a small ball of white flower paste to 2.5 mm (1/8 inch) and cut four medium-sized leaves and a small circle. Glue the leaves around the circle to form a base. Make a hole in the centre.

12   Attach ribbons, loops, a rose and leaves to the top of the heart with royal icing.

13   Pipe a small quantity of royal icing into the hole in the base and carefully position the heart by inserting the spaghetti into the hole. Support in

place, upright with foam, for 36 hours until completely dry.

ASSEMBLING THE CAKE

14   Trim the cake boards with the white ribbon, securing with double-sided tape. Secure the cake top ornament to the top tier with royal icing or leave free-standing. Arrange the cakes off-set on a perspex cake stand.

2

Hold the stencil against the cake board and, using the stippling action, apply the diluted red colour.

2

Use a sharp scalpel to etch around the edges of the stencilled shapes to highlight and define.

SUMMER POPPIES WEDDING CAKE

This two-tiered cake with its wonderful tangled mass of Iceland poppies conjures up an immediate atmosphere of hot summer days. Use the poppies from pages 88–9 (you will need 12 of the full flowers and about 14 buds but it's always best to make some extra).

15 cm (6 inch) and 30 cm (12 inch) oval cakes (use mixture for 15 cm and 30 cm round cakes)

3 kg (6 lb) champagne-tinted sugarpaste
tangerine, red and green petal dust
clear alcohol
2 kg (4 lb) marzipan
1 tablespoon royal icing

EQUIPMENT

23 cm (9 inch) and 40 cm (16 inch) oval
cake boards
firm and fine paintbrushes
border stencil design
scalpel
narrow red ribbon and wide orange ribbon
3 small perspex discs
small candle holder, pillars or cake stand
2 mounds of soft sugarpaste or florist's staysoft
12 Iceland poppies, assorted colours (pages 88–9)
and about 14 Iceland poppy buds

COLOURING THE CAKE BOARDS

1   Cover both cake boards with champagne sugarpaste and leave to dry. Using tangerine petal dust and a firm paintbrush, colour the area of the boards that will be exposed once the cakes are positioned. Use a stippling action with the brush to achieve a more interesting texture and to adhere a strong colour to the boards. Overdust with red petal dust using the stippling action again (some of the tangerine base colour should show through).

2   Dilute a little of the red petal dust with a small amount of clear alcohol (if you have too much alcohol the finished result will be patchy and very sticky). Place the border stencil on top of the dusted board and, using the stippling action again, apply the diluted red colour. (It is your choice whether to use a very detailed or simple stencil. We have used a complicated stencil and picked out parts of the design.) Leave to dry. Using a sharp scalpel, etch around the edges of each of the stencilled shapes to highlight and define the design.

COLOURING THE CAKES

3   Cover the cakes with marzipan and leave to dry. Cover the cakes with champagne sugarpaste. Secure the cakes to the cake boards with a little royal icing and leave to dry for three days.

4   Using the same stencil as before, add a design to the top of both cakes. This time use the tangerine and red petal dusts mixed with alcohol to create the design. Add extra hand-painted details using a finer paintbrush and tangerine, red and green dusts diluted with alcohol.

5   Trim the base of each cake with two bands of red ribbon, securing with a small amount of royal icing. Trim the boards with the orange ribbon, securing with double-sided tape.

ASSEMBLING THE CAKE

6   Position one thin perspex disc on the centre of the bottom tier and place the candle holder on top. Position the smaller cake on top, making sure that the cakes are balanced.

7   Attach a mound of soft sugarpaste or florist's 'staysoft' on top of each of the remaining perspex discs. Place one at the back of each cake. Start to position the poppies and buds, inserting the end of each stem into the soft sugarpaste. Tangle the flowers and buds as much as possible and use the stems as part of the finished design. You will have to remove the top tier, probably, to complete the arrangement and then reassemble the cake afterwards. Stand back occasionally to check that the arrangement is well balanced.

SUGAR SWEET PEAS WEDDING CAKE

This exquisite three-tier wedding cake uses masses of the delicate sweet pea flowers from pages 84–7, with trailing stems and entwining tendrils. The actual cake has been kept very simple in form, with only bumble bees and delicate shading to break up the surface.

20 cm (8 inch), 25 cm (10 inch) and 30 cm (12 inch) oval cakes (use mixture for 20 cm, 25 cm and 30 cm round cakes)

2 tablespoons royal icing
3 kg (6 lb) marzipan
5 kg (10 lb) sugarpaste
small amount flower paste
plum, deep purple, pearl white and white petal dust

EQUIPMENT

20 cm (8 inch), 25 cm (10 inch) and 40 cm (16 inch) oval cake boards
narrow pale pink ribbon
narrow lilac ribbon
4 wooden cake dowels
2 long crystal pillars
18 stems of sweet peas (pages 84–7) and numerous stems of sweet pea foliage with tendrils
2 posy holders
bumble bee cutter

1　Attach the two smaller cakes to their cake boards with a little royal icing and cover with marzipan. Leave to dry and then cover with white sugarpaste. Cover the large cake board with white sugarpaste and secure the large cake to the board with royal icing. Leave to dry for three days.

2　Trim the base of each cake with the narrow pink ribbon, securing with double-sided tape. Trim the large cake board with the lilac ribbon, securing with double-sided tape.

ASSEMBLY

3　Insert four wooden dowels into the large cake, equally spaced so they will be covered by the cake above but off-set from the centre. Cut off the dowels level with the icing and place the middle tier, off-set, on top of the base tier. Insert the two crystal pillars into the back of the middle tier. Position the top tier on the middle tier, resting against the pillars.

4　Arrange the sweet peas and foliage into the crystal pillars behind the top tier, trailing them over the top of the small cake and then down over the middle tier. Insert a couple of posy holders into the bottom tier and arrange the remaining sweet peas in them. Try to make the arrangement as wild and informal as possible.

5　Cut out several small bumble bees from flower paste, using the bumble bee cutter. Stick in position with a little water. Dust with plum and deep purple, diluted with pearl white and white petal dust. Shade the cake edges with a pale mixture of the petal dust.

1 Prepare a scraper with two holes melted into the side so that you can make parallel lines on the cake.

2 Spread a small amount of icing across the top of the stencil and then smooth with a scraper.

4 Pipe in the outline of the collars and then fill in the shape with the runout icing. Dry under a lamp.

8 Attach two flowers to the runout sections of the collars. Remove the collars from the paper and attach to the cake with icing.

HONEYSUCKLE DREAM WEDDING CAKE

Stencilling is a quick way to decorate that produces fast, impressive results. Colour this cake with dusting powder or paint on the design with powder or paste food colouring mixed with a little clear alcohol. Coating with royal icing and runout collars are not for beginners.

18 cm (7 inch), 23 cm (9 inch) and 28 cm (11 inch) oval cakes (use mixture for 18 cm, 23 cm and 28 cm round cakes)

3.5 kg (7 lb) marzipan
3.5 kg (7 lb) royal icing
pink, yellow, brown and green liquid food colourings

EQUIPMENT
cake scraper
20 x 25 cm (8 x 10 inch), 25 x 30 cm
(10 x 12 inch) and 32 x 38 cm (13 x 15 inch) oval cake boards
large honeysuckle stencil
small honeysuckle stencil
paintbrush
numbers 0, 1 and 2 piping tubes
number 51 leaf piping tube
narrow maroon ribbon
3 tilting cake stands

COVERING THE CAKES

1 Cover the cakes with marzipan and leave to dry. Apply two coats of white royal icing to the top and sides. Prepare a cake scraper with two holes melted into the side, 2.5 cm (1 inch) from the bottom and 2.5 cm (1 inch) apart. (You may need to rub away the melted plastic from the base of the holes with sandpaper.) Apply a third coat of icing and use the scraper to smooth it around the side to create a pair of parallel lines. Coat the boards with royal icing while the sides are still wet and later apply the final top coat. Leave the cakes to dry.

STENCILLING

2 Using the large honeysuckle stencil, apply the design to the top of the largest cake. Place the stencil on the iced surface of the cake and hold it in place. With a palette knife, spread a little icing across the top of the stencil and smooth with a scraper. Remove the stencil without distorting the design. Stencil the second tier in the same way, but mask off a portion of the design with tape. To decorate the top tier, mask off the whole pattern except for the largest flower. Apply the small stencil design to the edge of the cake boards, front and back. Leave to dry.

3 To colour, put the stencil back on the cake, pressing it down around the raised design. Paint on the colour with a mixture of food colouring and clear alcohol (don't put too much on your brush or the colours will bleed). Colour the board decoration in the same way, carefully replacing the stencil. Colour all the cakes and boards, then leave until completely dry.

RUNOUT COLLARS

4 Trace the collar patterns on page 299, which will frame one half of the top of the cake. Lay them on a flat surface and secure a piece of non-stick baking paper on top. Pipe in the outline of the collars with a number 1 tube and white royal icing and fill in this shape pattern with white runout icing (see page 68). Dry under a lamp for 30 minutes, by which time a shiny crust will have formed on the surface. Leave the collars to dry completely in a warm place.

5 Trace the flower patterns on page 299 and secure under non-stick baking paper. Prepare more runout icing, with the consistency thick enough to be able to hold its shape without an outline. Put in a paper piping bag without a tube and cut a small hole in the end, about the size of a number 2 tube. Pipe bulbs for the centre of each flower and leave under a heat lamp to form a shiny crust.

Pipe alternate petals, using the same piping bag, applying extra pressure at the outside tip of each one. Make sure they are anchored well to the bulb in the centre. Allow these to form a crust under a lamp before piping in the remaining petals. When dry, overpipe the centres with tiny bulbs using a number 0 tube. Make at least 51 flowers: 12 for the top tier, 15 for the middle and 18 for the base tier; plus four for the base and middle collars and two small ones for the top collar.

DECORATING THE BOARDS

6 To make templates for the board linework, cut out the tracings of the collar patterns from step 4, following the cake line to make the inside edge of the templates. Place the templates around the end of each cake. If they will not lie flat, cut them in half at their central point, to improve the fit. Pipe a line around the template at each end of the cake, joining at the centre of each side, using a number 2 tube. Then overpipe the linework using the same tube.

PIPING

7   Pipe the detail around the base of the cake using white royal icing and a number 51 leaf tube. Overlap each leaf slightly, working in opposite directions from the central point on each side of the cake. Lift the tube away from the surface after each leaf to avoid them running into each other. Take the piped flowers and carefully remove them from the paper. Pipe small bulbs of icing onto the parallel lines on the sides of the cakes. Attach the flowers at intervals of approximately 2 cm (3/4 inch).

8   Attach two flowers to the runout sections of the collars. Remove the collars from the paper and attach to the end of each cake with royal icing.

9   Pipe a line along the inside edge and around the tips of the collars with a number 2 tube. Continue the piped line around the edges of the cakes not covered by the collars. Overpipe this linework using the same tube. Trim the cake boards with maroon ribbon, securing with double-sided tape. Position the cakes on three tilting cake stands, so that their designs are shown to best effect.

see templates page 299

CELEBRATION CAKES

Christening, engagement, Easter, Mother's Day, wedding anniversaries, Valentine's Day, coming of age... the list of things to celebrate is endless. For a cake decorator each of these special days is an occasion for imagination and experimentation. We've included some simple cakes that are perfect for beginners (like our colourful heart-shaped Valentine or the Boxes of Gifts piled up high) but most of the christening cakes, with their delicate frills and paintwork, are beautiful creations for very special celebrations.

BOXES OF GIFTS

Spectacular for almost any occasion—birthday, wedding or even a christening—this colourful centrepiece is surprisingly easy to make. You can use all one type of cake or alternate the layers between fruit and mud cakes.

2 Plug any holes in the cake with icing to give a smooth surface. To cover the cake, roll the icing over the pin, then re-roll over the top of the cake.

7 Cut out tiny daisies from the darker yellow icing and stick them to the yellow-tinted cake with water or egg white.

8 To make a bow, cut two strips of dark orange icing, then trim the corners, fold in half and support with cotton wool until dried.

8 Wrap a small strip of icing over the centre of the join to make a bow.

---

30 cm (12 inch), 25 cm (10 inch), 16 cm (6¹/2 inch), 12 cm (5 inch) square cakes

1 tablespoon royal icing
90 g (3 oz) apricot jam
4.5 kg (9 lb) sugarpaste
food colourings
12 wooden cake dowels
1 egg white

EQUIPMENT

36 cm (14 inch) square cake board
large piping tubes

1 Cut three cardboard squares the same size as the three smaller cakes. Trim the tops off the cakes so they are similar heights. Turn the cakes upside-down and secure on the cardboard and cake board with a little royal icing. Warm the jam, strain and brush over the cakes.

COVERING THE CAKES

2 Knead 1.75 kg (3¹/2 lb) of the sugarpaste on a work surface dusted with icing sugar. Tint the icing pale pink. Roll out the icing to about 5 mm (¹/4 inch) thick and large enough to cover the largest cake, dusting the bench and rolling pin with icing sugar to prevent sticking. Use a little icing to fill in any holes in the cake, to ensure an even surface. Roll the icing over the rolling pin and re-roll over the top of the cake. Gently press over the cake, using the palms of your hands dusted with icing sugar. Smooth and trim any excess. Add more pink colouring to the leftover icing to tint it dark pink and wrap in plastic.

POSITIONING THE DOWELS

3 Insert four wooden dowels into the centre of the largest cake, equally spaced so they will be covered by the cake above. Cut off the dowels level with the icing.

4 Knead 1.25 kg (2¹/2 lb) of the sugarpaste and tint pale blue. Roll out to cover the 25 cm (10 inch) cake. Tint the leftover icing darker blue. Insert four wooden dowels into the cake, equally spaced so they will be covered by the cake above. Cut off the dowels level with the icing.

5 Knead 750 g (1¹/2 lb) sugarpaste and tint pale yellow to cover the 16 cm (6¹/2 inch) cake. Keep a little pale icing and tint the rest darker. Insert four dowels into the cake and cut off level with the icing.

6 Knead 500 g (1 lb) of the sugarpaste and tint pale orange to cover the smallest cake. Tint the leftover icing darker orange.

ADDING THE DECORATIONS

7 Place the cakes on top of each other. Roll the darker icing out on a surface dusted with icing sugar, to about 3 mm (¹/8 inch) thick. Cut small hearts from the pink icing and stick onto the pink cake with a little water or egg white. Cut strips from the blue icing and stick onto the blue cake. Using a cutter or knife, cut daisy shapes from the dark yellow icing and stick onto the yellow cake. Use a large piping tube as a cutter to make small rounds of pale yellow icing for the centres. Use another piping tube to cut rounds of dark orange icing and stick them to the orange cake.

MAKING THE BOW

8 Re-roll the remaining dark orange icing and cut into 3 cm (1¹/4 inch) wide strips. Stick to the cake to form a flat ribbon. Re-roll the remaining icing and cut two strips. Trim the corners from the ends of the strips, fold in half and support with cotton wool. Wrap a small strip of icing over the centre of the join for the centre of the bow. Place in the centre of the 'ribbon'. Remove the cotton wool when set.

STAR OF THE SHOW

This is an easy cake, decorated with cut-out stars and plenty of glitzy ribbon. The texture of the stars is made with crumpled foil.

1   Cover the cake with marzipan and leave the cake to dry.

2   Colour 315 g (10 oz) of the sugarpaste with a little violet food colouring and use to cover the cake board. Leave to dry.

MAKING THE STARS

3   To make the stars, roll out 60 g (2 oz) white sugarpaste. Lightly press crumpled foil or greaseproof paper over the icing to give a textured surface. Dip the star cutters in a little cornflour, then cut out several stars in each size. Place on a sheet of non-stick baking paper. Colour another 60 g (2 oz) sugarpaste deep blue and another 60 g (2 oz) a slightly darker shade of violet. Make more stars in these colours and leave to dry overnight. Use the remaining sugarpaste to cover the cake.

4   Secure the cake to the board with royal icing, positioning so that the tips of the star are in line with the points on the hexagonal board. Press the cord around the base of the cake and leave to dry.

5   Use the silver colouring to paint the white stars. To arrange the ribbon, twist one of the wired ribbons around the fingers to coil it. Gently pull the ends apart. Twist the wires together at one end and tuck just under the cord around the base of the cake.

ADDING THE RIBBON

6   Tuck the other end of the ribbon under the cord on the other side, cutting off a little ribbon if it is too long. Use the same technique for the other wired ribbon, laying it across the first.

7   Arrange the cut-out stars over the cake and around the board to decorate, securing with a little royal icing. Trim the board with ribbon, securing with double-sided tape.

3
To create texture, press crumpled foil over the sugarpaste before cutting out the stars.

25 cm (10 inch) star-shaped cake

750 g (1¹/₂ lb) marzipan
1.5 kg (3 lb) sugarpaste
violet and blue food colourings
2 tablespoons royal icing
silver liquid colouring

EQUIPMENT
28 cm (11 inch) hexagonal or round silver
cake board
small, medium and large star cutters
fine purple, silver or blue haberdashery cord
fine paintbrush
wired blue ribbon
wired silver ribbon
narrow blue or lilac ribbon

EASTER BASKET

This quick and easy Easter cake uses bought chocolate eggs wrapped in ribbon. The cake mix is baked in a wide shallow ovenproof bowl to make a basket. Use the quantity of cake mix specified to make a 20 cm (8 inch) round cake.

Pipe short lengths diagonally over the side of the cake to make a basket.

Madeira mixture for 20 cm (8 inch) round cake
750 g (1½ lb) chocolate buttercream
12 large chocolate eggs

EQUIPMENT

3.5 litre heatproof bowl
22 cm (9 inch) round cake board
number 2 piping tube
narrow yellow, green and burgundy ribbon

1   Preheat the oven to 160°C (315°F/Gas 2–3). Grease and line the base of the bowl with a circle of non-stick baking paper. Spoon the cake mix into the bowl and level the surface. Bake for 1½–1¾ hours, or until a skewer inserted into the centre comes out clean. Leave to cool in the bowl.

2   Remove the cake from the bowl, remove the paper from the base and trim the domed top level. Transfer to the cake board, securing with a little buttercream. Using a palette knife, spread about half the buttercream over the top and side of the cake, smoothing down lightly.

3   Place some of the remaining buttercream in a piping bag fitted with a number 2 tube. Starting around the top edge of the cake, pipe short diagonal lengths of icing to create a rope pattern. Pipe more bands of rope under the first, working down to the base of the cake. Finish by piping a further rope band inside the top rim.

4   Cut lengths of ribbon to decorate the eggs, either tying them in bows or securing the ends with melted chocolate. Arrange the eggs in the basket.

ART DECO ROSES

This teardrop-shaped cake was inspired by the 1900s fashion for stylised flower decoration and we kept our icing colours a little muted to match that theme. We used a set of stainless steel rose petal cutters and a ribbon cutter, but you can manage with a sharp knife or scalpel.

25 cm (10 inch) teardrop-shaped cake (use mixture for 25 cm round cake)

1.25 kg (2¹/₂ lb) marzipan
1.25 kg (2¹/₂ lb) sugarpaste
250 g (8 oz) flower paste
lavender, green, blue and pink paste food colours
edible glue
250 g (8 oz) royal icing

EQUIPMENT

36 cm (14 inch) oval cake board
numbers 1, 1.5 and 2 piping tubes
tracing paper, pencil and scriber
stainless steel rose petal cutter set
narrow pink ribbon and very narrow purple ribbon

1   Cover the cake with marzipan and leave to dry. Cover the cake with sugarpaste and leave to dry for 24 hours. Cover the cake board with sugarpaste and leave to dry for 24 hours.

DECORATING THE BOARD

2   Divide the flower paste into four portions and colour them lavender, pale green, pale blue and pale pink. Cover with plastic wrap when not using.

3   Roll out and cut strips of blue flower paste with a sharp knife or ribbon cutter and fix them to the board with edible glue, following the design on the cake shown, or making your own pattern.

4   Secure the cake to the board with royal icing. Using a number 2 piping tube and royal icing, pipe a snail trail around the base of the cake.

CAKE DECORATION

5   Make a paper template of the cake and sketch or trace on to it your chosen design, showing the positions of the appliquéd flowers and leaves. The template we have used is on page 295. Put the template on the cake and mark lines with a scriber.

6   Place the cake on a tilting turntable or stand, and tilt it away from you. Roll out and cut more strips of blue flower paste and fix to the sides of the cake with edible glue, turning the cake as necessary.

7   Roll out the pale pink and lavender flower paste and cut out petal shapes. Using the different-sized cutters, cut the petals into shaped pieces. Attach to the cake with edible glue. Plan the shape of each flower before securing it to the cake.

8   Cut out more petal shapes of green flower paste and attach to the cake for leaves. Keep all the appliqué pieces as flat as possible with the edges clean and sharp. Press them gently into position without denting the paste.

9   Using deep lavender coloured royal icing and a number 1.5 piping tube, pipe in the stems of the flowers and leaves. Using a number 1 tube, overpipe the edges of the flowers and leaves. Trim the cake board with the pink and then the purple ribbon, securing with double-sided tape.

NOTE   It is easier to decorate a cake like this if you have a tilting turntable. If you don't, a pile of telephone directories will bring the cake up to a good height for working on.

3

If you have one, use a ribbon cutter for cutting the blue flower paste. If not, use a scalpel or knife.

7

Cut petal shapes from the lavender paste, using the different sized cutters. Plan the shape of the flower before sticking to the cake.

9

Using the deep lavender royal icing, pipe in the flower stems and overpipe the edges of the flowers and the leaves.

see template page 295

TRAINS AND TEDDIES CHRISTENING CAKE

This very pretty christening cake is an easy starting place for newcomers to sugarpaste modelling. The train and building blocks are very simple shapes to mould, with the teddies needing a little more care. The icing looks just as effective tinted pale blue or yellow.

5

Shape the teddies' bodies, heads, arms, legs, ears and muzzles in different tints of sugarpaste.

7

For the train carriages, cut neat blocks of sugarpaste and position them behind the engine.

22 cm (9 inch) and 15 cm (6 inch) round cakes

2 kg (4 lb) sugarpaste
pink food colouring
1.5 kg (3 lb) marzipan
1 tablespoon royal icing

EQUIPMENT
30 cm (12 inch) round silver cake board
4 wooden cake dowels
large and fine paintbrushes

1   Reserve 185 g (6 oz) of the sugarpaste. Colour 60 g (2 oz) of the remainder bright pink. Colour another 185 g (6 oz) a paler shade of pink. Colour the remaining sugarpaste very pale pink.

2   Cover the cakes with marzipan, allowing 500 g (1 lb) for the small cake and 1 kg (2 lb) for the large cake. Secure the large cake on the cake board with a little royal icing.

3   Reserve 60 g (2 oz) of the palest pink icing. Use the remainder to cover the cakes, allowing 500 g (1 lb) for the small cake and 1 kg (2 lb) for the large. Leave to dry for three days.

POSITIONING THE DOWELS

4   Insert four wooden dowels into the centre of the largest cake, equally spaced so they will be covered by the cake above. Cut off the dowels level with the icing. Lift the smaller cake onto the large one. Use a little white sugarpaste to cover the edge of the cake board.

MODELLING THE DECORATIONS

5   Make a sugarpaste rope by twisting lengths of white and palest pink icing and secure around the base of each cake with a little water. To make a teddy, roll two balls of icing, one slightly smaller than the other. Gently press the smaller one on top of the larger, securing with a little water. Shape two flattened rounds of paste. Halve one and position for ears; position the other for a muzzle. Shape the arms and legs and secure to the body. Use a contrasting colour to make the paw pads and the centres of the ears. To complete the teddy, paint faint features on the head with a fine paintbrush and diluted pink colouring. Repeat to make more teddies.

6   To make building blocks, simply mould neat cubes of sugarpaste.

7   For the train, shape and position the engine and carriages and then add tiny white wheels, securing with water. For the train 'steam', use thinly rolled white sugarpaste cut to shape with a template or cloud cutters if you have them.

8   Arrange the decorations on the cake while still soft, securing with water or a little royal icing.

SAINT VALENTINE'S DAY

Use any type of cake except a fruit cake—a fruit cake will crumble at the edge when you try to cut it into shape.

20 cm (8 inch) round cake

50 g (1³/4 oz) butter
120 g (4 oz) icing sugar
3 teaspoons liqueur (Cointreau, Grand Marnier etc)
red food colouring
500 g (1 lb) sugarpaste
1 tablespoon royal icing

EQUIPMENT
heart-shaped cutters

1   Draw around the base of the cake tin and cut out a 20 cm (8 inch) circle from a piece of paper. Fold the circle in half and draw on half a heart shape using the fold as the middle of the heart and the outside edge as the edge of the heart. Cut along this line and then unfold the paper to make a heart-shaped template.

2   Cut the domed top off the cake to give a flat surface. Turn the cake upside down and use the template to cut the cake into a heart with a serrated knife. The cake should cut easily, leaving a clean edge.

3   To make the pink buttercream, beat the butter until soft, add the sifted sugar and continue beating until light and fluffy. Add the liqueur and a few drops of colouring and beat well.

4   Cut the cake in half horizontally. Spread the bottom layer with a third of the buttercream and sandwich the halves together. Spread the remaining buttercream over the cake in a thin layer, to help the next layer of icing stick.

5   Knead the sugarpaste until smooth on a surface dusted with icing sugar. Remove a small piece of white paste and set aside. Add a couple of drops of food colouring to the rest of the icing and knead well. Pull off a piece the size of a golf ball and add another few drops of food colouring to make it darker than the first. Continue doing this until you have three or four different shades of icing set aside with the small white piece. Tint the remaining icing pink and use to cover the cake. Leave to dry.

6   Roll out the balls of white and coloured icing and use the cutters to make heart shapes of varying sizes and tints. Attach to the cake with dots of royal icing.

Fold the paper circle in half, draw half a heart on one side and cut out.

Put the paper template over the cake and cut with a serrated knife.

2

Make a template a little higher than the side of the cake and cut out the textured pastillage.

5

Pipe the inscription on the gift label and then thread a little gold thread through the hole.

6

Secure the pink bow and the gift tag to the box with a little melted chocolate.

BOX OF CHOCOLATES

This cake is a chocoholic's dream, but obviously you can change the contents to suit the recipient... try toffees, fudge or jellies. If you have time, fill the box with home-made truffles. The cake needs to be a sponge, as it's cut into shape.

18 cm (7 inch) square chocolate genoise sponge

200 g (6$^1/_2$ oz) black-tinted sugarpaste
375 g (13 oz) buttercream
440 g (14 oz) ivory-tinted pastillage
185 g (6 oz) dark chocolate, melted
2 tablespoons royal icing
black food colouring
125 g (4 oz) pink-tinted pastillage
assortment of chocolates or sweets

EQUIPMENT

28 cm (11 inch) square cake board
ribbed rolling pin
numbers 1, 4 and 43 piping tubes
10 cm (4 inches) gold thread
narrow pink ribbon

SHAPING THE CAKE

1   Roll out the black sugarpaste and cover the cake board. Cut the cake in half horizontally and sandwich with a little of the buttercream. Make a 15 cm (6 inch) square template from thin card or paper and place on top of the cake. Use a sharp knife to slice the cake at an angle from the template edge to the outside base edge of the cake, giving the cake sloping sides. Reserve the template for later use. Spread the top and sides of the cake with the remaining buttercream and secure on the board.

MAKING THE BOX

2   Make a template of the side of the cake, adding a little extra height to the top. Roll out the ivory pastillage and texture the surface with the ribbed rolling pin. Cut out four side shapes, ensuring the ribbing runs in the same direction on all four sides. Press onto the sides of the cake—the extra height on the sides should create a box effect. Cut out a square lid from the textured paste, using the cake cutting template, and leave to dry.

3   Roll out the ivory pastillage trimmings thinly and cut out a rectangle for the gift tag. Cut a hole in the tag, using a number 4 tube, for the tie.

EDGING THE BOX

4   Add a few drops of cold water to the melted chocolate to thicken it slightly. Using a number 43 piping tube, pipe a shell border around the top and base edges and corners of the box. Pipe around the edge of the box lid.

5   Using a number 1 tube and black royal icing, pipe an inscription onto the gift tag. Knot the gold thread through the hole.

6   Roll out the pink pastillage thinly and cut out a square with the cake top template. Lay the square crossways on top of the cake to look like tissue paper lining. Arrange the chocolates in the box and attach the gift tag and a pink bow, securing with melted chocolate. Trim the cake board with ribbon, securing with double-sided tape.

FLORAL BASKET

This cake would be a real treat for Mother's Day, a birthday or Easter. The decorative technique used is quilting (for extra hints and instructions on sugar embroidery, see pages 58–9), which does require a stitching wheel.

18 cm (7 inch) round cake
1 kg (2 lb) marzipan
1 kg (2 lb) sugarpaste
cream, yellow, orange, peach, green and brown food colourings
500 g (1 lb) firm-peak royal icing

EQUIPMENT

25 cm (10 inch) round cake board
closed-curve crimper
large petunia cutter
leaf cutter
basketweave rolling pin
straight scallop-edged cutter
stitching wheel
narrow brown ribbon

1   Cover the cake with marzipan and leave to dry. Tint 600 g (1¼ lb) of the sugarpaste cream and use to cover the cake and board. Crimp the edge of the board with a closed-curve cutter while the icing is still soft. Impress flowers and leaves at random on the top and slightly over the edge of the cake, using the large petunia and leaf cutters. Leave to dry for three days.

2   Using white royal icing, pipe the pads separately on the centres and petals of the flowers, and on the leaves. Do not pad any sections placed over the curved edge or on the side of the cake. Leave to dry.

BASKETWEAVE

3   Colour small amounts of sugarpaste yellow, orange, peach and green, and the remainder brown. Roll out the brown paste to 0.5 cm (½ inch) thick and emboss with a basketweave rolling pin.

4   Cut the basketweave into strips 5 cm (2 inches) deep and scallop the top edge. Secure these around the cake with a little water, with each join lying at the end of a scallop.

5   Large stitch with the stitching wheel along the top edge of the scallop and vertically down the basketweave between each one.

QUILTING

6   Tint half the yellow, orange, peach and green paste with white paste to give two shades of each. Cut out the shapes, using the same cutters as for the impressions, and smooth the edges. Moisten and position over the padded areas.

7   Small stitch all around the edges and in lines out from the centres of the flowers. Vein the leaves.

8   Cut out small brown circles for the centres of the flowers, attach and crisscross with small stitches. Trim the board with ribbon, securing with a little double-sided tape.

Impress the top and side of the cake with the cutters. Pipe the centres of the shapes on top of the cake.

Place the scalloped basket-weave around the cake, then stitch around the top edge and down between the scallops.

CRADLE GARLAND CHRISTENING CAKE

This flowers on this cake are not wired, which makes them easier to make. Several techniques are used for the decorations: brush embroidery, appliqué, modelling and painting, none of which are difficult but do require care and time and a little previous experience.

7 First attach the ribbon tails to the cake, then secure the ribbon loops on top of them. Add a ball for the centre of the bow.

10 For the rosebuds, cut out two petals, then ball and soften the edges. Place slightly overlapping on top of each other.

23 cm (9 inch) oval cake (use mixture for 23 cm round cake)

1.25 kg (2¹/₂ lb) marzipan
1.25 kg (2¹/₂ lb) sugarpaste
30 g (1 oz) royal icing
30 g (1 oz) modelling paste
30 g (1 oz) flower paste
assorted dusting powders
assorted paste colours
edible glue
piping gel

EQUIPMENT

28 cm (11 inch) oval cake board
scriber
fine paintbrush
ball tool
number 2 piping tube
miniature plunger cutter
rose petal cutters
small daisy cutter
silk stamens
tweezers
narrow pink ribbon

1 Cover the cake with marzipan and leave to dry. Cover with white sugarpaste and secure to the board with royal icing. Cover the board with sugarpaste. Leave to dry for three days.

GARLAND

2 Trace the garland template on page 295 onto non-stick baking paper and scribe onto the cake. Do not mark on the ribbon bows or rose petals. Paint the small leaves in different shades of green.

CRADLE

3 Trace the cradle, drapes and bow templates onto thin card. Colour a grape-sized piece of modelling paste pale blue. Roll out the paste thinly and cut out with the inner cradle shape template. Secure to the cake top with a little water.

4 Cut out the pillow shape from white modelling paste, the baby's head from flesh-coloured paste and bed cover from white paste. To colour the paste for the cradle, add champagne, brown, and peach petal dusts. Roll out a little more thickly so that it sits higher than the previous shapes. Secure the pieces to the cake top with a little water.

5 To make the drapes at the top and side of the cradle, roll out the paste as thinly as possible. Cut out and ball the edges so that they are really fine. For the top frill, roll the edge with a cocktail stick. Fold the edges under and secure in postition with water.

6 For the side drapes, again ball the cut edges. Turn the outer edges under and make folds. Arrange around the cradle and secure in place. Attach the bottom of the drapes below where the bow will be. Thinly roll out some white modelling paste. Cut a scalloped edge with a cocktail stick and attach to the bottom of the coverlet and the top of the cradle edge.

BOWS

7 For the bows, cut out the two tails using the template on page 295 and soften the edges with a ball tool. Butt against the drape and twist and curl. Make the loops using the template. Soften the edges. Glue together and attach between the tails. Make a small ball for the centre of the bow and flatten into place. Make a further bow for the top of the cradle. Paint small blue spots on the coverlet. Paint on the baby's hair and add a few strands on the pillow. Paint on the features with diluted food colouring.

8 Colour a third of the royal icing green. For the larger rose leaves, add ¹/₄ teaspoon of piping gel to the royal icing. Fill the piping bag and outline the leaf. Draw the icing towards the middle of the leaf with a fine paintbrush. Clean the brush and draw it down the centre to form the vein.

ROSES AND ROSEBUDS

9 For the roses, use rose petal cutters of various sizes. Colour a grape-sized piece of flower paste pale pink. Roll out very thinly. Ball the edges to give a natural look and secure in place with water.

10 For the rosebuds, cut out two petals, then ball and soften the edges. Place both petals, slightly overlapping, one on top of the other. Colour a grape-sized piece of paste with grape colour. Roll out thinly. Cut out the daisy shape. Cut out each petal

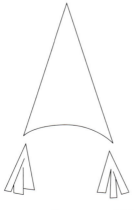

see templates page 295

individually and soften the edges with a ball tool. Curve slightly on foam and secure to the cake.

FORGET-ME-NOTS AND DAISIES

11   Colour a small grape-sized piece of paste pale blue. Roll out thinly and cut out florets with a small plunger cutter. Remove the centre with a number 2 piping tube. Glue in place. Paint on the stems and calyx with green and dot each forget-me-not with an orange centre. Dust each rose centre with pale green. Define the edges of petals with dark pink dust. Pipe on the daisies with a number 2 piping tube. Give each a warm yellow centre.

12   Using silk stamens, dust the tips brown and the cottons yellow. Cut them quite short. Pipe a bulb of pale yellow/green icing in the centre of the rose. Draw each stamen against the thumbnail to curve it. Insert into the icing with tweezers. Attach a pink bow to the bottom of the garland.

FINISHING TOUCHES

13   Pipe a snail trail of white royal icing around the base of the cake with a number 2 piping tube. Add further buds and smaller flowers to fill any gaps. Secure two rows of ribbon around the base of the cake, securing with royal icing.

KEY TO THE DOOR

Gold-edged filigree work gives an interesting finish to this 18th or 21st birthday celebration cake. Filigree work is piped with royal icing but is a random pattern and not difficult—practise on paper or spare icing before you start.

28 cm (11 inch) square cake

1.5 kg (3 lb) marzipan
500 g (1 lb) royal icing
cornflour
2 kg (4 lb) sugarpaste
blue, green and gold food colourings

EQUIPMENT

33 cm (13 inch) square gold cake board
number 1 piping tube
medium star piping tube
fine paintbrush
wide gold ribbon

1   Cover the cake with marzipan and secure to the cake board with a little royal icing. Dust the top, to within 2.5 cm (1 inch) of the edges, with cornflour. Brush the rest of the cake with egg white or clear alcohol as usual before covering it. Cut out a 23 cm (9 inch) square of non-stick baking paper.

REMOVING THE CENTRE PANEL

2   Cover the cake with sugarpaste, reserving the trimmings. Once the sugarpaste is completely smoothed around the edges and sides of the cake, lay the square of non-stick baking paper over the top, securing it at the corners with pins. Using a sharp knife, cut right through the sugarpaste around the paper. Lift out the central square of white sugarpaste. Remove the paper and pins.

3   Knead the white sugarpaste square and trimmings together and colour with equal quantities of blue and green colourings. Roll out and cut out a 23 cm (9 inch) square, reserving the trimmings. Brush the empty panel on top of the cake with clear alcohol and lay the square of coloured sugarpaste over the top of the cake, so that it fits neatly into the space. Smooth the edges lightly.

4   Use the coloured sugarpaste trimmings to make the key using the template, right, to cut out the shape. Leave overnight to harden.

PIPING FILIGREE

5   Put a little royal icing in a paper piping bag fitted with a number 1 piping tube and pipe thin wavy lines over two-thirds of the coloured sugarpaste. Pipe long, continuous, curvy lines, keeping the tube about 1 cm (1/2 inch) above the cake and breaking off frequently to rest your hand and change position.

6   Using more royal icing and a medium star tube, pipe a shell border around the edge of the coloured paste and around the base of the cake. Leave overnight to harden.

FINISHING TOUCHES

7   Using gold food colouring and a fine paintbrush, carefully paint over the piped icing. Paint the edges of the key with a little gold colouring. Leave to dry for several hours.

8   Wrap the ribbon around the sides of the cake, cutting off the excess and securing with a dot of royal icing. Shape the remaining ribbon into a bow and secure to the top of the cake with a dab of royal icing. Lay the key over the bow, securing with a small dot of royal icing.

NOTE   The little key is made from sugarpaste, using a template to cut out the shape. Alternatively, a real key can be used.
    Gold food colouring can be difficult to find. If so, use gold lustre powder mixed with water or clear alcohol.

5

Pipe thin wavy lines over two-thirds of the coloured paste, keeping the tube about 1 cm above the cake and breaking off frequently to rest your hand and change position.

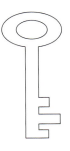

template actual size

MOUSE IN A CRADLE CHRISTENING CAKE

A sprig of summery apple blossom suspends this baby mouse, but you could vary the flowers to suit the season—catkins or lilac for spring, fir cones for autumn or holly with berries for a winter baby. This is a cake for those with experience in decorating.

3 Colour the modelling paste brown to make the cradle and mark in the basketwork with one petal of a blossom cutter.

4 Roll out a sausage of paste and then flatten and cut out an arc shape to make the rim of the hood. Mark in the basketweave with the blossom cutter.

20 cm (8 inch) round cake

1 kg (2 lb) marzipan
cornflour
1 kg (2 lb) sugarpaste
500 g (1 lb) pastillage
chestnut, paprika, cream and blue food colourings
2 tablespoons royal icing
60 g (2 oz) modelling paste
blue dusting powder
small spray of seasonal flowers

EQUIPMENT

28 cm (11 inch) round cake board
12 cm (5 inch) round plaque cutter
scriber
small blossom plunger cutter
anger tool
ball tool
cotton or white stamens
carnation cutter
numbers 1 and 2 piping tubes
fine paintbrush
short length of narrow blue ribbon
ribbon insertion tool or scalpel

1 Cover the cake with marzipan and leave to dry. Dust a 12 cm (5 inch) round on the top with cornflour. Brush the rest of the cake with clear alcohol as usual before covering it. Cover the cake with blue sugarpaste. Using a plaque cutter, remove the centre round while the sugarpaste is still soft. Smooth any marks and secure on the board with royal icing. Cover the board with blue sugarpaste. Leave to dry for three days.

2 Using the same cutter, cut out a plaque from the white pastillage. Leave to dry. Trace the template, opposite, onto non-stick baking paper.

MAKING THE PLAQUE

3 Transfer the design to the plaque with a scriber or pin. Colour modelling paste brown for the basket. Roll out finely and cut out the inside of the hood. Create a woven effect by pressing curved marks with one petal of a small blossom cutter. Mark so that the indentations fan out and are not in straight lines.

4 Roll out a thick sausage shape. Flatten with a rolling pin and cut out an arc shape. Round the outer edges with your fingers so that they curve and touch the base of the plaque. Push the inner edge of the hood against your thumb with an anger tool. Mark again with the blossom cutter. Roll out two thin strips of paste, twist them together quite tightly and secure to the edge of the hood with water.

5 To make the pillow, take a small ball of white modelling paste and flatten with your thumb. Square off the sides and tweak out the corners. Using a ball tool, indent and flatten for the mouse's head. Attach to the inside hood of the basket.

MOUSE

6 To make the mouse, colour some sugarpaste light brown and make a ball, then a cone. Indent an eye with the end of an anger tool. Make a hole in which to place the upper ear. The ear on the underside of the head is made by making a small ball, then a cone. Flatten it by pressing between your thumb and forefinger.

7 Make the upper ear from two slightly larger balls of paste, one brown, one a fleshy pink. Flatten both balls as before. Place the pink flattened ball slightly below the brown one so that the pink is edged with brown. Squeeze the bottom edge together and cut away the excess. Moisten the base and place in the ear.

8 Use a scalpel to mark fur on the mouse. Make whiskers from cotton stiffened with sugar syrup or use white flower stamens.

BASKET AND COVERS

9 To make the bedspread and lower basket, roll out paste so that the lower edge is quite thick. The paste should become thinner as you roll away. Mark quilt lines on the bedspread when it has been pushed into shape. Place over the base of the basket and butt it up to the bottom edge of the plaque. Curve around the bedspread. Mark basket lines as before.

10 Use a carnation cutter (or garrett frill cutter) for the lace frill. Cut out the lace holes with piping tubes. Frill the bottom curved edge to make the straight piece of paste curve.

11 Insert the narrow blue ribbon into the lace while the paste is still soft, to look as if it is woven through the lace, using a scalpel or ribbon insertion tool. Dust the coverlet with a darker blue dusting powder in the corners and add lines. Attach lengths of ribbon to each side of the basket with royal icing and join together above the basket.

FINISHING TOUCHES

12 Attach the spray of flowers to the plaque with royal icing, placing it over the join in the ribbon. Make a small bow and attach to the branch where the ribbon meets the branch. Using a fine brush and diluted food colourings, paint small flowers or dots over the blue sugarpaste and board and leave to dry. Tint the remaining royal icing pale blue and, using a number 1 tube, pipe a snail trail around the base of the cake. Trim the cake board with the pink ribbon, securing with double-sided tape.

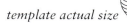

template actual size

BRODERIE ANGLAISE CAKE

This delicate cake would make a perfect centrepiece for many occasions. It is royal iced to give a clean sharp-edged base and the broderie anglaise requires a steady and experienced hand with the piping bag. For more details on broderie anglaise, see page 55.

20 cm (8 inch) round cake

1 kg (2 lb) marzipan
1.5 kg (3 lb) royal icing
yellow food colouring

EQUIPMENT

28 cm (11 inch) round silver cake board
number 1 piping tube
medium star tube
wide yellow ribbon
8 small yellow silk roses
8 small yellow bows

1   Cover the cake with marzipan and secure to the cake board with a little royal icing. Leave to dry.

2   Colour 1 kg (2 lb) royal icing the palest shade of yellow and spread three coats of icing over the cake. Leave overnight to harden.

MARKING THE SCALLOPS

3   Cut out a 28 cm (11 inch) circle of non-stick baking paper. Fold it in half, then into quarters. Fold once again to create a cone of eight layers of paper. Trace the template on page 299 onto a piece of non-stick baking paper, then trace it onto one of the end sections of the cone. Cut out the shaded areas of the template through all the layers of paper. (The outer shaded area forms the template for the board; the inner shaded area is for the top of the cake.)

4   Open out the outer template and lay it on the board around the cake. Secure it in place with pins. Place a little royal icing in a paper piping bag fitted with a number 1 piping tube and pipe scallops on the board, around the template. Remove the template.

5   Unfold the small template and lay it on top of the cake. Secure with pins. Mark the scalloped border with icing in the same way. Remove the template. Pipe a line of icing 5 mm (1/4 inch) inside the top edge of the cake.

BRODERIE ANGLAISE

6   To create the broderie anglaise pattern, pipe circles at regular intervals around the top of the cake in groups of three, then pipe further individual circles between the groups. Repeat on the cake board within the marked scallops, to make a similar design around the base of the cake.

7   Place half of the remaining icing in a bowl and thin with a little water until it becomes completely level when left to settle in the bowl for several seconds. Colour the icing a slightly darker shade of yellow and put in a paper piping bag. Snip off the end of the bag and gradually fill the outline with the thinned icing, easing it into the corners with the tip of a cocktail stick. Fill the outline with as much icing as it will hold without flooding over the piped outline. Fill the scalloped areas around the base and on top of the cake. When flooding a large area with icing, work on 10 cm (4 inch) sections at a time so that the icing does not form a crust before you have had time to ease it into the corners. Leave the icing for several hours to harden.

8   Place a little white icing in a piping bag fitted with the piping tube and pipe small circles to emphasize the broderie anglaise work. Finish off with leaf outlines.

FINISHING TOUCHES

9   Pipe decorative loops of icing around the scalloped edges.

10   Put more white icing in a piping bag fitted with the medium star tube. Pipe a shell border around the top and base of the cake.

11   Wrap the yellow ribbon around the cake and secure with a dot of icing. Place the roses and bows at the point of each scallop around the top and side of the cake, securing with dots of icing.

4

Lay the template on the board around the cake. Pipe scallops around the template and then remove.

6

Pipe circles around the top of the cake in groups of three, then pipe further groups between them.

8

Emphasise the broderie anglaise by piping white icing around the edge of the circles. Pipe leaf outlines to finish.

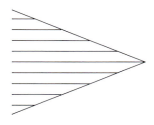

see template page 299

FRILLED CRADLE CHRISTENING CAKE

The charm of this cake lies in the delicacy of the rows of garrett frills and the precision of the paintwork, which is suitable for experienced sugarcrafters. We've used alphabet cutters for the writing, which is an easy alternative to piping if you're not confident.

5   To make the blanket, roll pea-sized balls of different shades of sugarpaste and flatten and curve slightly.

7   For the corner frills, attach the darkest pink garrett frill to the base.

7   Build up the frills in graduating shades of pink from dark to light.

8   Alphabet cutters are a quick and easy alternative to piping letters.

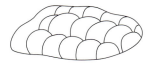

see templates page 289

---

20 cm (8 inch) square cake

1 kg (2 lb) marzipan
1 kg (2 lb) sugarpaste
1 tablespoon royal icing
claret, paprika and melon food colourings
60 g (2 oz) modelling paste

EQUIPMENT
28 cm (11 inch) square cake board
numbers 1 and 2 piping tubes
scriber
garrett frill cutter
narrow pink ribbon
alphabet cutters

---

1   Cover the cake with marzipan and leave to dry. Cover the cake with sugarpaste and secure to the board with a little royal icing. Cover the board with sugarpaste. Leave to dry for three days. Pipe a snail trail around the base of the cake with a number 2 piping tube. Trace the templates of the cradle, pillow and blanket on page 289 onto non-stick baking paper. Transfer the outlines to the top of the cake with a scriber.

PILLOW

2   Use a grape-sized piece of sugarpaste to make the pillow by pinching, flattening and pushing the paste into shape—use a piece of tracing paper over the pattern as a guide. Roll out some modelling paste very thinly and wrap around the pillow. Leave one side open and curl the paste backwards with your fingers to give a natural effect. Secure the pillow in place with a little royal icing and indent an area for the baby's head.

BABY'S HEAD

3   Make the baby's head by following the modelling instructions on page 95. Remember that only the upper part of the face need be visible. Make two small indentations for the closed eyes and two nostrils with the end of a cocktail stick. Make a tiny ear by using a small ball of sugarpaste and forming a small ridge around the top edge. Flatten the base for the lobe and make a small hole in the ear with a cocktail stick. Secure the head into the indented area in the pillow with a little water.

4   Make the cradle by rolling out some sugarpaste 5 mm (1/4 inch) thick. Cut out the shape from the template. Smooth the cut edge with the fingers until rounded and secure in place.

BLANKET

5   Colour two small grape-sized pieces of modelling paste in two pale shades of claret, one slightly darker than the other. To create the padded effect, roll a pea-sized piece of pale pink paste into a ball, flatten and curve slightly. Attach to the cake surface. Make another shape from the darker pink and push into the previous shape, then repeat using the paler colour. Continue until the blanket is complete. When dry, paint a tiny pattern on each square and fine pink lines on the side of the pillow.

FRILLED CRADLE

6   Make a small garrett frill (following the instructions on page 55) and secure around the base of the cradle. Make more garrett frills and gradually work up the cradle until complete. Make a tiny frill around the top of the cradle facing the opposite way. When dry, paint pink dots onto the frills. Finally, attach a piece of narrow ribbon onto the top seam between the final garrett frill and the inward-facing frill with small dots of royal icing. Attach two tiny bows and two tails to the ribbon.

CORNER FRILLS

7   Pipe a snail trail around the base of the cake. Colour some sugarpaste in three shades of pink. Make four garrett frills from the darkest pink and secure to the base of the cake in each corner. Make four garrett frills in the lighter shade of pink and secure above the first frills. Finally, make four frills from the lightest pink and secure above the others. When all the pink frills have been attached to the corners of the cake, secure one final white frill all around the cake. When dry, paint with tiny pink dots to match the cradle.

8   Pipe small dots of royal icing with a number 1 tube on the top edge of the top frill and around the top of the pillow. Paint in the baby's features with diluted food colouring. Colour some royal icing with light brown food colour and pipe hair onto the baby's head. Stamp out the word 'Congratulations' with alphabet cutters and secure to the cake.

TEMPLATES

Unless stated, the following templates are shown actual size. For those that need to be enlarged, the percentage of enlargement is indicated by the design. This is easiest to do by using a photocopier. If you do not have access to a photocopier, you will need to trace the design onto squared paper to enlarge.

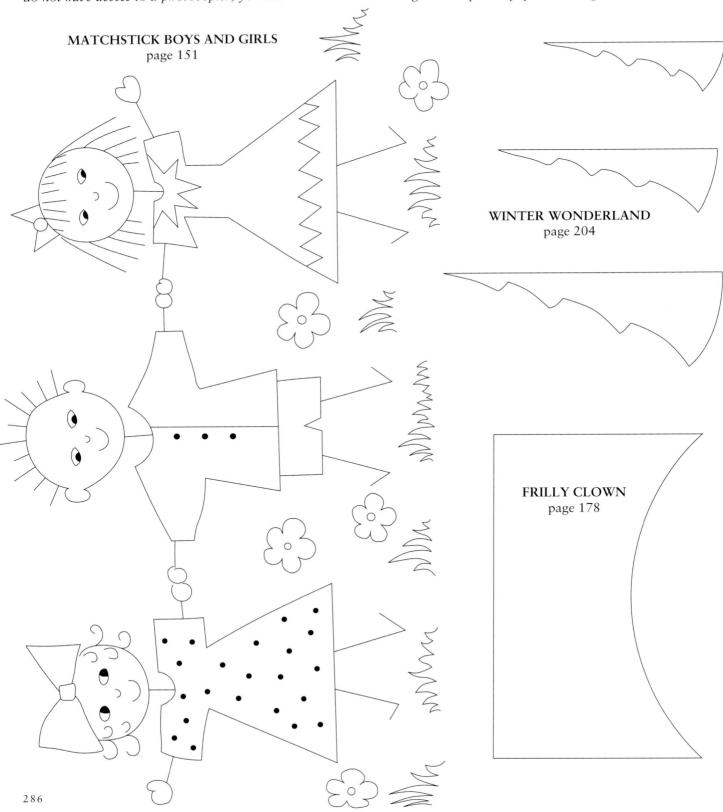

MATCHSTICK BOYS AND GIRLS
page 151

WINTER WONDERLAND
page 204

FRILLY CLOWN
page 178

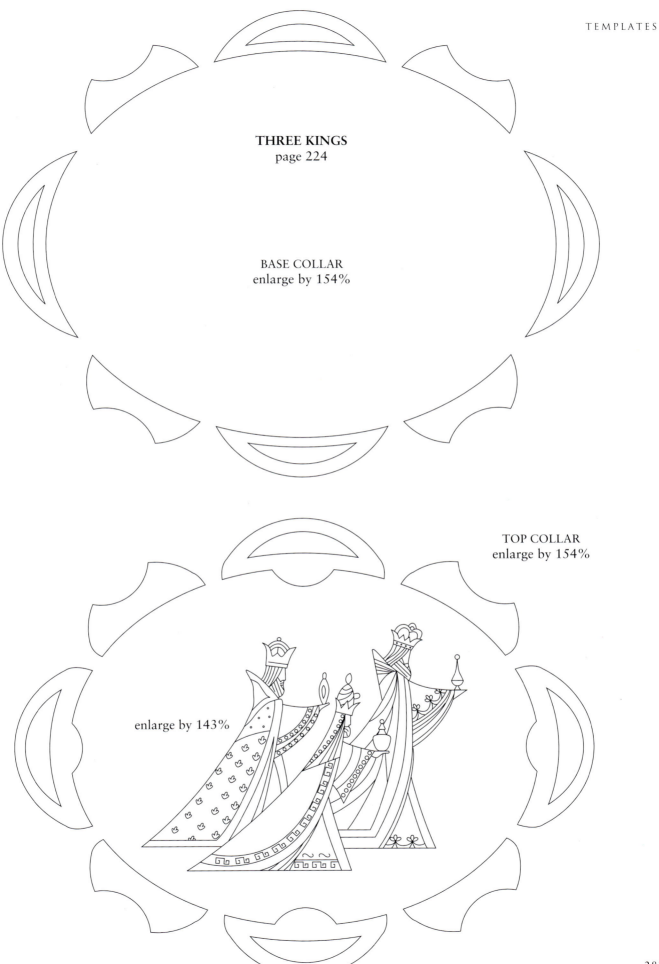

THREE KINGS
page 224

BASE COLLAR
enlarge by 154%

TOP COLLAR
enlarge by 154%

enlarge by 143%

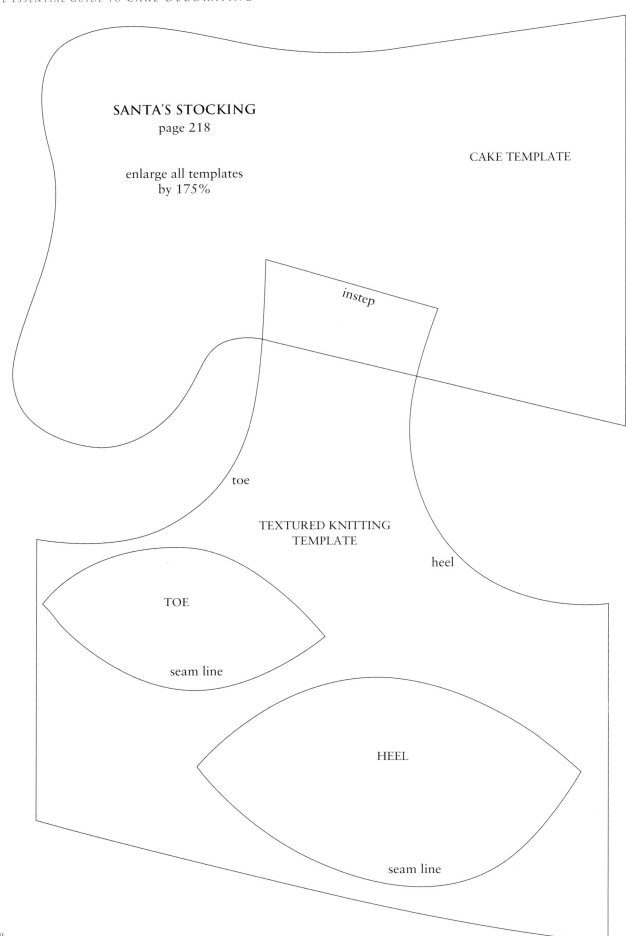

SANTA'S STOCKING
page 218

enlarge all templates
by 175%

CAKE TEMPLATE

instep

toe

TEXTURED KNITTING
TEMPLATE

heel

TOE

seam line

HEEL

seam line

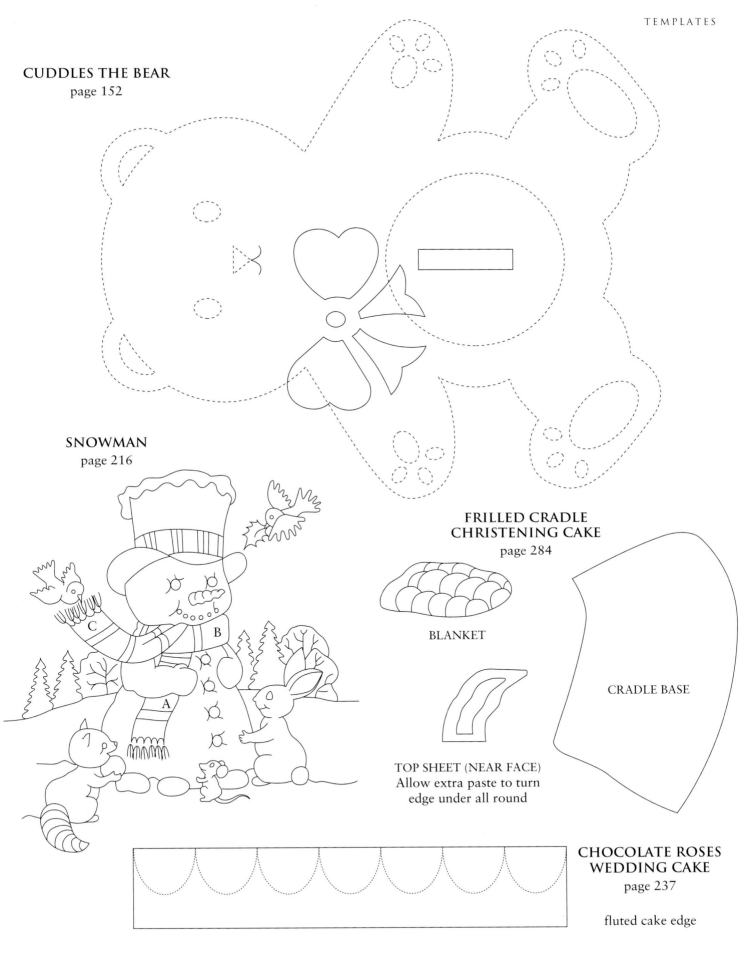

CUDDLES THE BEAR
page 152

SNOWMAN
page 216

**FRILLED CRADLE
CHRISTENING CAKE**
page 284

BLANKET

TOP SHEET (NEAR FACE)
Allow extra paste to turn
edge under all round

CRADLE BASE

**CHOCOLATE ROSES
WEDDING CAKE**
page 237

fluted cake edge

NOAH'S ARK
page 186

TREES

END
DESIGN

TOP RAMP

enlarge by 126%

SIDE RAMP

enlarge
by 126%

CAKE PATH

enlarge by 126%

BOARD PATH

enlarge by
126%

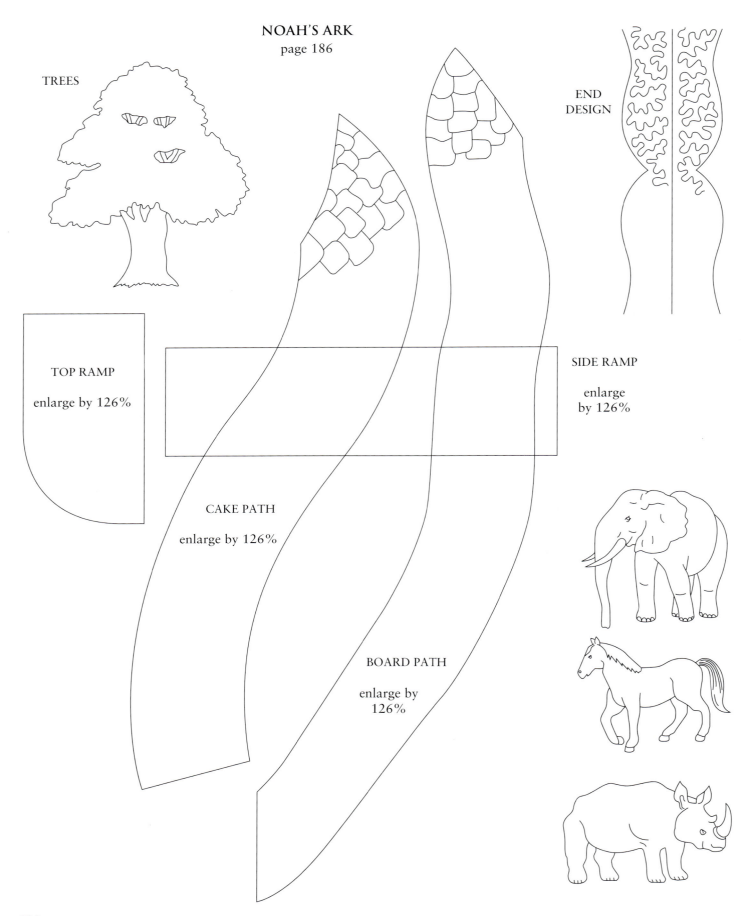

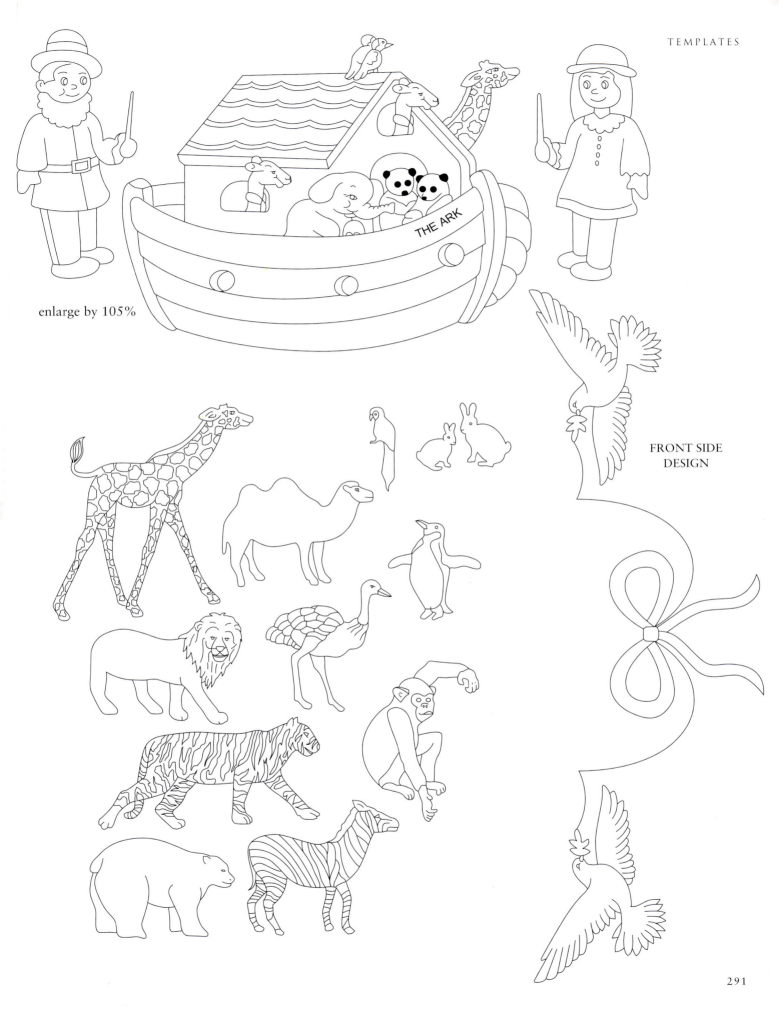

enlarge by 105%

THE ARK

FRONT SIDE
DESIGN

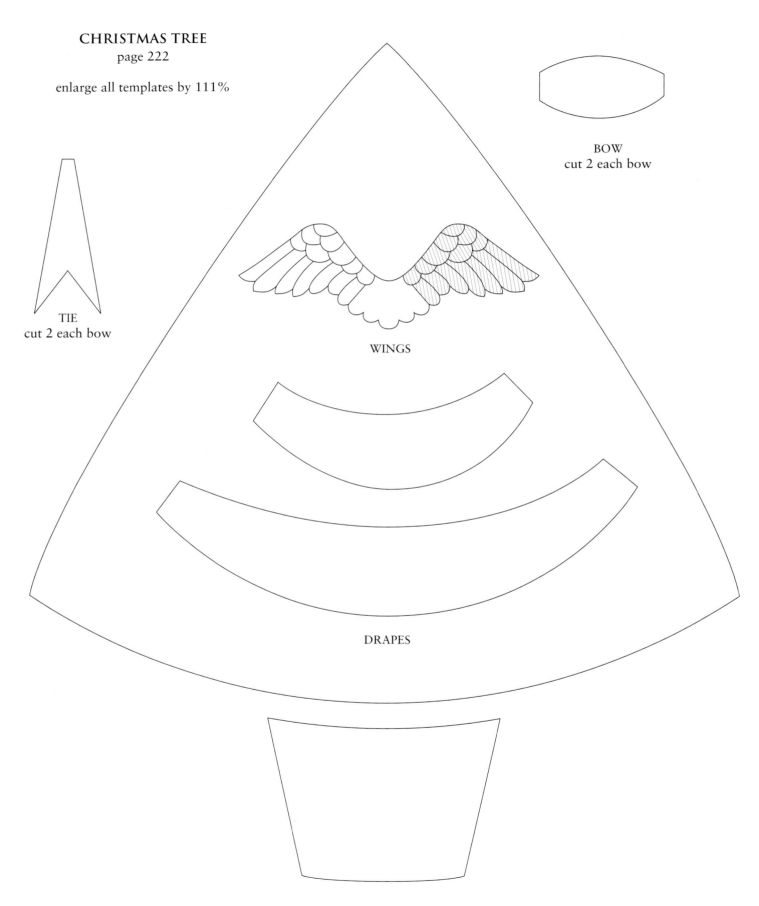

CHRISTMAS TREE
page 222

enlarge all templates by 111%

BOW
cut 2 each bow

TIE
cut 2 each bow

WINGS

DRAPES

PASTORAL PEACE
page 220

enlarge by 111%

overlapping base shape

**SNAKES ALIVE
NUMBER TWO**
page 155

enlarge by 215%

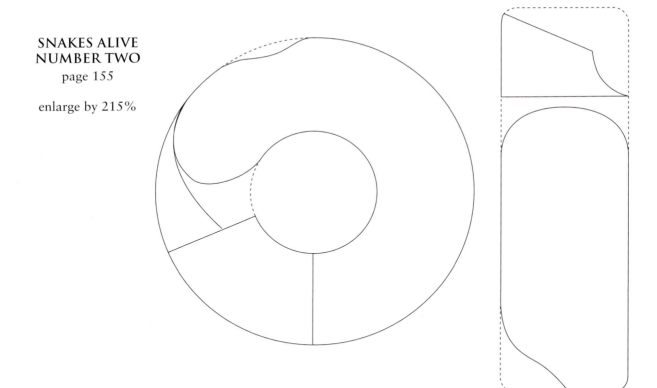

AT LAST I AM TEN
page 163

enlarge by 266%

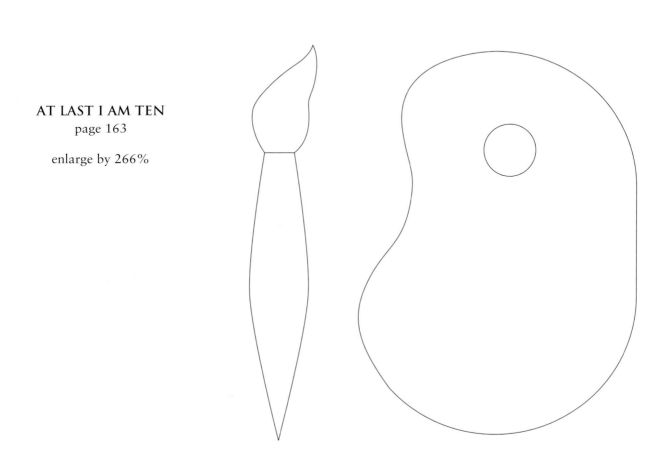

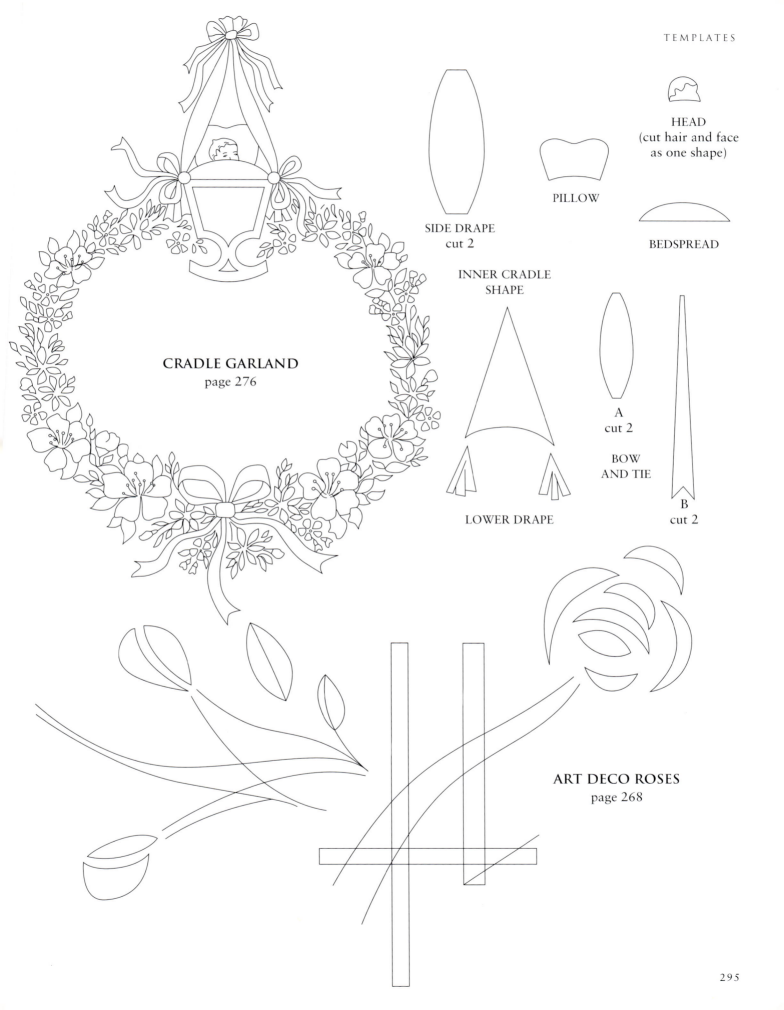

HEAD
(cut hair and face
as one shape)

PILLOW

SIDE DRAPE
cut 2

BEDSPREAD

INNER CRADLE
SHAPE

A
cut 2

BOW
AND TIE

B
cut 2

CRADLE GARLAND
page 276

LOWER DRAPE

ART DECO ROSES
page 268

WOODCUTTER'S COTTAGE
page 177

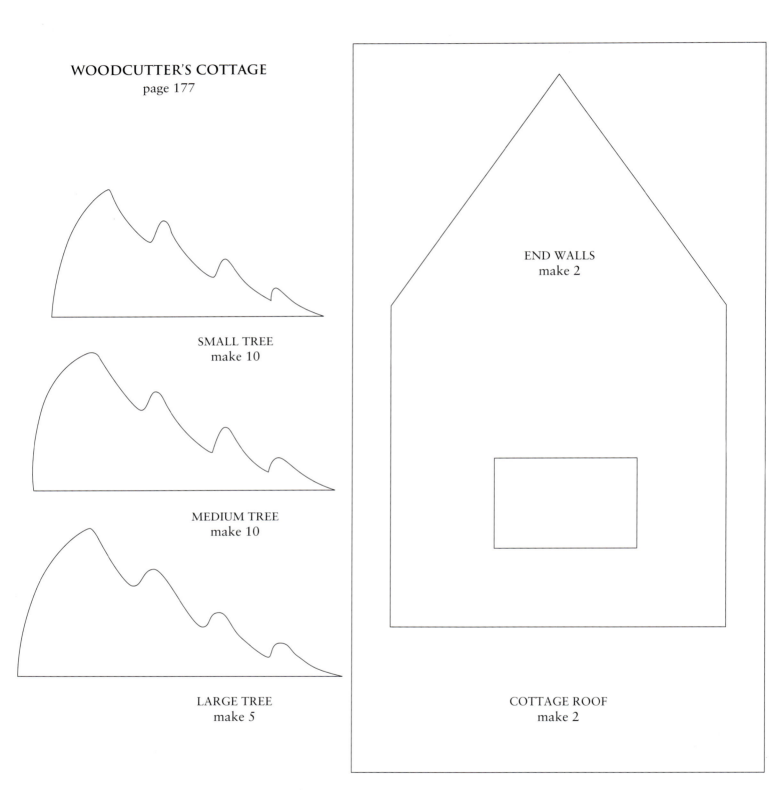

SMALL TREE
make 10

MEDIUM TREE
make 10

LARGE TREE
make 5

END WALLS
make 2

COTTAGE ROOF
make 2

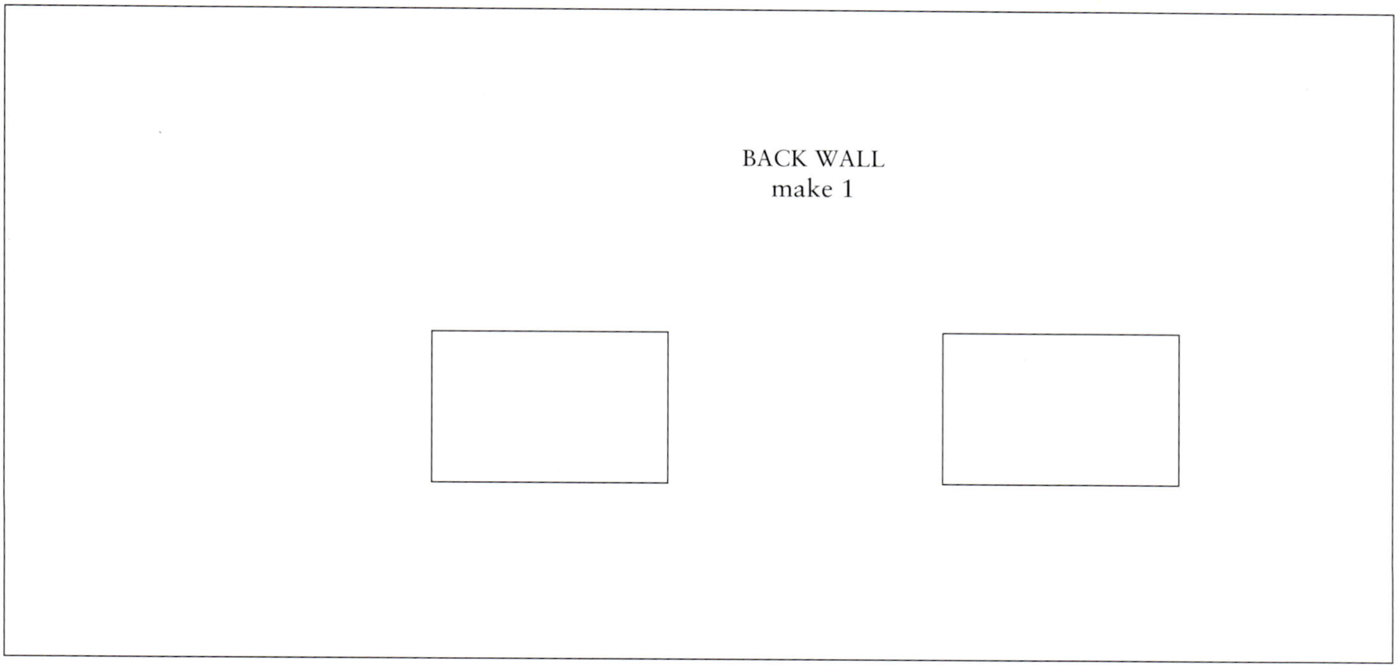

BACK WALL
make 1

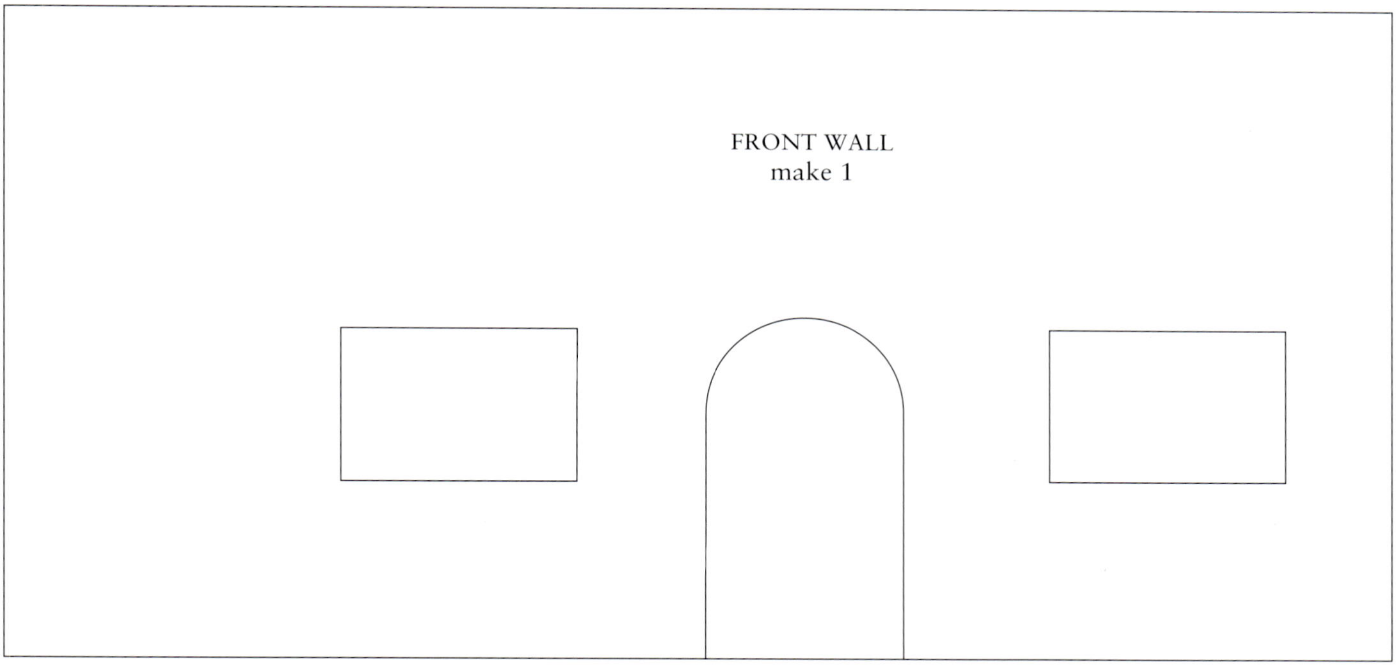

FRONT WALL
make 1

DOOR
make 1

SHUTTERS
make 12 of each

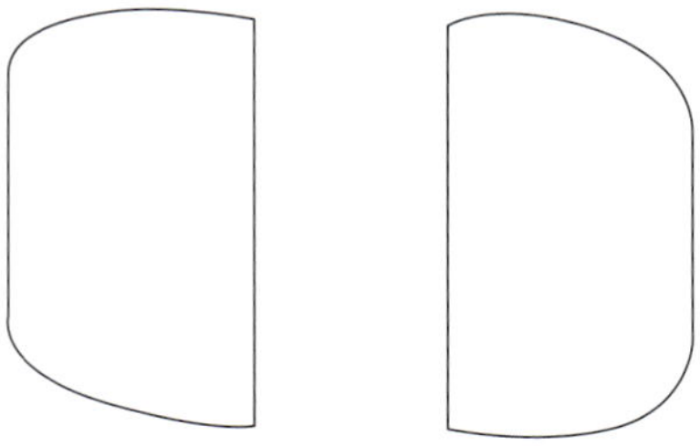

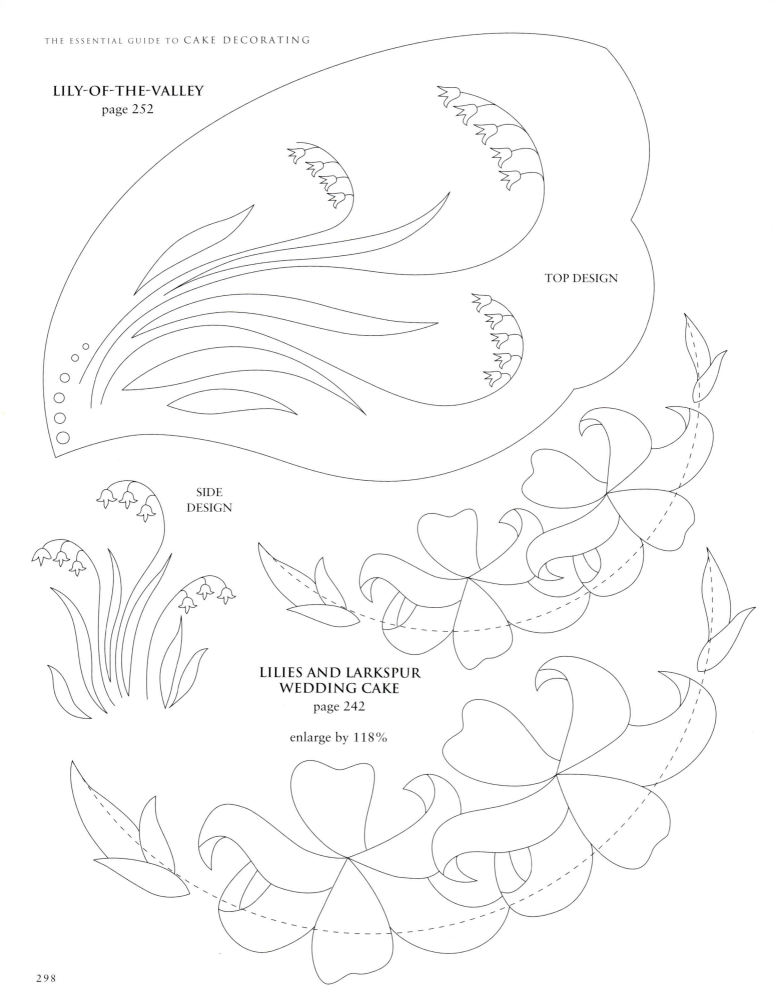

LILY-OF-THE-VALLEY
page 252

TOP DESIGN

SIDE
DESIGN

**LILIES AND LARKSPUR
WEDDING CAKE**
page 242

enlarge by 118%

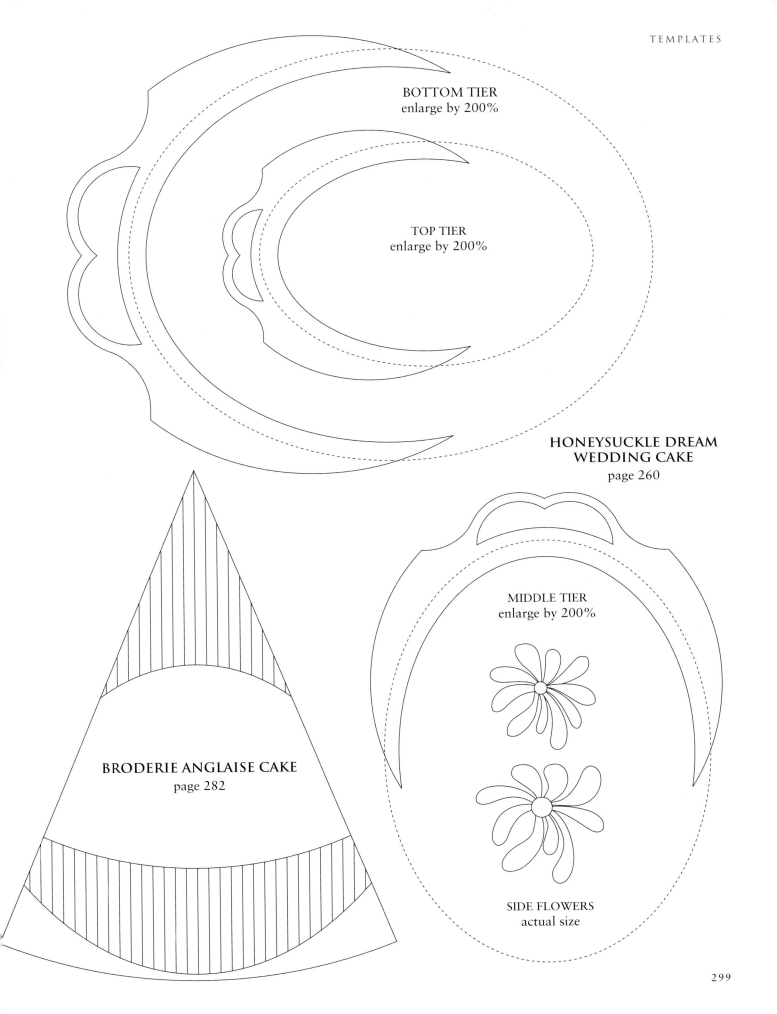

BOTTOM TIER
enlarge by 200%

TOP TIER
enlarge by 200%

HONEYSUCKLE DREAM
WEDDING CAKE
page 260

MIDDLE TIER
enlarge by 200%

BRODERIE ANGLAISE CAKE
page 282

SIDE FLOWERS
actual size

**ROSEBUD
WEDDING CAKE**
page 250

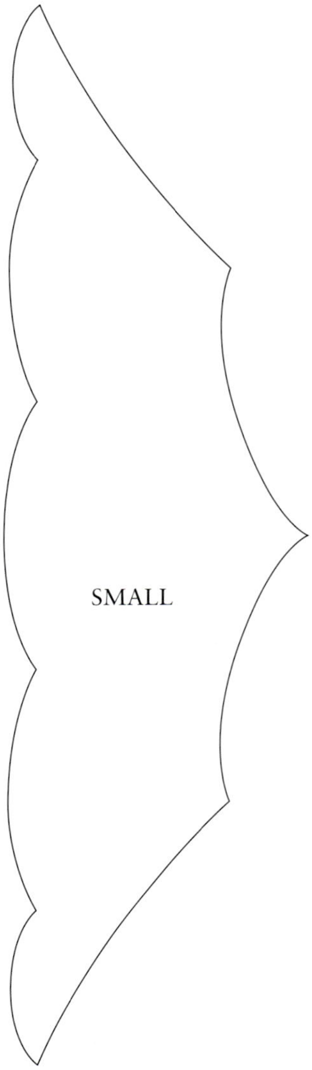

SMALL

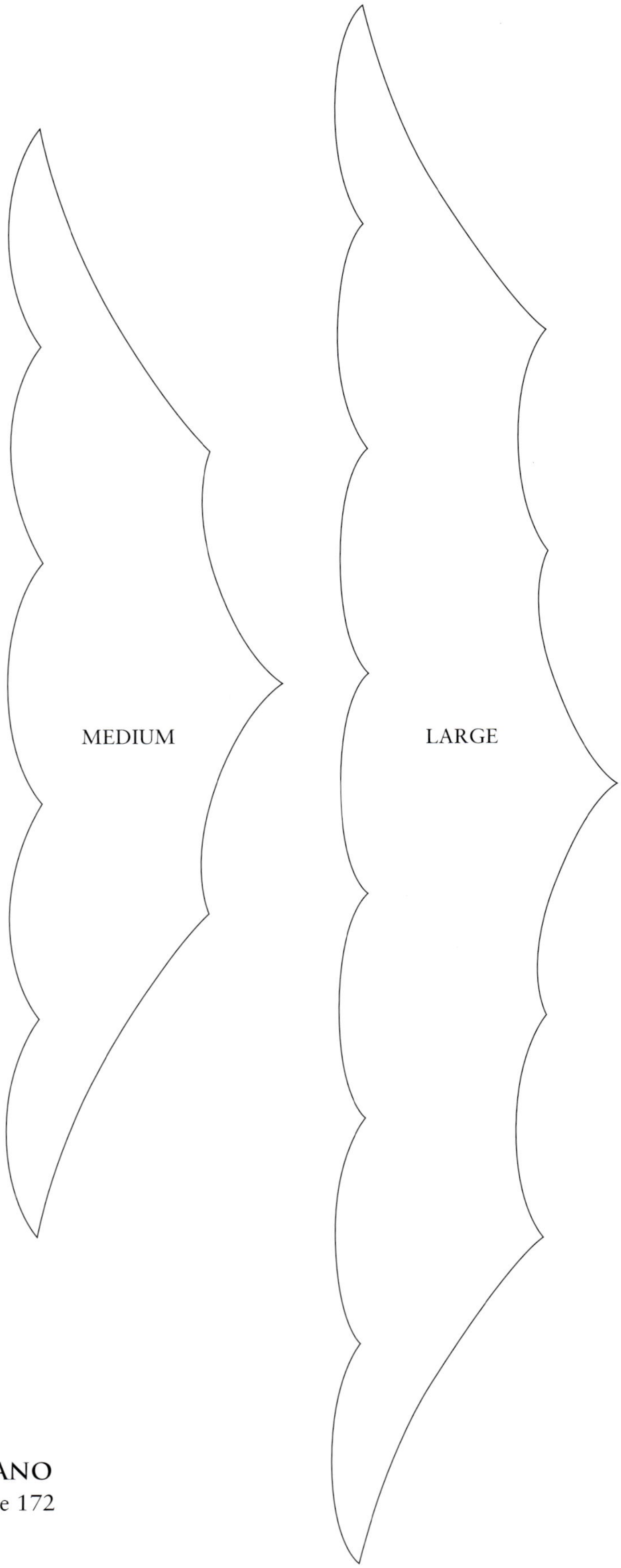

MEDIUM

LARGE

PIANO
page 172

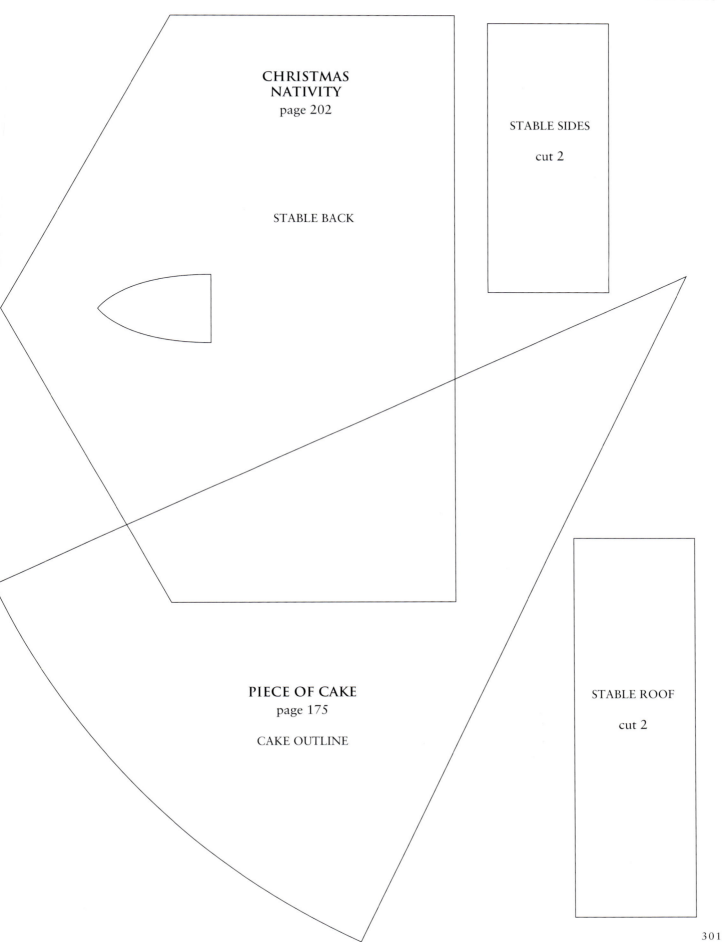

**CHRISTMAS
NATIVITY**
page 202

STABLE SIDES

cut 2

STABLE BACK

PIECE OF CAKE
page 175

CAKE OUTLINE

STABLE ROOF

cut 2

INDEX

A

accessories, 100
albumen powder, 10
Almond and apple
    gateau, 109
almond icing *see* marzipan
alternating shells, 65
animals, 98, 99
appliqué, 57
apricot glaze, 10
arms, 95
Art deco roses, 269
At last I am ten, 163
Autumn gold chocolate wedding
    cake, 241

B

backgrounds, 102, 103
Baggy trousers clown, 182
ball tool, 10, 15
bark, tree, 103
bas-relief, 57
bas-relief paste
    see modelling paste
basketweave, 10, 65
blossom, 78
blossom cutters, 10
blossom tint *see* petal dust
bodies, 94
books, 100
bouquet, teardrop, 91
bows, 101
Box of chocolates, 272
Boxes of gifts, 264
bricks, 102
bridgework, 10
broderie anglaise, 10, 55
Broderie anglaise cake, 283
Broderie anglaise wedding
    cake, 249
brush embroidery, 10, 73
bulb, 64
Bunny cake, 146
Buttercream, 10, 36

C

C scroll, 65
C shape, 64
cake boards, 46, 48
cake boards, covering, 46, 47
cake dowels, 10, 16, 48, 49
cake pillars, 10, 17
cake tins, lining, 38, 39
calyx, 10
Cappuccino truffle cake, 119
Carol singers, 207
Carrot cake, 29
celpad *see* foam pad
celsticks, 14
chalks, dusting, 17
Cherry millefeuille, 120
Chocolate cake, 30
chocolate decorations, 116, 117
Chocolate frosting, 36
Chocolate ganache, 37
chocolate, Modelling, 34
Chocolate mud cake, 31
Chocolate roses wedding
    cake, 237
Chocolate sugarpaste, 33
choir boy, 96
christening cakes
    Cradle garland christening
        cake, 276
    Frilled cradle christening
        cake, 284
    Mouse in a cradle christening
        cake, 280
    Trains and teddies christening
        cake, 270
Christmas nativity, 202
Christmas roses, 211
Christmas tree, 222
Christmas trinkets, 101
Classic sponge, 26
clay gun, 11
clear alcohol, 11
cobbles, 103
Coconut cake, 28
collar, 11

(continued)

colouring, 52, 53, 62
Cornelli and roses wedding
    cake, 254
cornelli work, 11
cornflour, 11
covering cake boards, 46, 47
covering cakes with
    marzipan, 40, 41
covering cakes with royal
    icing, 44, 45
covering cakes with sugarpaste,
    42, 43
Cradle garland christening
    cake, 276
cranked palette knife, 11
crescent, 91
crimpers, 16
crimping, 11
Cross-stitch building blocks, 181
crust over, 11
Cuddles the bear, 152
curved former, 11
Custard meringue gateau, 134
cutters, 11
cutters, flower, 17
cutters, leaf, 12, 17
cutters, petal, 17
cutters, plunger flower, 17

D

daffodil, 78
daisy, 79
Devil's food cake, 132
dog, 98
doll, rag, 96, 97
Dream castle, 171
dresden tool, 11
duck, 67, 99
dusting chalks, 17
dusting powder *see* petal dust

E

earth background, 102
Easter basket, 267
edging, 54

edible glue, 11
elephant, 99
embossing, 11, 54
embroidery, 72, 73
extension work, 11, 75

F
fairy, 97
Father Christmas, 96
feet, 95
filigree, 11, 73
firm-peak icing, 11
First birthday blocks, 154
Five down on the farm, 158
flat icing, 11
fleur-de-lys, 65
flooding *see* runouts
floorboards, 102
Floral basket, 275
florist's tape, 12
florist's wire, 16
flower cutters, 17
flower cutters, plunger, 17
Flower paste, 12, 35
flower pot, 100
flower spray, 90, 91
flowers, 7891
flowers, inlay, 103
foam pad, 15
fondant icing *see* sugarpaste
Frangipani wedding cake, 228
Frilled cradle christening
     cake, 284
Frilly clown, 178
Frosted fruits, 197
frosting, Chocolate, 36
fruit, 101
fruit cake, Glacé, 25
fruit cake, Light, 23
fruit cake, Rich, 22

G
ganache, 12
ganache, Chocolate, 37
Garlands and tulle wedding
     cake, 234
Garrett frill, 12, 55
Gateau tiramisu, 111
Genoise sponge, 27
Glacé fruit cake, 25
Glacé icing, 37
glass-head pins, 12, 15
grass, 102
gum arabic, 12
gum tragacanth, 12

H
hand-painting, 53
hands, 95
hats, 100
heads, 95
heat lamp, 12
hogarth spray, 91
Holly garland, 201
Holly in the Christmas snow, 215
Honeysuckle dream wedding
     cake, 260

I
icing, Glacé 37
icing, Royal, 13, 32, 44, 6275
icing ruler, 12
icing smoother, 14
inlay, 12, 56
inlay flowers, 103
ivy leaves, 79

J
Jewelled boxes, 198
Jungle cake, 164

K
Key to the door, 279

L
lace, 74
lace mould, 17
leaf cutters, 12, 17
leaf veiner, 12, 16
leaves, ivy, 79
leaves, rose, 83
leaves, sweet pea, 87
Lift off at nine, 162
Light fruit cake, 23
Lilies and larkspur wedding
     cake, 242
Lily-of-the-valley wedding
     cake, 253
line, 64
linework, 64
lining cake tins, 38, 39
liquid glucose, 12
Love's dream wedding cake, 246

M
Madeira cake, 24
marble, 103
Marble glazed cake, 127
marbling, 12, 52
Marzipan, 12, 32, 40
marzipan, covering cakes
     with, 40, 41

Matchstick boys and girls, 151
metal ruler, 14
mini rolling pin, 14
Mistletoe garland, 194
Mocha gateau, 113
modelling, 94–103
Modelling chocolate, 34
Modelling paste, 12, 34
modelling tools, 14
mouse, 98
Mouse in a cradle christening
     cake, 280
mud cake, Chocolate, 31

N
Noah's ark, 186
non-stick baking paper, 12
nozzle *see* piping tube

P
paint brushes, 16
palette knives, 15
Passionfruit and lemon curd
     sponge, 114
paste, Flower, 12, 35
paste, Modelling, 12, 34
Pastillage, 12, 35
Pastoral peace, 221
Patch, 142
paving, 103
Peach and orange mousse
     cake, 123
Pears with a spun toffee halo, 138
petal dust, 12
petal cutters, 17
Piano, 172
Piece of cake, 175
pig, 99
pillars *see* cake pillars
Pink lazy daisy, 110
piping, 6275
piping bags, 15, 63
piping gel, 13
piping tube, 16, 63
plaques, 13
plunger flower cutters, 17
pond, 103
poppies, 88, 89
posy, 90
pressure piping, 13, 66, 67
Pussy cat, 148

Q
quilting, 13, 58
quilting wheels, 15

R
rabbit, 66
Race you four it, 157
Racing at eight, 161
rag doll, 96, 97
reindeer, 67
return, 90
ribbed board, 13
ribbed rolling pin, 13, 14
ribbon insertion, 13, 59
ribbon loops, 90
Rich fruit cake, 22
rocks, 103
roof tiles, 102
rose leaves, 83
Rosebud wedding cake, 250
roses, 66, 8083
rosette, 65
Royal icing, 13, 32, 44, 6275
royal icing, covering cakes
        with, 44, 45
runout, 13, 68, 69
runout collars, 70, 71

S
S scroll, 65
Saint Valentine's day, 271
sand, 102
Santa's stocking, 218
scribers, 13
sea, 103
Seventh heaven, 160
shell border, 65
shoes, 100
smocking, 13, 59
smoother, 13
snail trail, 13, 64
Snakes alive! Number two, 155
snow, 102
Snowman, 216
soft-peak icing, 13
soldier, toy, 97

sponge, Classic, 26
sponge, Genoise, 27
sponging, 53
Spotted collar cake, 137
Spotty snake, 145
spray, flower, 90, 91
spray, hogarth, 91
Springtime daffodils wedding
        cake, 245
stamens, 13, 16
star, 65
Star of the show, 266
Stencilled boxes wedding
        cake, 233
stephanotis, 79
stitching wheels *see* quilting
        wheels
stone, 102
Striped chocolate curls cake, 131
Sugar sweet peas wedding
        cake, 259
sugar syrup, 13
Sugarpaste, 13, 33, 42, 5259
sugarpaste, Chocolate, 33
sugarpaste, covering cakes
        with, 42, 43
Summer fruits cake, 128
Summer poppies wedding
        cake, 256
Sunflower faces, 168
Sweet fig and chocolate cake, 124
sweet pea leaves, 87
sweet peas, 8487

T
tailor's wheels *see* quilting wheels
teardrop, 64
teardrop bouquet, 91
teddy bear, 67, 98
Teddy bear cake, 167
Teddy bears' picnic, 190
Teddy with a big blue bow, 189

Third bird-day, 156
Three kings, 224
Tiered Christmas cake, 208
tiers, 48, 49
ties, 100
tiles, roof, 102
tip *see* piping tube
tools, 100
Toy box, 185
toy soldier, 97
Trains and teddies christening
        cake, 270
Travelling trucks, 147
tree bark, 103
tube *see* piping tube
tube embroidery, 72
turntable, 13, 15
twisted rope, 65

U
Under the sea at six, 159
utensil, 15

V
veining tools, 13, 15
Victorian lace wedding cake, 238

W
White chocolate cream gateau,
        106
White Christmas, 212
White ivy, 231
window, 103
Winter wonderland, 205
Woodcutter's cottage, 177
wooden cake dowels
        see cake dowels
Wrapped presents, 230

Z
zigzag, 64